NINE GREAT AMERICAN MYTHS

NINE GREAT AMERICAN MYTHS

WAYS WE CONFUSE THE AMERICAN DREAM WITH THE CHRISTIAN FAITH

PAT APEL

Wolgemuth & Hyatt, Publishers, Inc.
Brentwood, Tennessee

Unless otherwise noted, all Scripture quotations are from the Holy Bible, New International Version. © 1973, 1978, 1984 International Bible Society. Used by permission of Zondervan Bible Publishers.

Wolgemuth & Hyatt, Publishers, Inc.
1749 Mallory Lane, Suite 110
Brentwood, Tennessee 37027

Library of Congress Cataloging-in-Publication Data

Apel, Pat.
  Nine great American myths : ways we confuse the American dream with the Christian faith / Pat Apel.—1st ed.
      p.   cm.
  Includes bibliographical references and index.
  ISBN 1-56121-064-1
  1. United States—Civilization. 2. National characteristics, American. 3. United States—History—Religious aspects—Christianity. 4. Christianity—United States. 5. Christianity and culture. I. Title. II. Title: 9 great American myths.
  E169.1.A577 1991
  261'.0973—dc20   91-17582
                                                                   CIP

To Katherine, Therese, Mary, and Jeep.
May He who began the good work
carry it on to completion.

CONTENTS

— ACKNOWLEDGMENTS

The idea for this work arose in conversations with Dr. Willem VanGemeren, Professor of Old Testament at Reformed Theological Seminary. The idea was developed in joint research and writing. American mythology then became the main theme of a course at RTS entitled *Interpretation and Communication in the American Context*.

I thank Professor VanGemeren for his invaluable assistance in this work, and I thank each of the students in that course who patiently listened to us "test" the ideas and contributed greatly in insight as well as illustrations for the American myths. I would also like to thank student assistant Scott Lindsey for his encouragement in this matter. It seems that he had a word of encouragement each time the project looked like it had come to a dead end. Likewise, I thank Mike Hyatt for his interest and encouragement over the months and years that we developed the ideas contained in this book.

Last but not least, I would like to express my appreciation to my wife, Katherine, and our children, Therese, Mary, and Jeep, for putting up with me during this entire period of our lives. Their patience came through love and understanding.

PAT APEL
Hazlehurst, Mississippi
1991

INTRODUCTION

This book rests on three premises. The first is that each culture has a set of traditions, myths, or legends that comprises a cultural worldview and guides the thoughts and conduct of the people. This phenomenon exists in each culture, including the American culture.

The second premise is that we are unable to separate ourselves physically from the culture in which we live. In this country we must live as Christians and as Americans. To do one to the exclusion of the other is to ignore the command to be the salt and light of the earth. We are unable to separate ourselves from our culture for we must view the world around us, to borrow a metaphor from John Calvin, through the lenses of our culture. That is, we are all subject to our cultural worldview. Calvin points out that, for Christians, Scripture provides the lenses which correct the astigmatism of our worldview.

The third premise is that the worldview of each culture is or has been contrary to the tenets of the Christian faith as set forth in the Bible. God gives us His grace so that we can recognize that Scripture is given for the purpose of discerning that the machinations of humankind are not the purposes of God; that holiness and community are given to overcome the sense of alienation and hopelessness pervading our culture; and that prayer is given that we may come closer to God, knowing Him and His will.

One purpose of this book is to identify several of the myths or traditions which collectively comprise the various strains of the American worldview, to discuss the crises in our decade resulting from the changes in those myths, and to offer some thoughts concerning the Christian faith and the American Dream.

In his fine history of Christianity, Justo L. Gonzalez suggests:

Without understanding the past, we are unable to understand ourselves, for in a sense the past still lives in us and influences who we are and how we understand the Christian message. . . . The notion that we read the New Testament exactly as the early Christians did, without any weight of tradition coloring our interpretation, is an illusion. It is a dangerous illusion, for it tends to absolutize our interpretation, confusing it [our interpretation] with the word of God. . . .

One way that we can avoid this danger is to know the past that colors our vision. *A person wearing tinted glasses can avoid the conclusion that the entire world is tinted only by being conscious of the glasses themselves.* (emphasis added)[1]

In the United States, the American Dream still lives within us and influences our lives far beyond recognition. We can prevent this cultural worldview and its many progeny from coloring our interpretations by being conscious of the tinted glasses we wear and by testing those interpretations with the glasses of Scripture.

A second purpose of this book is to create with the readers a dialogue which will open windows upon our culture—windows through which the reader can discover more about culture, Scripture, and, eventually, his or her beliefs. This is the goal. I recognize that there are those who do not share these observations of the world and, thus, will not agree with much of what is said. That is the purpose for dialogue—not to instruct others but to learn from this undertaking and to share whatever benefits may be found.

I recognize that many of the statements herein are generalizations which, if subjected to rigorous cross-examination, could be interpreted in a different light. This is the problem of all generalizations, one that must be recognized and, if possible, avoided. But if this book is to accomplish its goals, generalizations must suffice where specifics may be more appropriate, and vagueness must creep in where eloquence is lost.

I hope that those who read this work will consider these ideas and be led to think as seriously about Scripture and contemporary culture as they do about their own experience and beliefs and conduct. It has been said that to gain understanding of the full meaning of our present situation is to enjoy uninterrupted dialogue between the wisdom of yesterday and the wisdom of tomorrow. To forget the wisdom of yesterday is to drown ourselves in a chaotic sea of individualism. To ignore the wisdom of tomorrow is to bury ourselves in the shallow grave of the mistakes of our ancestors.

PART 1

AN AMERICAN VISION

1

AN AMERICAN IMAGE

We [Americans] suffer primarily not from our vices or our weaknesses, but from our illusions. We are haunted, not by reality, but by those images we have put in place of reality.

DANIEL BOORSTIN, *The Image*

I f you were Pilgrim in John Bunyan's classic, *Pilgrim's Progress*, and if you were to begin your journey from where you are right now and proceed, like Pilgrim, along your own path to the Celestial City, what would you see? Remember, much of what you would see in your journey through life would be of your own making. You determine your goals and aspirations; you determine your occupation and recreation; you pick your spouse, your home, your car—all this is within your power.

Or is it? How do we determine the things we choose for our own lives? As we take our separate ways toward the Celestial City, who determines the criteria we use to make our selections? Why do you drive a car to work rather than a camel? Why wear business clothing instead of robes? Perhaps your circumstances dictate many of the things you do on your pilgrimage.

In the United States we are restricted by circumstance, custom, or tradition to a limited number of things we may do. Granted, within those restrictions, there are a wide variety of options. But, just the same, the general pilgrimage of each of us is similar. What are the restrictions? We might call them, collectively, *Americanism*.

Theodore Roosevelt once said that Americanism is an issue of principle, of idealism, of character; it is not a matter of birthplace or creed or line of descent.

At about the same time, Nobel Prize-winning American playwright Eugene O'Neill wrote: "We talk about the American Dream, and want to tell the world about the American Dream, but what is that Dream,

---

"The Bible from cover to cover decries the building of material kingdoms on this earth."

---

in most cases, but the dream of material things? I sometimes think that the United States, for this reason, is the greatest failure the world has ever seen."[1]

These two national assessments, by men who interpreted American life with the artist's eye, see the American journey quite differently. Roosevelt saw the material dimension of life yet spoke of the spiritual. O'Neill saw the spiritual dimension of America yet spoke of the material.

Americans, citizens of one of the world's largest melting pots, can see glimpses of truth in each of the statements while recognizing that neither statement is altogether accurate.

From another perspective, in these two statements lurks something that, on the surface, eludes most Americans. The import of these two statements lies in their biblical roots. It is difficult for those familiar with the Bible to reflect upon the Roosevelt quote without eventually thinking of Isaiah or Romans. No doubt Roosevelt saw the biblical proposition that acceptance into the Israelite faith or the Christian faith was not based merely upon ancestry and fleshly descent.

Likewise, the Bible from cover to cover decries the building of material kingdoms on this earth. Perhaps O'Neill, no stranger to biblical imagery, saw in America the shadows of the eighth century B.C. Hebrew temple worship which paid homage to God then scurried from high place to high place to bow at the altars of the foreign and man-made gods, not the least of which was materialism. Perhaps O'Neill lamented in America the lost promise of the biblical dream of a just and compassionate society unblemished by greed or lust.

The quotations by Roosevelt and O'Neill bring us to the question: What makes an American distinctly American? Birth, wealth, politics, race, creed, principles, ideals?

WHAT MAKES AN AMERICAN?

Think for a moment.

If you were relaxing in the terminal at Heathrow Airport in London watching the streams of passengers flow by, could you pick an American out of the crowd? How would you tell an American from all the others?

Some people may be recognized by their clothing. An orthodox Jew, for example, may wear a skullcap or a beard to designate his faith. An Indian may wear the robes of his native country.

We may try the caricature test. A Russian, by caricature, is blond and stout. In 1979, shortly after the Afghanistan invasion, three Russians from the Soviet Embassy—two were economic officers, introduced as husband and wife, and a third, a young political officer—came to speak to a graduate seminar in Soviet politics. I do not know whether it was their complexion (light and rosy) or their clothing (a rough imitation of collegiate America reminiscent of the early Steve Martin skit on "two wild and crazy guys"), but I was convinced that I could spot them as Russians in any crowd. The young man, big and blond with wavy hair combed straight back, scowled like a big bear, like Brezhnev at age twenty-five.

We had the opportunity to meet socially after the class, and later that evening several class members took him to some of the watering holes in Nashville to hear country music. Disappointed that these taverns sold only beer, the young Russian resolved the matter with a big grin.

"In our country, like yours," he said to the students as he produced a bottle of Russian vodka from his coat, "we are often required to go outside the system to solve our problems."

Surely, he would fit the caricature held by his own people as much as he would ours.

The German, by caricature, is stern, regimented, cold. Molded by American television, our German is bald, wears wire-rimmed spectacles, a dark jacket, and carries a luger. He is cast as the German SS officer who pursued Harrison Ford in *Raiders of the Lost Ark*. We could spot him on any movie or TV screen through any amount of popcorn and soft drink.

But what about the American? A white man in a business suit and briefcase—"the ugly American"? A young student in jogging clothes returning from vacation—the college student touring Europe to find him/herself? A slender black man with a fedora which gives him a 1920s air—the presence of the American military overseas?

Such a question draws smiles, blank stares, knowing nods. Many American images come to mind: historical images, like Washington crossing the Delaware, or the drum, fife, and bugle corps; social images, like the American family as portrayed by Norman Rockwell, or a mime on the San Francisco streets; economic images, like Donald Trump on his yacht at the 1988 Republican Convention, or the homeless in New York or Chicago or Nashville on any given day; political images, like John F. Kennedy and "Camelot," or George Bush and Iraq; religious images, like Jerry Falwell and the Moral Majority, or a church service on a Harlem street.

I remember vividly one hot morning in 1968, while visiting in Shelbyville, Tennessee, an elderly gentleman asked if I had watched the Democratic presidential convention the night before. When I said I had not, he began to describe in the most amazed and unbelieving tones a scene he had obviously never seen before. It was, no doubt, a scene many of us had never seen before. As he described what he had seen through the narrow and fallible eye of the television news, he began to ask, like many others across the nation, what was going on? Who was doing what to whom?

Who, in fact, is the American in the images of the 1968 Democratic Convention? The long-haired demonstrator rampaging in the streets? The helmeted police officers subduing them? Mayor Daley muttering an obscenity at the speaker on the platform, broadcast on national television? The citizen at home who watched the whole thing in utter amazement? We do not know the answer but we know that we're not content to pick just one or the other.

THE IDENTITY OF AMERICANISM

Yet, even with the diversity reflected in our culture, all who are Americans have something in common. Americans see the world around them through a set of spectacles, lenses if you will, which are peculiarly

American. Granted, those lenses may be tinted by the fact that the viewer is male or female, white or black, rich or poor, but, nonetheless, the American view of the world is interpreted by the fact that the viewer is an American.

Chrysler Motor Corporation advertises that pride is back, born in America. They say that, of course, to sell cars. But the reason they can sell cars with that jingle is that there is a little bit of that in all of us. How many Americans can watch the Olympics and see Old Glory raised and hear the Star-Spangled Banner without a lump in their

---

"[It is] a man-made set of beliefs and rules and myths which perpetuate our culture and identify us as Americans."

---

throats? Pride is not back in America; it never left. Our pride is embodied in the common images we hold of ourselves and evoked in the sacred myths of our past and present.

In America our common bond is not in race or birthplace or line of descent, as Roosevelt suggested, but in our worldview, our creed, if you will. Each American has a common interpretation of our culture and the world which forms a worldview of Americanism, a man-made set of beliefs and rules and myths which perpetuate our culture and identify us as Americans.

G. K. Chesterton wrote:

America is the only nation in the world that is founded on creed. That creed is set forth with dogmatic, even theological lucidity in the Declaration of Independence. . . . It enunciates that all men are equal in their claim to justice and that governments exist to give them that justice, and that their authority is for that reason just. It certainly does condemn anarchism, and it does also by inference condemn atheism, since it clearly names the Creator as the ultimate authority from who these equal rights are derived.[2]

So, think again for a moment. What are the distinctives that make us American? Most Americans, diverse though they may be, can spell out the planks of the platform. We ought to live in a democracy, enjoy religious freedom, have the right to vote, work in a relatively free enterprise system, own private property, pursue happiness, have equal opportunity for all in the workplace, exercise freedom of speech, press, and expression. In short, we ought to be free to live our lives in a manner consistent with Western political traditions as they developed during and after the Protestant Reformation.

Yet there is more to the creed of Americanism than a simple and common political belief. Americans tend to view their history in a similar way. Americans see themselves as a people who are special, who have a certain prerogative in the world which leads them to a certain self-interpretation of uniqueness. Our ancestors believed that we were a people chosen by God and led on a mission from the Old World to conquer a promised land and to serve as a beacon of freedom to a decadent world.

Our worldview is so strong that you can take the American out of America but you cannot take America out of the American. Black writer and philosopher, James Baldwin, fled to Paris in the 1950s to escape what he saw as American oppression and racism. He wanted to be free to express himself as a black writer and a human being. But he found something quite different. He ran headlong into the brick wall of the Parisian culture. Everywhere he turned he saw the customs and myths and mindset of a nation many centuries older than his own. Rather than finding freedom, he found something he was not bargaining for—his own Americanism. He was as American, he said, as any Texas GI.[3]

CONCLUSION

Roosevelt was right to a certain extent. Americanism is a question of principle, of idealism, of character; it is not a matter of birthplace or line of descent. But he is wrong when he says that it is not a matter of creed. Americanism is a matter of creed! He may be calling it principle and idealism and character, but if that is not a creed, what is?

In that vein, O'Neill is right also. Surely, a part of principle, idealism, and character—a part of the creed—has to do with accumulation of material wealth. But to the extent that O'Neill mentions it, it marks a dangerous shift in the description of our creed, a change in the course of the social history of the United States, and an alteration of the original purpose for coming to this continent.

"We live not in America but in our own description of America."

James Cornman, in his text, *Philosophical Problems and Arguments: An Introduction*, writes, "Every period of intellectual history has some dogma which is regarded at the time not as dogma, but merely as what is evident."[4]

Centuries from now, historians will look back at the "American Empire" just as we look back at the Hittite Empire, the Roman Empire, or the British Empire. They will search for the "dogma which was regarded in our time not as dogma, but merely as what is evident." They will systematize the principles, the idealism, and the character which made the American Empire cohesive and compare the American worldview to those of the other great empires. They will describe our culture and think their descriptions accurate.

But what about our descriptions? We are not in the future. We are merely evaluating ourselves through a set of lenses based upon the principles, idealism, and character which, we contend, shows us the "what is evident" and which establishes our worldview.

Poet Wallace Stevens said, "We live not in the place but in the description of the place." We live not in America but in our description of America.

As we lonely pilgrims in this world make our way toward the Celestial City, we stop and gaze at the landscape of our culture. Yet we see not the landscape but the image of that landscape that our worldview gives us. That image is comprised of the worldview with which we have grown up, the stories which have taught us who we are, and the creed which makes us Americans.

2
AN AMERICAN DREAM

Obsessed by a fairy tale, we spend our lives searching for a magic door and a lost kingdom of peace.

EUGENE O'NEILL, *More Stately Mansions*

There is a wonderful story about a Greek man who brought his wife to America in the years after World War II and settled in a Southern city. They spoke little English—let alone any Southern—but they managed to open a restaurant. The location was great, the atmosphere good, and the people friendly. But times were tough in that town, and the Greek, virtually penniless when he arrived in America, went broke quickly. To complicate matters, his young wife was pregnant with their first son.

At the end of his rope, he worked up the courage to walk up the street to the local Presbyterian church and ask several of the elders if they would lend him enough money to make one more go of his business. He vowed they would get their money back, even if he had to mow their lawns.

Doctors, lawyers, and businessmen who had just returned from the war and who were picking up the businesses they had left four years earlier scraped deep in their pockets to come up with what he needed. The Greek worked twenty hours a day to make ends meet. As time went by, more people came to the restaurant and more sons to the family.

Today, over four decades later, the Greek has retired and his sons run the corporation that runs the chain of restaurants. The Greek and his lovely wife occasionally fill in as greeters at one of the restaurants, and the greeting which comes from his smiling lips as the patrons enter the door is, "God bless America."

The story of this Greek is a success which we, in America, like to hold out to others because it represents the best of what we, as individuals and as a nation, like to think about our country—the dream of success, the hope for the future. It represents our viewpoint on what our culture *should* offer to each individual.

"DREAMS ARE WHAT GUIDE US"

On the twenty-fifth anniversary of the assassination of John F. Kennedy, "CBS Evening News" closed its broadcast with a eulogy of the slain president which ended: "Heroes are what inspire us; dreams are what guide us."

A poetic close, no doubt, but this epigram revealed a more persistent truth than was intended. The framework of belief arising from cultural viewpoints or worldviews sets the criteria for "heroes" and provides the ultimate truth for the dreams which guide our conduct. JFK, with the help of press agents and favorable news reporters, was portrayed as living the American Dream, embodying the "American Creed." As a popular hero, he was a mirror of the popular mind.

Behind every popular view, there is always a story. And in America there is always a dream. The importance of the story of the Greek is not in what happened to the immigrant who came to these shores but what could happen to any immigrant or native on these same shores. It is the dream that guides us. The importance of the story of JFK is not in the caliber of his performance as chief executive or in his martyrdom but in the reassurance that anyone can achieve a dream. It is the dream that guides us.

Stories and dreams have been the acculturating factor in every civilization since the beginning of time. Something inherent in the human mind compels each of us to set out the story of life, even if we do so around a campfire or chronicle events in the family Bible. We are storytellers; that is how we learn about history and about our cultures and about ourselves. Each of us sits on a parent's lap and hears about life. The stories may begin with "eensie-weensie spider" or its cultural counterpart and progress through "I shall not tell a lie" to the birth of great nations. But the stories are there in every civilization. As human beings, we are all dreamers, and we like to tell those dreams in our stories.

Bill Moyers, in his discussions with Joseph Campbell, an authority on mythology, said:

> Myths are stories of our search through the ages for truth, for meaning, for significance. We all need to tell our story and to understand our story. We all need to understand death and cope with death, and we all need help in our passages from birth to death. We need for life to signify, to touch the eternal, to understand the mysterious, to find out who we are.[1]

Sociologically, the stories provide an education for the new members of the culture. Beyond that, the stories provide a common bond which cements the individuals in the culture into a body. It tells them

---

"Something inherent in the human mind compels each of us to set out the story of life"

---

who they are, what they want, how they get it. This is as true in America as in any other culture—from ancient Egypt to the Greeks and Romans to the medieval English to the twentieth-century Germans.

These stories explain our creed and provide our worldview. These are the stories which enable individuals to experience meaning in the culture at large. In these stories, the thousands of scattered and seemingly unrelated details of ordinary life are assembled into a complex, meaningful whole. Even the most trivial elements are somehow woven into the story like a huge, continuous, multicolored tapestry.

Stephen Ausband writes:

> No society has existed that did not need some sort of structure, a system of belief, by which it could ask and answer questions about its relationship to the universal. Myths die as societies change, but the

need for the myth does not die because man's need for order does not change or die.[2]

The stories which comprise the American Dream are the stories which provide for us a sense of order and identity. They maintain and continue our perceptions of the sacred and pass them on to the new-comers to our culture as well as to new generations.

Richard Slotkin writes about the American myths:

> The stories [are] drawn from history [and] have acquired through usage over many generations a symbolizing function that is central to the cultural functioning of the society that produces them. Historical experience is preserved in the form of narrative; and through periodic retellings those narratives become traditionalized. . . . they are re-duced to a set of powerfully evocative and resonant "icons"—like the landing of the Pilgrims, the rally of the Minutemen at Lexington, the Alamo, the Last Stand, Pearl Harbor, in which history becomes a cliché. . . . the range of reference of these stories is being expanded. Each new context in which the story is told adds meaning to it, be-cause the telling implies a metaphoric connection between the storied past and the present—as, for example, in the frequent invocation of Pearl Harbor in discussions of the need to prepare for nuclear preemp-tive strikes; or the invocation of "Munich-style appeasement" when discussing the possibilities of negotiating with our adversaries.[3]

Slotkin continues,

> These [stories] not only define a situation for us, they prescribe our response to that situation. At the very least, they tell us how we ought to value the situation—whether we are to identify with it or against it, whether our attitude to the "Lone Ranger" and the "Last Stand" is hostile, friendly or satirical. But they are also ideologically loaded for-mulations, "enlisting" us, morally and physically, in the ideological program.[4]

The Greek did not just come upon his dream of building a restau-rant business in the United States out of the blue. He had heard the stories of literally decades of immigrants who had come to the "Prom-ised Land" and transformed rags into riches. The dream motivated him and motivated his twenty-hour workdays. His success is simply a retell-ing of the same story which had been lived out by generations of people before him.

Those beliefs, myths, or legends are passed from one generation to another so that they provide a model for the conduct of those in the culture. The stories, myths, or legends then comprise the worldview held by that culture.

The purpose here is not to distinguish between the technical definitions of *myth*, *legend*, and *tradition*. That is for the social scientists whose study involves those technical differences. G. B. Caird, professor at Oxford, notes seven basic definitions of *myth* used by various disciplines in the social sciences.[5] He discards, as do Professors Ausband and Slotkin, the definition which holds myth to be merely falsehood. Myth is not necessarily false but is the embodiment of the traditions and beliefs of the culture. Professor Caird concludes: "Faced with an array of opinion, we shall be wise to conclude that myth has a complexity which defies all attempts of the foolhardy to reduce it to a single origin or function."[6]

My purpose is not to define *myth* but to show that such a phenomenon exists and that it affects the way we live our lives.

THE POWER OF WORLDVIEW

The worldview held by the culture dictates the actions of the individuals within that culture. We do many things in life because they are expected of us—expected of us because the culture holds certain things sacred. These things are held sacred because we hold that view of truth,

---

"Myth is not necessarily false but is the embodiment of the traditions and beliefs of the culture."

---

and any conduct other than what is expected would be considered abnormal. Now, we are not talking simply about how we dress or the material things that we have. Cultural worldviews address issues far more fundamental and far less obvious than fashion or fad.

The power of cultural worldview has been in each culture in each age. A cultural worldview with France at the center of the world aroused a young woman (many would say a child) in the fifteenth century to take up the sword in defense of what she saw to be the country chosen of God to establish His kingdom here on earth.

"Those who wage war against the holy realm of France," cried Joan of Arc, "wage war against King Jesus."

We are not convinced in the twentieth century that the holy realm of France in the fifteenth century was the equivalent of the kingdom of God. But Joan of Arc and many other French people—then and perhaps today—were convinced. They shared a cultural myth which held that God had elected France as a unique people with a mission to be the light to the world and to conquer the oppressors from across the English channel.

The underlying beliefs of Joan of Arc were no different from those of the radical Muslims in Iran or the Bolsheviks in Russia or the British mercantilists in the eighteenth century. Each culture has had its representatives who see God's hand exclusively guiding what they do and what they have.

Is ours any different? There is no question that many Americans have been convinced that God has anointed the United States to be the light of the world. Future historians may ask whether we are any more accurate in our belief than Joan of Arc was in hers.

The invisible hand of cultural worldview can also be more subtle and mundane, manifesting itself in the minor details of our lives. When we think of computers we generally think of the Japanese. Yet recent surveys show that computers are used much more broadly in the United States than in Japan, where many of them originated. In 1989 there was only one desktop computer for every twenty-seven workers in Japan. In the United States, the ratio is one to six; most are used for administration rather than instruction.[7] In using a computer there is a sense of isolation, a sense of being alone with the computer, an interaction which excludes everyone but the user. For the American, that's great. Individualism is held as a sacred tenet of the American culture, and a computer is conducive to that self-image.

But the Japanese are a people who believe in the value of teamwork, a sacred tenet in the Japanese culture. The Japanese work together, live closely together, relax together—they do very little individually. Individualism, in the American sense, is not a valued trait in the Japanese view of themselves. "Computer assisted instruction is a system designed for individual study," the *Tribune* quotes Professor Takashi Sakamoto of the Tokyo Institute of Technology. "It is an alien concept here and not originally Japanese. It has been difficult for Japan to accept."[8]

The use of the computer, which requires individual rather than team work, is frowned upon. And that cultural worldview is reflected in the frequency of computer use in the country. The power of the Japanese worldview touches each aspect of Japanese life. That power is exercised in Japan, and in America, on a daily basis.

In the end, it is the stories and myths we tell and believe about ourselves that guides what we do and how we think.

Robert Fulghum writes about what he calls "The Storyteller's Creed":

I believe that the imagination is stronger than knowledge.

That myth is more potent than history.

That dreams are more powerful than facts.

That hope always triumphs over experience.

That laughter is the only cure for grief.

And I believe that love is stronger than death.[9]

Imagination and myths, dreams and hope, laughter and love—surely in the human existence, like it or not, they guide our thoughts and our actions far more vividly and directly than anything else.

THE "TRUTH" OF WORLDVIEW

The issue is not *whether* these stories are true; the issue is rather *how* these stories are true.

Our worldview is not entirely based upon fact, and its function is not reliant upon fact. The American Dream is not perpetuated by seeking factual historical accounts. Like a "docu-drama," it may be based upon an actual occurrence but there the resemblance stops. Diligent research would often show that there is little similarity in fact between the "docu" and the "drama."

The American Dream is perpetuated by perception, by stories, by myths which make up our worldview. Whether George Washington actually chopped down a cherry tree is of little relevance. The myth is not told to inspire Americans to join the Sierra Club; it inspires us to honesty. Perhaps our questioning the factuality of the story is a comment upon our cultural view of honesty and truth. Be that as it may, we are more concerned here with perceptions, for it is what we perceive that counts. In this context, the message is what we receive, not what was sent.

A retired missionary friend, now a seminary professor, married a Canadian some forty years ago. After they had served extensively over those years in Africa and South America, she decided that she would become a U.S. citizen. A well-educated woman who had served in the mission field as a nurse, she studied diligently for the exam, reading everything she could on American history and political processes.

When the day finally came and she raised her right hand and gained American citizenship, she was elated. But after the celebration, something nagged her. Her husband, sensing something was amiss, questioned her.

Embarrassed, she denied that anything was wrong. But finally, due to his persistence, she relented.

"I enjoyed that study about politics and history," she said. "But the problem is that what they were teaching us about the history of the United States, well, . . . my goodness, none of that is true."

Her husband, a veteran of a variety of cultures, smiled knowingly. The "facts" she had studied in her preparation for American citizenship were not so believable to a person growing up north of the border and watching the daily reality of American life.

The goals we pursue in our lives are based upon perception. As a result, there are many interpretations of the historical basis of the American Dream. One of the shortcomings of the American Dream is our efforts to interpret our world so that we may appropriate its benefits for our own personal gain.

The Greek historian Herodotus, in the fifth century B.C., said that very few things happen at the right time, and the rest do not happen at all; the conscientious historian will correct these defects.

While we smile at the historian's jab at his chosen profession, we are reminded that history is, after all, written by human beings who carry to their task the baggage of their cultural biases. In our case, the American Dream operates as the "conscientious historian" in our lives by providing us with the correction of the defects in our life stories.

AN AMERICAN WORLDVIEW: THE AMERICAN DREAM

As we move into our third century, the communications media has given us many examples of the American Dream: the opportunity for each individual to make it on his own, to be free to do what he wants in life, to be happy, to achieve his goals, to go as far as he can on his own merit. It is, in other words, an expression of what we as Americans want for ourselves.

Reader's Digest, in the January 1990 issue, gives several examples of the fulfillment of the American Dream in the editorial article, entitled "Freedom on the March." The article celebrates the American nation by describing a poor, black teenager from the inner city of Detroit, a Vietnamese who came to America after the fall of Vietnam, a Mexican who emigrated to the United States, a black police officer—each has "made it" in his own way. Each is a "success story" to be celebrated and to signify the greatness of America. Each is an example of the American Dream. Very few of us could read this celebration without feeling the pride in our hearts that America is, indeed, "filled shore to shore with millions of the world's common people, many of whom, in another place, or another time, would have remained peasants or serfs."

The editors of *Reader's Digest* then treat us to their own version of history: "We have been booted out of or dragged from or have fled every nation on earth, our only baggage mankind's most dangerous notion: we can choose our own destinies."

Do not think that the power of this story to motivate Americans is lost on those whose job it is to exploit the American fantasy. Advertising agencies across the nation splash red, white, and blue across the commercial advertising of their clients in an effort to associate the products of their clients with the dreams and aspirations of Americans.

Citicorp, a New York banking concern, has saturated the market with a picture advertisement of several people of varying nationalities

standing in what appears to be a courtroom, right hand raised as if taking the oath of citizenship. Behind the eager and grateful faces of these
newcomers hangs a picture of George Washington. This celebration is
all under Citicorp's banner and a statement which suggests that
Citicorp has an integral part in all this.

The editors of *Reader's Digest* explain in their article that "It is far
too rarely noted that the astonishing collective achievements of this
land have their deepest roots in the plain, unassuming lesson parents
and teachers have repeated again and again to young children: Do
what's right. Tell the truth. Help your neighbor. Learn as much as you
can. . . ." There are several other "lessons" with the caution that these
are not simple truths but "represent the distilled wisdom of human experience, born of enormous struggle and sacrifice."

These, of course, are the basis of the American Dream, the stories
passed on from generation to generation which reflect the values and
lessons "parents and teachers have repeated again and again to young
children." The parents and teachers did not simply say "Do right!" or
"Tell the truth," but they told stories which conveyed those messages to
the next generation and which showed models of Americans to be ad-
mired and imitated. They told stories like the local story of the Greek
who built a successful restaurant chain.

We come to the question: What is the American Dream? Just as we
can say that most Americans will agree to the general specifications of
our "creed," we can say that most Americans will agree to the basic
components of the American Dream.

The American Dream is the multicolored tapestry comprised of the
many myths and stories of those who have come before us and, through
struggle and sacrifice, have made it possible for us to create our own
"success story." It is the worldview comprised of the myths and stories
which have portrayed the description of the place in which we live.

As we move into the third century of our nation's history, we can
see many examples of those stories of success in the entertainment
media. Often they have a great deal of tension. The movies *The Green
Berets* and *Platoon* appear to reflect differing views. Billy Graham and
Donald Trump seem to have differing worldviews. What we learn in
school, in church, and by experience seems to be in tension with other
stories in our culture. Yet, beneath the contexts, the varying myths of

the American worldview have the same foundation and the same themes and tenets.

The American Dream has the same basic components as it did when the Puritans brought it to this continent centuries ago. They believed they were chosen by God and led on a mission from the Old World to conquer the New.

Over the years the American worldview has been personalized. Now individuals adapt to themselves the basic components of the American Dream. Each sees himself in some ways elect or unique, as having a specific mission to enter a certain field—restaurants, politics, athletics—and to conquer that promised land. Granted, there are those who seem to have missed the American Dream. But it is not because

---

"The American Dream is the multicolored tapestry comprised of the many myths and stories of those who have come before us and, through struggle and sacrifice, have made it possible for us to create our own 'success story.'"

---

they have not had the dream. Rather they have not, in one way or another, reached the expectations to which they think they are entitled in the Dream.

The strength of the American Dream, and its ultimate weakness, is its adaptability to many contexts.

CONCLUSION

Nigerian novelist Chanua Achebe recently said that all societies need drummers and warriors and storytellers. Drummers, Achebe contended, arouse the populace and unite them behind the causes. Warriors fight for the causes and enforce the results of the causes. But storytellers are the most important, he said. Storytellers "make us what we are; they create history."[10]

In the next several chapters, we shall examine a number of the historical myths which have made us what we are, which have created history. These stories provide the continuing and changing contexts of the American Dream. Each is based on a foundation of uniqueness, exclusive mission, and conquest.

These myths are not, by any means, the only myths in our history. Nor are they without a great deal of inner tension. But, they give us an insight into what motivates men like the Greek businessman mentioned earlier, the young man or woman who ventures onto Wall Street, and each of us who has grown up in this country. When we gain that insight, we are better able to understand the cultural baggage we carry with us through life and which colors our view of the world around us.

3

THE MYTH OF OUR CHRISTIAN ORIGINS:

In the Beginning

Purity of the soul cannot be lost without consent.

SAINT AUGUSTINE

H.L. Mencken once described the Puritans as a people who have a haunting fear that someone, somewhere, is having a good time. We often speak mockingly of the Puritans who came to this country seeking religious freedom. Our public schools, harsh and unrelenting mirrors of our secular culture, tend to follow the cultural whim in portraying the Puritans as long-nosed, sour-faced, black-clothed, colorless, mirthless disciplinarians who would rather crack the back of a hand with a ruler than eat.

On the other hand, in evangelical circles we often hear the nostalgic cry to turn back the clock to the golden days of the Puritans, as if they had some magical way to deal with the problems of their time. We think of their faith and their spirituality and the quality of their churches, and we wistfully mutter, "This nation was founded as a Christian nation."

In the past two decades historians and sociologists have rediscovered the Puritans and written of them in a light which reflects their bold individualism and their courageous defiance of tyranny—traits most Americans like to claim for themselves.

The Puritans brought the Reformation to America and laid the foundation of our modern culture. They are our link between the birth of our country and the culture of Western Europe as it developed through the Renaissance and the Reformation. Their imprint on every facet of American life is indelible.

In the 1830s, French sociologist Alexis de Tocqueville, while visiting the United States, observed, "I think I can see the whole destiny of America contained in the first Puritan who landed on these shores."[1]

James Reichley, a fellow of the Brookings Institution, writes in *Religion in American Public Life* that "the single most influential cultural force at work in the new nation was the combination of religious beliefs and social attitudes known as Puritanism."[2]

THE FOUNDATION OF THE AMERICAN DREAM

The American Puritans saw themselves as chosen of God to leave Europe on an exodus to the New World and there to conquer the promised land much like Joshua had done centuries before. They saw this as a great and exclusive mission given to them alone, led by the hand of God and inspired by the Holy Scriptures.

That view of the call of God to perform the holy mission of conquering the promised land is the bedrock of the American Dream. The Puritan experience, drawing upon the biblical metaphors of uniqueness, exclusive mission, and conquest, created the context from which all other American myths arose. Granted, it has been distorted and profaned, but it has survived over the generations.

Sacvan Bercovitch writes:

> The *same Puritan myth, differently adapted* encouraged [Jonathan] Edwards to equate conversion, national commerce, and the treasures of a renovated earth, [Benjamin] Franklin to record his rise to wealth as a *moral vindication* of the new nation, [James Fenimore] Cooper to submerge the historical drama of the frontier in the heroics of American nature, [Henry David] Thoreau to declare self-reliance an economic model of "the only true America," Horatio Alger to *extol conformity as an act of supreme individualism* and [Herman] Melville, in *Moby Dick*, to create an epic hero

who represents in extremes both the claims of romantic isolation and the thrust of industrial capitalism. (emphasis added)[3]

Each generation's version of the American Dream and each of the myths which comprise the American worldview have their origins in the Puritan worldview. Each generation has "differently adapted" the Puritan myth to itself. But the Puritans were the first to envision the American Dream, and their vision has come down to all of us.

THE PURITANS IN THE OLD WORLD

The Puritan myth began in the England of the Reformation when James I (1566–1625) had succeeded in uniting the kingdoms of Scotland and England. At that time, there were various factions in the land who thought that the church and the state should be separate, that the monarchy was impeding the Reformation, and/or that the church should purify itself. Those factions which sought to separate completely from the Church of England were called Separatists.

Others, consistent with the Reformed tradition, merely wished to reform the church, to purify it from its errant ways. They were called Puritans.

The vast majority of English society considered both of these groups dissidents of the worst order because they criticized, among other things, the lavishness and opulence of the Church of England and

"The Puritan experience, drawing upon the biblical metaphors of uniqueness, exclusive mission, and conquest, created the context from which all other American myths arose."

thought that members of the clergy should not be openly and publicly drunk and cavorting in brothels. These dissidents were not the cowardly conformists portrayed by our secular persuaders. They were, if anything, somewhat stubborn and independently minded citizens who were unable to agree with each other on many things; let alone with what they perceived to be a Scot usurper and his apostate church.

James I, in opposition to these groups of Separatists and Puritans, authorized the English translation of the Bible, which is now called the Authorized Version (1611), or the King James Version, in an effort to stifle and suppress the Tyndale version and the Geneva Bible which were used by the Puritan communities. The Geneva Bible, which was often called the "fig leaf" Bible because it was the first to translate the attempts of Adam and Eve to cover themselves in the Garden of Eden as the putting on of fig leaves, had been translated and accepted in Protestant circles in Switzerland during the early Reformation.

Over the years, the Puritans united, rebelled, fought the monarchy, and eventually several of their number were forced to flee England.

Among the community which remained in England was the family of John Bunyan (1628–1688). Bunyan, born at approximately the time the first waves of Puritans were coming to the New World, was a lay preacher with very little formal education. He fought in Cromwell's army in the civil wars against the monarchy and was later imprisoned by the English government for his Puritan preaching.

Offered freedom if he would decline further preaching, he gave his now famous reply, "If I am freed today I will preach tomorrow." Remaining in prison, Bunyan proved his literary genius with *Pilgrim's Progress, Grace Abounding to the Chief of Sinners,* and later with *The Holy War,* a volume said to be the best allegory ever written—the best, that is, after *Pilgrim's Progress.* Bunyan's written legacy of Puritanism is only one evidence of its strong influence upon the culture of Western civilization.

The Puritans frequently met opposition from the Anglican church and its congregations for the language they used in describing themselves and their relation to God. That they applied metaphors from the Old Testament as models for their conduct came under criticism by their contemporaries, particularly the hierarchy of the Anglican church.

This language of metaphor used by the Puritans, commonly referred to as the language of Canaan, described the tribes of Israel in the Exodus, the wilderness, and the conquest. In this metaphorical language, they clearly saw themselves in the same circumstances as the Israelites—chosen of God and sent upon an exclusive mission to conquer the promised land. They perceived that they were living in the last days when the Millennium had come to earth. Therefore, the kingdom of God was theirs to build and enjoy.

It is not difficult to understand, then, in the face of the open and flagrant application of this language to themselves, that others in Elizabethan England might raise their eyebrows at the Puritan view. The logical extension of the metaphor, of course, was that everyone else occupied the role of the Egyptian slavemasters. The vast majority in Elizabethan England approved, openly or tacitly, the liturgies of the Anglican church and scoffed at the simple worship services of the Puritans.

The poem, "The Mad Zealot," is an example of that contemporary criticism:

> In the holy tongue of Canaan,
> I plac'd my chiefest pleasure,
> Til I prickt my foot
> With a Hebrew root,
> That I bled beyond all measure.[4]

Another contemporary critic wrote:

The whole gang [of what he called Nonconformist Phrasemongers, i.e., the Puritans] thought God was fulfilling Prophesies, and making good the Revelation, and they must help and be instrumental to him in this Generation-work: Else they might be shut out of the land of Promise, and not enter into the New Jerusalem. . . . Nay, *those whom you count the soberest persons were so drunk with this conceit* that they fancied themselves or their Friends to be Angels powring out Vials, or some such thing. (emphasis added)[5]

The Puritans, through their use of this language, carved out a position in society for themselves. And, of course, others objected to the Puritans' view of their unique role.

THE "SCRIPT" FOR THE DREAM

The Puritans landed on this continent with a worldview drawn from their Judeo-Christian heritage. The Puritan worldview rested upon three legs (as did the worldview of the Israelites centuries before):

1. They saw themselves as unique, the elect of God.

2. They believed that they had received an exclusive mission from God to conquer the promised land.

3. Their lives were dedicated to the conquest, the accomplishment of that exclusive mission.[6]

Of course, they did not arrive at their worldview out of the clear blue sky. Their worldview was the result of studied attention to the Bible and the immediate history of the Puritan factions, in addition to the results of the study of Scripture throughout the history of Christianity.

Over the previous sixteen hundred years, there had been a running debate—indeed, there still is—about the nature of Scripture. On one end of the debate, it is argued that Scripture is merely the record of the historical events in the Judeo-Christian heritage. The events which were recorded were just that—events.

On the other hand, the method of interpretation common in the Middles Ages included allegorizing, the search for a deeper meaning in a text when that meaning is not readily apparent. In the method of allegorizing, the historical aspects of Scripture, if any, were of little relevance when pitted against the overwhelming role of Scripture as God's message to the present-day reader.

The debate, of course, was and is not simple. There have been theological heavyweights on both sides taking a variety of positions ranging from absolute historicism to absolute allegorism.

A third approach involved the application of Scripture as typology. This interpretation saw the narratives of Scripture as historically based, yet providing a typology or metaphor for the reader to guide his conduct. An example of this would be when the Apostle Paul in his letter to the Galatians cites Hagar and Sarah and says, "These things may be taken figuratively. . . ." (4:24). While this is not exactly typology in the strict sense of the word, it reflects the use of previous events to illustrate a theological truth. This was the approach of the Puritans.

Scripture, as we can see from the debate over allegory and history, is written not in the technical or scientific language that we find in some segments of our culture but often in a poetic language more common in the Ancient Near East. It draws pictures for us, paints portraits of the world around us. The language is rich in literary device and relies heavily on metaphor to convey the images the authors wish to create.

The use of metaphor and simile adds fuel to the fire of the debate over the historical interpretation versus the typological and allegorical interpretations of Scripture. For example, the literary devices of simile and metaphor are sometimes intended to be taken only descriptively. The

---

"Scripture, as we can see from the debate over allegory and history, is written not in the technical or scientific language that we find in some segments of our culture but often in a poetic language more common in the Ancient Near East. It draws pictures for us, paints portraits of the world around us."

---

young shepherd in the Song of Solomon is not a young stag nor a gazelle on the hills, but he is *like* one—suggesting the response in the reader or listener of beauty, grace, and a sense of awe. To say that the maiden is a rose of Sharon, a lily of the valley, is not to say that she is a flower but to suggest that she is beautiful, *like* those flowers.

While the Puritans tended toward the literal in their interpretation of Scripture, they picked out of Scripture the message they thought God was delivering to them through His Word. The Exodus and the conquest became the theological framework of the early Puritans and the explanation of the sacred purpose of their culture.

JOHN WINTHROP—THE AMERICAN NEHEMIAH

Most notable among those who took the Scripture to heart and lived by it was Massachusetts governor John Winthrop (1588–1649). It is much more than coincidental that Cotton Mather entitled his biography of John Winthrop, *Nehemias Americanus*.[7]

The image of Nehemiah—the man who left his exalted position as cupbearer for the king of Persia to lead the faithful remnant of Israelites back to the ruins of Jerusalem—gave the newcomers a model with which to meet their own wilderness. His actions were a road map for their actions.

But Nehemiah, like Winthrop many centuries later, stands for more than just leadership, more than just political savvy. Nehemiah was a spiritual man who prayed for God's wisdom before seeking the king's permission to return to an Israel ravaged by war and left for dead. It was a great tribute to Nehemiah's loyalty that the king granted his request and provided materials for the rebuilding of Jerusalem.

Nehemiah rebuilt the walls in the face of hostile enemies. Nehemiah divided the force of men into workers, and guards who stood on the wall with sword in hand while the walls were being completed in record time despite the anger of pagan Canaanite neighbors. No overruns on this public project. The job was done quickly and efficiently, and the walls were prepared for battle. And, to paraphrase Proverbs 21:31, the victory was to the Lord.

Nehemiah is presented as a model in Christian businessmen's studies today to provide the right combination of spirituality, reliance upon the strength and will of God, and self-motivation. Nehemiah provides the model for leadership to be practiced outside the walls of the church. Frankly, we admire Nehemiah today because he is the guy who took the bull by the horns and got things done in Jerusalem. Winthrop was seen as the latter-day Nehemiah, the strong-willed man who was able to take the bull by the horns and accomplish things. But his efforts were dictated—even his opponents, no doubt, would have conceded—by his overriding goal to promote the common good. Winthrop set the tone for America when he wrote, "We must delight in each other, make others' conditions our own, rejoice together, mourn together, labor and suffer together, always having before our eyes our community as members of the same body."[8]

Nehemiah believed himself and his people elect of God with a mission to go on an exodus from exile to the wilderness which was the original Promised Land. There his mission was to reconquer Jerusalem. Nehemiah adopted the typology of Moses and Joshua, and Jerusalem was rebuilt.

Winthrop was a man who trusted God, who considered himself called of God and sent upon a mission. Again, the typology of the conquest permeates his thought and conduct. He went on to be the twelve-time governor of the Massachusetts Bay Colony and one of the chief architects of the Puritan, and eventually American, worldview.

Winthrop, like Nehemiah, became much more than a leader to his people; his story became a guide for the conduct of generations to follow.

"Frankly, we admire Nehemiah today because he is the guy who took the bull by the horns and got things done in Jerusalem."

THE PURITAN MYTH

When any community creates a sacred purpose, it must then have sacred stories of some sort to explain those sacred purposes. The Puritans, and Winthrop in particular, taking their role models from Scripture itself, became the early standard for those following them in conquering the New World.

Samuel Eliot Morison wrote that "Puritanism was a cutting edge which hewed liberty, democracy, humanitarianism, and universal education out of the black forest of feudal Europe and the American wilderness."[9]

Later, a Roman Catholic scholar, Christopher Dawson, was to observe,

The modern Western beliefs in progress, in the rights of man, and the duty of conforming political action to moral ideals, whatever they may owe to other influences, derive ultimately from the moral ideals of Puritanism and its faith in the possibility of the realization of the Holy Community on earth by the efforts of the elect.[10]

From our vantage point, we may hear people snicker about those who, as H. L. Mencken said, fear that someone, somewhere, is having a good time. Yet we must recognize that the Puritans had the dream to come and settle in the New World, to conquer the frontiers that God had given them, and to build a holy community on earth. That dream, of course, has been shared by millions over the generations since the first Puritans.

The Puritans, in applying Scripture to themselves, gave us the foundational myth by which we view the American Dream. By the 1840s, the "Puritan myth, differently adapted" led Americans to see themselves as called upon to fulfill a "Manifest Destiny." That destiny, and the great expansion westward which resulted, was used by the American apologists to excuse the incidents like the Trail of Tears and the slaughter of natural resources so that the mission could be accomplished. Following this distortion into later decades, it was our duty to fight "the war to end all wars," to provide an arsenal for democracy, and to be the policemen of the world. That foundation was so great and so lingering that it came to a head in the 1960s as America ventured into Vietnam. It was that sacred cultural belief that Henry Kissinger, in the 1960s, described as "the universal American sense of moral mission."[11]

The Puritan myth sends us on our "moral mission." But our orders for that mission are not directly from the Puritans. Our orders are "differently adapted"; our orders are those we wish to receive, those we see through glasses of our own making, those we interpret with our changing worldview. In the final analysis, the identity of the Puritans themselves has little impact upon the American Dream. We rest upon the foundation that they built; yet, each generation sees in them a different strength or a different weakness. The importance is not the Puritans themselves but the legacy they left us—a legacy which we differently adapt to meet our needs. To that extent, at least, we are a nation of Christian origins.

But, you say, if only that were true, if only we could go back to our Christian roots. If only nonbelievers would buy into that.

The point is that Christians and non-Christians alike have bought into this myth, and it is palatable to both. Our culture has perpetuated this basis of the American Dream through the generations. Variously interpreted, it says that we are unique; that we have received by virtue of that uniqueness a specific mission in life; and the mission is the conquest of our individual promised lands. Those promised lands include all frontiers before us—physical, material, spiritual, all things in our way.

The Puritan foundation is palatable to all. When Senator Albert J. Beveridge said some years ago that God has marked the American people as His chosen nation to lead in the regeneration of the world, he could include all, believers as well as unbelievers, within the parameters of "American people."

But what God was he invoking? Granted, he was speaking from the Puritan tradition. But the question is: Is that god the God of the Christian church? Is that god the God of the Bible, the God who revealed Himself to the Israelites, the God we call LORD? As we view our culture and our creed, that is the question we must face.

Just as we see that the images of the Puritans, rather than the factual accounts, are what guide us, we see that the Puritan myth has been differently adapted to fit the circumstances of each generation. But when we invoke the spirit of the Puritans, are we invoking the spirit of the Puritans to support our own human interests rather than seeking the God of the universe? Are we simply invoking the Puritan myth?

Such is the danger of a worldview. This danger plagued the Israelites, the Greeks, the Romans, the Mongols, the British, the Germans, and now, the Americans.

4

THE MYTH OF RESTORATION AND THE NEW BEGINNING:

Morning in America Again

Do not say, "Why were the old days better than these?" For it is not wise to ask such questions.

ECCLESIASTES 7:10

The Puritans were a people who set out to find a new beginning. They sought a perfection here on earth which they thought was promised to them in Scripture. They were a people about whom Fitzgerald's narrator in *The Great Gatsby* spoke, as he stared at the deceased Gatsby's boarded-up and abandoned mansion on Long Island:

Gradually I became aware of the old island here that flowered once for Dutch sailors' eyes [those who transported the Puritans from Holland to America]—a fresh, green breast of the new world. Its vanished trees, the trees that had made way for Gatsby's house, had once pandered in whispers to the last and greatest of all human dreams; for a

37

transitory enchanted moment man must have held his breath in the presence of this continent, compelled into an aesthetic contemplation he neither understood nor desired, face-to-face for the last time in history with something commensurate with his capacity to wonder.

Those Dutch sailors and their Puritan passengers pursued on this continent the last and greatest of human dreams—the restoration to perfection in the promised land.

The image of the restoration and the new beginning has been stamped into the American Dream so that *newness* is sacred, whether it is needed or not. We hear it in political rhetoric, in advertising, in all facets of life. To start over again—whether by moving to a new country or across town, whether by changing jobs or careers, whether by electing a new politician or rehabilitating a convicted one—seems to be as American as apple pie and baseball.

The myth of the restoration and the new beginning is the other side of the coin of the Puritan myth. The myth tells us that our uniqueness and our exclusive mission to conquer our own promised land inherently includes a new beginning and in that new beginning a hope of restoration to perfection.

THE FORCE OF FANTASY

Ernest G. Bormann, in his book, *The Force of Fantasy*, set out to study how the sacred language of the Puritans was adopted into secular use. He expected to find a change from the Puritan rhetoric in the seventeenth and eighteenth centuries to a secular rhetoric which arose after the influence of the Puritans subsided. To his great surprise, the professor of Speech Communication at the University of Minnesota discovered that the secular rhetoric in this country went back to the Great Awakening and ultimately to Puritan sermons.

Bormann confirms what other students of the Puritan movement had said for some time. The Puritan language of metaphor had received new uses in political and economic speech, in artistic expression, and in commercial advertising, but the Puritan imagery—what he calls "fantasy types"—remained constant in the soul of America. The Puritan beliefs have been the spawning ground of the myths of the American Dream.

Bormann sought to identify the original American *fantasies*, meaning the process of developing and sharing symbols among Americans that creates a coherence, an emotional bond, and a shared memory. Bormann writes:

> An example of sharing a group fantasy is the inside joke. The inside joke is a communication incident in which a speaker alludes to a previously shared fantasy with a nonverbal signal or sign or verbal code word, slogan, label, name of the hero or villain or story summary. This brief and cryptic message sparks a response appropriate in mood and tone to the original sharing response when group members first created the consciousness associated with the fantasy.[1]

"To start over again—whether by moving to a new country or across town, whether by changing jobs or careers, whether by electing a new politician or rehabilitating a convicted one—seems to be as American as apple pie and baseball."

An example of fantasy on the national level might be the Marine Corps monument in Washington, D.C., depicting the flag-raising on Iwo Jima. The monument and the newsreel of Marines raising the American flag on the South Pacific island of Iwo Jima has stirred Americans since it actually happened in the Second World War. The picture of those Marines causes in most Americans a shared emotional response similar to the flag-raising at the Olympics.

Bormann confirms that human beings do not see life around them in the abstract but only through stories acted out by real or fictitious characters. Thus, *The Scarlet Letter* could convey a message much stronger than a dozen sociological studies of intolerance in colonial America. Likewise, *Uncle Tom's Cabin* portrayed slavery with a poignancy far beyond the efforts of decades of abolitionists both in the United States and abroad. Today, when we think of the oppression by the government of George III which led to the American Revolution, we do not think of abstract terms or spreadsheets, but of the Boston Tea Party.

The factuality is of little consequence when considering the impact of these stories upon the culture and the cultural worldview. The stories or myths themselves are interpretations of life and, as such, influence the present worldview of our culture. The story itself, as it is retold again and again, is reinterpreted and differently adapted to our present circumstances.

The Puritan group fantasy, according to Bormann, allowed the Puritans to look beyond the extreme hardship of everyday life, of shortages of food and clothing and shelter, and of life in an extremely hostile environment. This vision focused upon each daily detail so that the group and the individuals of the group considered themselves God's agents in the undertaking. A common theme was the goodness of the new beginning—a goodness which overshadowed the hardships. This theme of goodness has been shared by subsequent generations of immigrants to these shores.

THE PERFECT CREATION

In the case of the Puritans, the myth of restoration and the new beginning was founded upon the New World itself. In the isolation of the New World, the Puritan use of biblical language thrived. The restoration was biblical in origin, following, first, the themes of the perfection in the Garden of Eden, and second, the exodus from bondage into the perfection of the new garden, the Promised Land.

However, a new environment confronted the settlers. Coming from Europe where the environment was subdued, the Puritans landed in a world untouched by Western tradition. Yet they viewed this land as God's perfect creation, God's kingdom on earth, God's unblemished gift to them.

This view of the New World, as Robert Bellah writes, carried a broader perspective than the origin of the earth itself:

> According to John Locke, "In the beginning all the world was America." America stood for the primordial state of the world and was indeed seen, by the first generations of Europeans to learn of it, to be the last remaining remnant of that earlier time. The newness which

was so prominent an attribute of what was called the "new" world was taken not just as newness to its European discoverers and explorers but as newness in some pristine and absolute sense: *newness from the hands of God*. (emphasis added)[2]

For the Puritans, the new beginning in the perfect creation was perceived as coming directly to them from the hands of God. The sacred aspect of that newness and that pristine sense stayed with the American political rhetoric through the years and became a critical element of the myths of the American Dream.

DREAM OF PERFECTION

The other half of the myth of the new beginning is the theme of *restoration*. Among the grandest of fantasy types held by the Puritans, the restoration is found in the perfection of the new beginning. To be restored is to wipe out all the failures of the past, wipe the slate clean, and start over again without blemish. The Puritans sought that restoration in the perfect creation in the New World. Today, Madison Avenue flashes that perfection before us on the television screen and in the glossy magazines. We are restored to perfection when we use the product paraded before us.

Whether it is biological or sociological, we all have that yearning for some state of perfection which has been known or perceived to be in our past. Such a yearning, variously called *restorationism, primordialism,* or *primitivism,* has been found in all cultures and religions. Prevalent in the Protestant Reformation, the reformers wished to return the practice of religion to a pristine form of earlier years—return it to the days of the early church. In fact, John Knox once said of Calvin's Geneva, "never has there been a more godly school of saints since the apostles."

Restorationism as a tenet of the Christian faith is based in the Bible. All was well in the Garden of Eden as Adam and Eve lived with God. But after they fell, mankind struggled to re-enter the peace and rest of God, yearning for the time when man would be carried back into the Garden, and restored to the favors of God. The motif appears again in the Exodus and, nearly a millennium later, in the exile. The writings of the prophets are packed with the promises of God's restoration to His holy city, the New Jerusalem. Written in a language more beautiful and poetic than any before or since, the prophets Isaiah and Jeremiah wax eloquent as they weave messages of comfort with condemnation for sin and relay to the ages God's promises to draw His people back to Him like a hen takes chicks under her wings.

The Hebrews constantly sought *shalom* and *shabbat*—peace and rest. They were looking for God's peace and God's rest, concepts which shouted for God's presence and well-being.

The traditions of restorationism are found in the European Enlightenment and in the Muslim Enlightenment of the Middle Ages. In each of these, scholars and academicians sought truth in the writings of the ancient Greeks. Plato, Socrates, Aristotle, et al., resurged from obscurity to establish a way of thinking which was much more influential in academic circles the second time around.

In the American experience, the Puritans left the legacy of restorationism. Richard T. Hughes and C. Leonard Allen, in *Illusions of Innocence*, contend "that recovery of primal norms has been a fundamental preoccupation of the American people. In the quest for identity, both the nation and the nation's religious traditions have employed this perspective with striking regularity."[3]

I once had the opportunity to visit a church which had just opened the doors of a beautiful new facility. As we toured the buildings during the fellowship time between Sunday school and the church service, my host, an immaculately dressed businessman, commented with great satisfaction, "This church is more like the first-century church than any I've seen."

An image of the Apostle Peter in a navy blue suit, starched white shirt, and pink tie flashed to my mind. He drove to this complex in his Mercedes, no doubt. No, this wasn't Peter.

"How so?" I asked.

His eyebrows raised. "How so what?" he said.

"How is this church like the first-century church?"

"Oh," he said, having forgotten his own comment. "You know, in fellowship, in caring for one another. This is a good, growing church, lots of professionals."

I didn't push it any further other than to wonder how we could re-create the characteristics of the first-century church in our churches today. Sometime later I pondered my friend's comment again and recognized the yearning somewhere deep within each of us to return to the past, to restore those small town values, to move to a farm and enjoy the peace of the countryside, to do our own thing, to be free, or any of a number of such expressions which embody the same impulse.

But we have not found that perfection here on earth. The Bible does not say that it is within the power of man to erect that perfection here on earth; it is only within the power of God. Indeed, one of the fundamental themes of the Bible is that man's first sin was the effort to find perfection on his own.

Yet we see again and again in our history the efforts to return to the New Jerusalem, to restore ourselves to a time when we were in the presence of God. The Reformers tried it, the Puritans tried it, Manifest Destiny promised it, the New Agers have chanted it—yet, it does not come.

INDIVIDUAL THEMES

Within the myth of restoration and the new beginning are two themes which mark the early stages of a shift in focus in the American worldview from one which spoke of group aspirations to one which

> *"One of the fundamental themes of the Bible is that man's first sin was the effort to find perfection on his own."*

spoke of individual aspirations. This shift marks the fundamental tension in the American Dream—the tension between commitment to the common good, the group fantasy, and individual advancement, personal fantasy.

The two common themes which integrated the individual into this myth of restoration and the new beginning, as set forth by the Puritan preachers which Bormann studied, were the themes of the individual as *pilgrim* and as *soldier*.

The pilgrim gives himself to discipleship, self-sacrifice, and reflection on the road to sanctification. The characteristics of the pilgrim are more in accord with what we commonly think of as scriptural, that is, a love of God, a love of neighbor, a sharing of personal and spiritual matters for the common good. The theme of the pilgrim supplied the Puritans with a role model which sought after patience, faith, and perseverance in a land which often dealt harsh blows. The role model of the pilgrim allowed the Puritans an emotional response to those blows, which were like the obstacles on the road encountered by Pilgrim in John Bunyan's classic, *Pilgrim's Progress*. As the pilgrim picked his way through those obstacles, he matured and grew faithful in reliance on God's Word and God's promises. He came closer to the Celestial City.

On the other hand, the soldier portrays the road of discipline, militancy, and service as God's instrument for establishing His kingdom on earth. This theme allowed the Puritan to defend himself and fight his neighbors, either fellow Europeans or the Native Americans. The soldier swung God's sword; it was his duty. The theme of soldier provided an excuse when that sword was swung wildly and needlessly. The tension between these themes grew as a harsh environment required a variety of responses to a variety of contingencies.

Both themes are seen in our society today. We use these role models, these fantasies, to justify many of the things which were done throughout our history. The pilgrim theme prompted the settlers to sit down and thank God with the Indians on the day which became known as Thanksgiving. That picture, of course, is symbolized today in our celebration of the autumn and suggests emotional responses far beyond the picture itself. On the other hand, the soldier theme excused the Trail of Tears in which the Cherokee were moved off their land in Carolina and marched westward in an early American version of the Bataan Death March.

Each of those illustrations conjures up in Americans various images and emotional responses which are shared within groups. The more traditional have mental images of the Norman Rockwell paintings of the Indians and the settlers or of the family gathered around the dinner table at Thanksgiving. Those mental images explain our past as well as guide us in our conduct. Likewise, the Trail of Tears conjures up mental and emotional images which divide us emotionally as we identify with or against certain events in our past.

These were the ways in which the Puritans dealt with the newness of the New World. Today, as the context of those themes has changed, the individual uses them as his prerogative. The myth of restoration and the new beginning permits the individual to deal with hostility in life, to strike out on an exodus from the perceived bondage of individual

---

"This shift marks the fundamental tension in the American Dream—the tension between commitment to the common good, the group fantasy, and individual advancement, personal fantasy."

---

situations, and to seek the pristine and absolute newness from the hands of God or the gods of the culture. The myth encourages us that the promised land is there; we simply have to find it in our own restoration.

We see modern shadows of the pilgrim and the soldier in the movie hero, Rocky Balboa. In the movie *Rocky IV*, Rocky's Russian boxing opponent is a man of the most advanced technology. His training program is inside the newest gym with the most modern equipment. Everything is recorded and studied with computer-aided technology. His weight training is on the newest equipment, his breathing and heart rate constantly monitored. He is, in cinematic reality, the embodiment of human technology.

And, of course, we Americans, through our hero Rocky, are out to beat the Russians at their technological game. We can out-technology them any day. Right?

Wrong!

Rocky is not a business-suit executive working for IBM. Rocky is the symbol of American pride and power. He is our pilgrim who will go to the wilds in self-sacrifice.

Reminiscent of Jack London's novel, *The Call of the Wild*, Rocky takes to the hinterlands and trains in the open and hostile fields of the

Russian wilderness—no technological monitors for our hero. He has re-
verted to our beginnings. He is the frontiersman who trains by exercis-
ing not on a Nautilus machine but by lifting logs, not by running on a
computer-controlled treadmill but on the ice-covered trails of the
lonely Russian steppes.

Rocky is our soldier, the loner who will embrace nature to fight the
technological giants of the Soviet Union. As such, he symbolizes an
America longing for the simpler days when life and its philosophies did
not seem so complex. Rocky is the cinematic embodiment of our search
for restoration and a new beginning in the face of cold and uncon-
trolled technological advancement.

THE STRENGTH OF THE MYTH

What is the strength of the myth of restoration and the new beginning?
Enough that we hear talk of a new beginning in every political campaign
at all levels of government. Enough that we look for it in every area of our
personal lives, in the many things described as "life-changing." Enough
that it permits public figures to be granted a second chance upon public
confession—remember Billie Jean King and conversely, Richard Nixon
and Gary Hart in their refusals to confess.

Former UN General Secretary Dag Hammarskjöld wrote that "forgiveness is the answer to the child's dream of a miracle by which what
is broken is made whole again, what is soiled is made clean again."[4] In
restoration, like forgiveness, we are able to wipe the slate clean and
begin again. The new beginning lurks in each of us like a child's dream
to mend what is broken and soiled.

The strength of this myth should not be underestimated when
viewed by the clinical eye of our time. Like all generations of mankind,
we accept our view of the world as the truth and disregard everyone
else's as a set of beliefs based upon the mythology of that culture, even
if it is that of our own fathers. The very fact that we question the
existence of our cultural myths, as based upon the Puritan vision, is
evidence of its strong impact upon our culture.

The Puritan vision should not be considered an oddity, either in
the history of mankind or in the history of America. We must remember that in our own times very few questioned the tremendous mobiliza-

tion of this country for war in 1941 and the hardships it caused. On the contrary, most Americans felt that America was indeed the arsenal of democracy and had an exclusive mission to protect the free world and that America had as its manifest destiny the obligation of conquest over the fascists. Very few questioned whether this country should, when beckoned by JFK in 1960, commit all its power to the space race. Most held the conviction that it was our place in the world to lead the exploration of space and not merely stand by as the Russians launched another series of Sputniks.

The Puritans were simply looking at the front end of a cultural worldview that we still share today. Lest we take our commitment to the myth of the restoration and the new beginning lightly, think a moment about what the new beginning grants us and the consequences of its denial. The new beginning gives us a new lease on life; it gives us liberties which otherwise are unavailable.

In a conversation among seminary students, the topic turned to how this country developed, how we claimed our land, and what right we have to it. "We are quick to tell the Israelis to give back Jerusalem and the West Bank and the Sinai to the Palestinians and the Arabs," one brave soul contended. "Yet we do not want to give back the Great Plains or California or Texas or Florida to the Indians or to the Spanish. We have a whole lot less claim to them than the Israelis have to the West Bank. Our only claim to them is a man-made right of Manifest Destiny, the force of arms and time."

Well, it's different for us, we say! And, so we go on.

CONCLUSION

The myth of restoration and the new beginning has beckoned people to these shores for nearly four centuries. The myth, descending from the Puritans, draws each of us today and explains the hope that many seek in our dreams: the power to make broken things whole again and soiled things clean.

Yet in this myth were the seeds of the shift from collective commitment to individual advancement. For the Puritans, the new beginning was applied in the context of a collective movement. Today, the myth is applied in an individual context. The shift in context is the banner for the course of the American Dream, a course that would be marked by an increasingly individualistic contextualization in the myths of the American Dream. The Puritan myth was being adapted differently to meet changing contexts.

5

THE MYTH OF SACRIFICE AND DISSENT:

"I Regret That I Have But One Life. . . ."

Greater love has no one than this, that one lay down his life for his friends.

JOHN 15:13

As a child in elementary school, one of the most influential pictures impressed upon my mind was the painting of one man standing in the midst of three British soldiers who were about to hang him for espionage. Asked if he had any last words, so the story goes, Nathan Hale responded, "I regret that I have but one life to give for my country." The picture told the whole story.

That picture ranks right up there with other stories like the defense of the Alamo conducted by Davy Crockett, Jim Bowie, and a couple of hundred Tennessee volunteers. It is as striking as Custer's "Last Stand" or the surprise attack at Pearl Harbor.

Sacrifice: To give of one's self for the common good.

49

There is no doubt that in the early years of this country there was plenty of sacrifice to go around. The necessity for sacrifice, one of the major themes to grow out of the Puritan experience, is often contrary to the theme of material gain in the New World. Yet the phenomenon of death and failure had to be accounted for in the emerging American Dream.

However, *sacrifice*, after the Puritan times, began to take on a new meaning. *To sacrifice* meant that one may be injured standing up for his own beliefs, as reflected in the stories of Nathan Hale and the Alamo. As our nation progressed, *sacrifice* came to mean to hold on to one's views regardless of the opposition, necessarily ending dialogue and compromise. While Daniel Webster became the Great Compromiser, others shifted the focus of the myth of sacrifice and dissent from sacrifice in the context of the common good to sacrifice in the context of individual advancement and dissent from the growing institutions in the New World.

SACRIFICE FOR THE COMMON GOOD

SACRIFICE THE COMMON GOOD TO INDIVIDUAL ADVANCEMENT

DISSENT IN AMERICA

The "errand into the wilderness"—as the Puritans called it—certainly had within its theological and sociological roots the necessity for individuals in the community to look out for the common good. But this did not mean that independence was prohibited. Quite the contrary, such a venture took stout-hearted individuals.

Like Abraham coming out of Ur of the Chaldees, like the Israelites coming up out of Egypt, like the remnant returning from exile, the newcomers to the American shores had left their homes, extended families, possessions, in short, whatever fortunes they had accumulated in the Old World. They left all that to come to a wilderness, knowing it to be a wilderness and recognizing that the comforts and securities of their view of civilization were not present in the New World. They were pioneers. And like pioneers in all other eras, they needed a healthy dose of faith, strength, and independence to survive this errand.

But after them came waves of other pioneers from Europe and Asia and Africa, some voluntarily, some on the run, and some as slaves, both indentured and kidnapped. They adopted the language, metaphors, dreams, and myths of the other Americans. These myths gave all newcomers a common bond, a common language, and a common form of expressing their hopes and dreams.

The language and the dreams of the Puritans belonged to them, too. Bormann writes, "By sharing the drama of the founding fathers and *converting it to the salient American vision*, the immigrant could cut free from the Old World visions and become an adherent of the *unifying drama* of the founding of the new vision" (emphasis added).[1]

"As our nation progressed, sacrifice came to mean to hold on to one's views regardless of the opposition, necessarily ending dialogue and compromise."

That "unifying drama" carried on the view of sacrifice for one's beliefs and dissent from the established institutions, including the church and the state, which had characterized the original Puritan exodus from Europe. The new vision of the Puritan communities was one of freedom of worship and expression, freedom from the oppression of man-made institutions. The achievement of this freedom often required dissent and sacrifice.

THE DISSIDENTS

Nearly two centuries elapsed from the time the Puritans came to this country to the time Thomas Jefferson became president. The time between the landing of the Puritans and the writings of Jefferson is roughly equivalent to the time between Jefferson and the present. A lot happened in that time.

The New World was, indeed, the *Great Experiment*, and its lushness invited more experimenting. To the European Puritans, regimentation and compulsory conformity were not the order of the day. But, in America, the Puritan communities grew and overflowed into new communities with a variety of people. The Puritan beliefs expanded with a variety of themes, making it difficult to draw one picture and call it Puritan. To say that one description would do justice to all the Puritans and their progeny would be as inadequate as saying that one picture could describe "businessmen" for the last two hundred years. Businessmen have the same general characteristics, but it would take more than one picture to describe a livery stable owner in the nineteenth century and Howard Hughes in the twentieth century.

There is no question that the first Puritans sacrificed heavily to leave Europe and begin the "conquest" of the New World. That sacrifice began with the first dissent from the Church of England. Yet the myth of sacrifice and dissent, like the others, has been differently adapted over the generations so that the theme remains constant while the context changes.

To sacrifice implies giving up life, liberty, and property, or some other item of value, for the furtherance of the goal. To dissent, in this context, implies an entity which is oppressive. That entity may be religious, political, economic, social, or a number of other things. That entity must be viewed as authoritarian—the Church of England, governmental taxation, parental guidance, and an infinity of other circumstances. One or the other side must be intransigent. Anything less than intransigence allows dialogue, and dialogue, by this definition, renders this kind of dissent needless.

The myth of sacrifice and dissent must have an object as well as a subject. Just as the Church of England was the object of the sacrifice and dissent of the Puritans, so the Puritans became the objects of the myth of sacrifice and dissent of the next generations.

According to this myth, after seeking freedom from the oppression of the European monarchies, the Puritans, or, more appropriately, the generations after the Puritans, created a community marked by apparent intolerance. Granted, they believed that their interpretation and application of God's revelation to them was right because it had come through the illumination of the Spirit. Their theological perspectives, their traditions, and their respect for gifted ministers of the Word led to a certain degree of uniformity in worship, morality, and politics. Such an attitude led to hailing conformity as a virtue.

"Toleration," wrote John Cotton, "made the world anti-Christian." Nathaniel Ward, the self-titled Simple Cobbler of Agawam (prototype for all later rustic Yankee xenophobes), produced a more homely formulation: "My heart has naturally detested four things: the standing of the Apocrypha in the Bible; foreigners dwelling in my country to crowd out native subjects into the corners of the earth; alchemized coins; and tolerations of divers religions, or of one religion in segregant shapes."[2]

In their efforts to solidify their community, they were perceived as acting with pride and prejudice and as excusing their repressive measures as a fight for the purity of the church and of doctrine. Artemus

---

> *"Sacrifice and dissent was honorable for a good cause but took the name of intolerance and obstinacy when it was for the cause of the opposition."*

Ward, an American humorist of the nineteenth century, wrote, "We are descended from the Puritans who nobly fled from a land of despotism to a land of freedom where they could not only enjoy their own religion but prevent everybody else from enjoying his."[3]

The new groups of settlers, mere human beings, began to fuss with their neighbors, and out of that conflict grew several interpretations of exactly who were the chosen people. The new neighbors accused the established neighbors of religious oppression, and a growing intolerance developed. In response, the neighbors built fences and threw stones and called each other inhospitable names. They found themselves "sacrificing" for their newfound beliefs and "dissenting" from the beliefs of others. Sacrifice and dissent was honorable for a good cause but took the name of intolerance and obstinacy when it was for the cause of the opposition.

This myth provides an identity which is nearly as strong as the identity achieved by martyrdom—and it is a lot less painful.

Among those dissidents was Roger Williams.

ROGER WILLIAMS: CHURCH AND STATE

In Geneva, Switzerland, one of the original homes of the Protestant Reformation, the statues of the great Reformers are displayed on the public street in an informal "Reformation Hall of Fame." Roger Williams (1603?–1683), the founder of Rhode Island, is the only American among those great Reformers. Williams, one of the founders of the American Baptist tradition, came to Massachusetts in 1631 and very shortly thereafter became an unceasing foe of what he considered to be the oppression of the religious freedoms exercised by the Puritan communities, the people who had themselves fled England and religious conformity.

Whether Williams was a victim of that oppression or an instigator of it is a disputed matter best left to the interpretations of historians. There are those who contend that the activities of Williams and others precipitated the conflict. The point made here is that the American Dream contains the myth of sacrifice and dissent and that myth can be traced back to the Puritans and the Baptists. The myth of sacrifice and dissent has remained vibrant in the American worldview and is often reinterpreted and differently adapted to fit our needs and circumstances.

The Puritans saw the Baptists and their comrades as the "Separatists" in North America just as many of the Puritans had been dubbed "Separatists" in England. The Puritans sought to cleanse or purify the church of its dross and, in so doing, were not bashful about using the long arm of the law to help in this project.

In 1637, the Puritans tried before a court of law and expelled Anne Hutchison for claiming to have heard a direct revelation from God. She and others moved to what is now Portsmouth, Rhode Island, and paved the way for a large influx into that colony of Baptists, Quakers, and other "unbelievers."

"God requires not a uniformity of religion to be enacted and enforced in any civil state," Williams wrote. Such enforced uniformity "is the greatest occasion of civil war, ravishing of conscience, persecution of Christ Jesus in his servants, and of the hypocrisy and destruction of millions of souls."[4] Compulsory conformity to any religious doctrine, in any context, was, to Williams, simply a matter of "soul rape." Whether these words were the cry of a pure heart or the snarl of an intransigent and defiant spirit is debatable. The fact that it has been reported historically as honorable is a tribute to the strength of the myth.

In 1644, Williams began his own experiment by obtaining from the Parliament of England the authorization to found the Colony of Rhode Island. The Baptists in Rhode Island, despite their own theological problems, took for themselves the shroud of protector of religious freedom.

SOLOMON PAINE

Solomon Paine, a leader of the Separatists, wrote in 1752, that the cause of the separation of church and state is not the fact that there are hypocrites and sinners in the church which will taint the government, but

> it is their being yoked together, or incorporated into a corrupt constitution, under the government of another supreme head than believers, which will not purge out any of the corrupt fruit, but naturally bears it and nourishes it, and denied the power of godliness, both in the government and the gracious effects of it.[5]

Paine, like many other Separatists, was also concerned about the purity of the church. But his concern arose from the threat that unbelievers might take control of the church-state complex and oppress the rights and freedoms of the people to worship God, just as the Roman Catholics had oppressed the European Protestants years earlier. The Separatists argued that if God Himself did not compel human beings to a certain denomination, then far be it from mere mortals to do so. And therein they found the authority to sacrifice and dissent.

Paine and the other dissident Puritans, like Thomas Jefferson a few short years after them, believed in the doctrine of fallen man. Man, with his sinful nature, could not be given the authority to interfere with a matter so sacred as the nature of the worship of God. Throughout history, man had, through the machinations of government, been able to dictate to the populace how and when and why they worshiped God.

For true religious freedom, they proclaimed, there must be checks and balances on the power of fallen humanity. Those checks and balances were most protected in a system which was pluralistic, that is, in a system which allowed the free expression of religious beliefs. For an

individual or a group of citizens to dictate which system should be allowed, the Separatists contended, would violate the rights of all people
who sought religious freedom.

THE GROWTH OF THE REPUBLIC

New European communities developed in North America and took on
unique characteristics. In time, the communities in the New World out-
grew the "New Israel" status and were now made up of merchants, farmers, professionals, day laborers, drifters, and charlatans who saw the new
land as a place to develop, an empire to build, a harvest bank of dollars
with unlimited blank checks. America seemed to offer an opportunity as
yet unknown in the history of mercantilism.
  Bercovitch writes:

> Like the New Englanders, the Maryland and Virginia settlers regarded
> the continent with a wonder commensurate to the unique prospect
> before them. They personified the New World simultaneously as a
> nourishing mother and an undefiled virgin (a mixed metaphor that
> adds pungency to the later concept of the rape of the land)—provid-
> ing material plenty, perennial good health, and moral purity against a
> backdrop of Edenic lushness.[6]

The theology of an American moral mission which found its birth
in Puritan thought hopped the barnyard fence of the Puritan churches
and landed in greener pastures among the cultural and political trends
growing in the colonies. *Sacrifice* now called brave souls to venture west
in the New World to find the other myths of the American Dream.
  The newcomers shared the vision of America brought by the first
Puritans and continued in the generations thereafter. They bought lock,
stock, and barrel the biblical imagery of the New World but they applied that imagery to themselves in a sociological and political manner
as well as a religious manner. Keeping the biblical rhetoric, the new
nation viewed itself on an exodus from the political oppression of the
monarchs of Europe with a mission to conquer the new frontiers of
individual freedom.

THE WALLS OF SEPARATION

Within the myth of sacrifice and dissent is a strong separatist theme. Sacrifice and dissent were remedied, as the myth grew, not by resolution of conflict or by compromise but by separation. The commitment to the collective good became a commitment to an increasingly smaller collec-

---

"The theology of an American moral mission which found its birth in Puritan thought hopped the barnyard fence of the Puritan churches and landed in greener pastures among the cultural and political trends growing in the colonies."

---

tive; the circle of exclusivity was being drawn tighter and tighter. The commitment to the common good, once so pronounced in the Puritan myth, was being differently adapted, that is, contextualized. As time went by, it was taking a back seat to one's "convictions."

As the nation grew, the myth of sacrifice and dissent made it much easier for individuals to leave obligations and follow the exhortation prevalent in the nineteenth century to "go west, young man." The legend of Daniel Boone set the model for just such conduct.

Professor Slotkin writes:

> Essential to his character, and later to his legend, is a paradoxical blend of ambition and self-denial, self-indulgence and equanimity in the face of deprivation. Whenever he was disappointed in business or politics, Boone would simply retire to the woods and the chase: rather than contest his landholding against the lawsuits of newcomers, he deserted Kentucky for Missouri and for the pleasure of the pure freehold, of land won with the rifle.[7]

The example of Boone led many newcomers to sacrifice what they had and seek the new beginning in another locale.

The sacrifice involved was not necessarily for the common good but was often restricted to the good of the individuals involved. In Williams's case, it was restricted to the small group. In Boone's case, it was restricted to the individual. But the impact is much larger than small groups or individuals.

The legend in the nineteenth century concerning the life and death of George Armstrong Custer is a prime example. The story of Custer and his battle at the Little Big Horn colored the views of an entire nation toward its western borders.

Those who opposed Custer, that is, Sitting Bull and his army, did not necessarily think that Custer was sacrificing for the common good when he came to the Little Big Horn region—just as the Puritans, no doubt, did not think that Williams was sacrificing for the common good when he began his own colony in Rhode Island. But Custer's "sacrifice" solidified the resolve of the expanding nation to prosecute more vigorously the westward movement.

However, the popular cry for sacrifice for the common good was superficial at best. Under that banner was a strong theme of opportunity for the individual. The growth of the myth of sacrifice and dissent generated a westward advancement marked not by sacrifice for the common good but by a flood of individuals staking individual claims to the New World. Custer became a mythical hero whose sacrifice cried out to each myth-holder for a vindication marked by blood, money, and individual advancement.[8]

The walls of separation between Native American and Incipient American were established with a vengeance. Each side perceived itself to have sacrificed and neither would back up an inch. This developing myth of sacrifice as the rallying cry for intransigence would be replayed time and again for generations.

CONCLUSION

The theme of sacrifice and dissent was advanced by these incidents and differently adapted to the circumstances. One man's sacrifice called for another's resolve. One man's sacrifice is another man's obstinacy. Yet the myth comes into our cultural worldview as the sacrifice for the growth of the country, the sacrifice for personal beliefs, the courage to stand up and be counted.

This myth marks the continuing shift of the American worldview from the context of the common good to the context of individualism. The result is often a lack of dialogue among the various factions in the culture. Sacrifice, in its original view, may have been a necessary myth to explain the hardships in the "perfection" of the New World. But, as the myth grew and changed, it began to create walls of separation in a country made up of many diverse people.

COMMON GOOD   COMMUNITY
INDIVIDUAL   INDIVIDUAL

METAPHYSICAL
POLITICAL | ECONOMIC

6

THE MYTH OF POLITICAL EQUALITY

"All Men Are Created Equal"

The political is replacing the metaphysical as the characteristic mode of grasping reality.

HARVEY COX, *The Secular City*

One of the strongest myths of the emerging American worldview was the belief that in America each man was free to pursue life, liberty, and happiness in the way he saw fit. Each man could call on his Creator to bring him to the promised land and to conquer his personal New World. The fact that this did not include slaves, women, and those in the bottom caste was not important at the time. Each man had certain inalienable rights which restructured his relationship with the government and with the community around him.

This perception found its way into American life and into the documents which gave structure to the new government. And it grew on the heels of the myth of sacrifice and dissent to carve out a new mode of conduct for the individual American as he lived with his neighbors in the land of the free. The development of this myth over the generations has produced the most "rights-demanding" and litigious society in history.

61

THE REPUBLICANS

The republican ideology, as it arose from the Reformation and the Enlightenment, called for a government of laws which were passed, not by a monarch or any other absolute authority, but by elected officials. The republicans believed that representatives of the people should be elected to speak the will of the people and that government should be submissive to that will.

The early republicans were democratic to the extent that they believed that the people should be able to elect officials to govern the country. They believed, of course, in restrictions upon those who could vote. They did not believe in a pure majority rule but in an organized and duly constituted government. Republicanism called for an adherence to and a supremacy of the laws passed by the representative body. No person or group could be supreme to the laws of the land.

As republicanism was institutionalized in myth, however, it continued to individualize the American Dream. While the thrust of the Puritan myth addressed the collective body in the New World, the adaptation of the basic myth to the republican circumstances focused on the relationship of the individual to the collective body. The "truths" abroad in the land were self-evident, and they were fertilized with the infusion of the individualism of the Enlightenment.

Reichley writes:

> If Puritanism was the most important intellectual and cultural force shaping the American mind in the second half of the eighteenth century, the European Enlightenment was unquestionably the second. The Enlightenment itself had important roots in the individualism and rationalism fostered by Puritanism. Its main impact in America, however, came, as one writer observed, not through "the witch-hunting Puritans of New England" but through "the fox-hunting cavaliers of Virginia."[1]

The republican drama, with its cast of characters, has been repeated frequently in our schools, churches, families, and legislatures, and the emphasis is always the same: the myth is adapted for the individual and grants him political equality before all his neighbors.

THE MYTH OF POLITICAL EQUALITY

One of those Virginia cavaliers was Thomas Jefferson, a leading propo-
nent of the new republicanism and among the chief architects of the
republic. In Jefferson and his writings is a strand of the American
Dream which was directed to each newcomer and defined his relationship to the state and the community.

But who was Jefferson?

In 1988, a storm brewed over the Christmas exhibition of a cross on
a Jackson, Mississippi, government office building, a design made by
leaving certain lights on after working hours. The American Civil Liberties Union and a number of other citizens filed suit to stop the display
of this design.

This suit prompted a spate of letters, pro and con, to the local
newspaper. Many of the letters cited Thomas Jefferson as an authority
for whatever constitutional provision happened to be to the writer's liking. Founder of the nation, Deist, True Christian, slaveholder, aboli-
tionist, atheist, adulterer, and patriot were among the many characteristics attributed to Jefferson. In fact, the descriptions were so broad that
either Jefferson was a horrible schizoid or the writers of these letters
were a bit fuzzy on their history.

It calls to mind the quip from historians Will and Ariel Durant:
"History is mostly guessing and the rest is prejudice."

Viewing this many-faceted Jefferson, an amusing question popped
to mind: Would you want your daughter to marry a man like Thomas
Jefferson?

Most of us would answer quickly, "Why, of course!"

But do we know the historical Jefferson?

His life and attitudes give us keen insights into the interpretations
and applications of "political equality" in our own communities.

Jefferson was conversant in theological as well as political matters.
He held strong beliefs gained from the evolving Western theories of
government and ethics. The foundation for his beliefs rested in the
American myths.

Like Jonathan Edwards, Jefferson turned to the Old Testament for a
parallel to the role and destiny of America. "I shall need," he said in
his second inaugural address, "the favor of that Being in whose hands

we are, who led our fathers, as Israel of old, from their native land and planted them in a country flowing with all the necessaries and comforts of life." (emphasis added)[2]

Jefferson was a republican. No, he was not necessarily a forerunner of Reagan or Bush, nor was he a follower of the early leaders of the Roman republic. But he was a man who believed strongly in the right of the people to govern, the right of the people to be free from oppression, wherever that oppression might originate, and the right of the people to political equality.

The myth of political equality, as developed by Jefferson, held at its center the relationship between the individual and the group of which he was a part. The myth of sacrifice and dissent emphasized that same relationship, but the republican myth took it a step farther. Within the governmental framework was written a philosophy which focused on the rights of the individual as opposed to the rights of the community at large. Many have hailed this as a brilliant step—a step central to the development of this nation and the way future generations of Americans would view themselves in relation to their government and their neighbors.

However, as the myth has developed, political equality has been differently adapted to the individual context. Each person, according to the myth, becomes central to the governing system and may use the system to manipulate those around him in order to accomplish his mission. The court system is no longer a tool for conflict resolution but becomes a sword for personal advancement.

As the myth is differently adapted to the personal context, "my rights" become paramount to the rights of the community. The myth of political equality grants each individual a mandate to defend his piece of the earth from the perceived encroachment, however peaceful, of his neighbor. Such a view is fatal to a sense of community.

THE REPUBLICAN MYTH AND THE CHURCH

The myth of political equality had a tremendous impact on the views Jefferson, and others, held toward the government. The altered relationship, in many ways positive, altered the role of the church in the community by diminishing its cementing effect in the culture. The church and the government in past generations have tended to provide the mortar for the bricks of culture. They have had a socializing and acculturating effect. In the development of the myth of political equality, that role has lessened. The myth has impacted the institutional church

---

"The myth of political equality, as developed by Jefferson, held at its center the relationship between the individual and the group of which he was a part."

---

and initiated the trend known today as privatization of religion—the idea that religion is a private matter and, therefore, to be practiced privately rather than publicly in a body of believers. Government, then, must fill the gap of acculturation and socialization; the political replaces the metaphysical.

Even though he lamented "this loathsome combination of church and state," Jefferson believed that any republic was founded upon religion and could not survive without it. In 1781, he wrote, "Can the liberties of any nation be thought secure, when we have removed their only firm basis, a conviction in the minds of the people that these liberties are the gift of God?"[3]

Yet, the church in North America, as Jefferson saw it, was no longer the moral leader of the community that it had been in the time of Winthrop. The church was perceived by many as moralistic and oppressive as it sought to stave off influences from various sectors of the culture.

Jefferson's view presented the church no longer as a body of believers, whose emphasis was on the body of Christ, but as a gathering of citizens, whose emphasis was the correct government in which each individual could thrive separately. The myth, as designed by Jefferson, not only impacted the role of the church in America by asserting the privatization of religion but also served as a model in future years for the relationship of the individual to the government. The privatization of religion was a forerunner of the privatization of citizenship.

JEFFERSON THE THEOLOGIAN

The impact of the myth of political equality upon the conduct of individual citizens is best illustrated by Jefferson's view of the church. Jefferson's relationship to the church became a model of conduct for an individual's relationship to both church, the government and other institutions and groups in the culture. His conduct put Americans on a path of individualism in which political equality have come to mean: "my rights, right or wrong."

Jefferson's theological writings reflect the views of a man struggling to find his place in the universe. With his emphasis upon individual rights and freedoms, he seems to have resented the authority, assumed or otherwise, of the church.

> [Jefferson's approach] only could have been conceived in the midst of a deeply felt hostility against the orthodox Christian tradition. Jefferson bore the brunt of as much criticism as any major political figure up until the present. Certainly a major object of that criticism was Jefferson's suspect religious views. One who attacked Paul ("the first corruptor of the doctrines of Jesus"), Athanasius ("impious dogmatist"), John Calvin ("atheist") and other venerable purveyors of Christian tradition in his correspondence could hardly expect immunity from public condemnation.[4]

Jefferson was a learned man, but he had his prejudices. He believed that his reading of the Bible was closer to the intent of the text than anyone else's. He had little place for theologians and clergy in his republic. His distrust, in most respects, was not aimed at Jesus but at the church.

In an 1816 letter, Jefferson wrote,

> I am a real Christian, that is to say, a disciple of the doctrines of Jesus, very different from the Platonists, who call me infidel, and themselves Christians and preachers of the Gospel, while they draw all their characteristic dogma from what its Author never said nor saw. They have compounded from the heathen mysteries a system beyond the comprehension of man, of which the great reformer of the vicious ethics and deism of the Jews, were he to return on earth, would not recognize one feature.[5]

Jefferson himself edited a cut-and-paste Bible in which the Gospels were arranged in parallel columns in four languages: Greek, Latin, French, and English. What remained of the Gospels after Jefferson's shears were those portions which would not contradict Jefferson's view of reason—those portions shorn of the miracles and able to stand on their own in front of the critical eye of reason, as reason was seen and defined by the culture of that day.

The structure of Jefferson's Bible sets Jesus, as an individual, in opposition to the Jews, who are cast as the churchmen of that day. Jefferson suggests that the Jewish leaders were not purveyors of the truth but of falsehood and, by analogy, the churchmen of Jefferson's day, like the Jewish leaders, were also the purveyors of falsehood.

Lest there be any doubt about Jefferson's views toward the churchmen of his day, he wrote in 1820, concerning his Bible:

> I abuse the priests [churchmen], indeed, who have so much abused the pure and holy doctrines of their master, and who have laid me under no obligations of reticence as to the tricks of their trade. The genuine system of Jesus, and the artificial structures they have erected to make him the instrument of wealth, power, and preeminence to themselves, are as distinct things in my view as light and darkness: and, while I have classed them with soothsayers and necromancers, I place him [Jesus] among the greatest of the reformers of morals and scourges of priestcraft that has ever existed. They felt him as such, and never rested until they had silenced him by death. But his heresies against Judaism prevailing in the long run, *the priests have tacked about, and rebuilt upon the temple which he destroyed, as splendid, as profitable, and as imposing as that.* (emphasis added)[6]

Jefferson viewed Jesus as one who had come to reform the religiosity of the Jewish church of His day. It may not be too far wrong to suggest that Jefferson viewed himself in the same light. He was purifying government in the political arena. In the same manner, he was attempting to purify the church, to restore it to its roots, to cleanse it of the dross which had crept in over the centuries. In that sense, Jefferson was trying to restore the early purity of Christianity. However, he was overlooking the community of the early church and replacing it with a privatization in which the individual stood against the church as merely another organization from which to dissent and to establish individual rights. The result, of course, was the diminution of fellowship in the body of Christ.

Lest we judge him too harshly, we must recognize what he has done. The importance of Jefferson's work lies in its application of the growing American worldview to the church, the community, and the government. He has taken the cultural views of his day—those of the Enlightenment, those of an era of intense antiestablishmentarianism, those of intense iconoclasm in many disciplines—and he has applied them to theology. He was not, as some claim, an atheist or a deist. Indeed, as noted above, he protested that he was a "real Christian"—a character flaw many of us have today.

That Jefferson's cultural biases should have colored his theology should not shock us. Remember that most of Jefferson's writings concerning religion were after the American Revolution and the French Revolution, in which the French philosopher Voltaire declared the cathedrals liberated from God and converted to Temples of Reason. We should recall that many through the ages have done much the same, including such luminaries as Tertullian, St. Augustine, St. Thomas Aquinas, and John Calvin.

His view of the church illustrates the foundation of the myth which led to a reassessment of individualism in the new nation. Jefferson's conduct would provide a model which would guide conduct for centuries to come. However, the illustration applies not only to the church but—as it developed through the generations—to the government, the neighborhood, and eventually, the family. Jefferson's attitude of antagonism to the institutional church, justified or not, laid the groundwork for a spirit of antagonism toward all institutions. Political equality drew a line of antipathy between the role of the individual and the role of the group.

INDIVIDUALISM VERSUS COMMITMENT IN THE MYTH OF POLITICAL EQUALITY

The myths of the American Dream to this point had centered largely on the concept of the public good. They were traditions aimed at the group. The myth of political equality continued the shift of emphasis to the individual, yet it was seen as the only way to keep the collective body healthy and to promote the common good. Indeed, the preamble to the Constitution of the United States reads, "We, the people, in order to form a more perfect union . . . promote the general welfare,

---

"The new American man was a frontiersman who, at least in his own vision, had set out on his mission to conquer his promised land."

---

and secure the blessings of liberty to ourselves and our posterity, do ordain and establish this Constitution . . ." The preamble suggests that the goal of the Constitution is for the government to promote the common good.

Yet the individual had a new role in the developing American mythology, and that role was not subservient to any authority. The new American man was a frontiersman who, at least in his own vision, had set out on his mission to conquer his promised land.

Many might say that this is a tenet of Protestantism, that the disregard of tradition solely because it is tradition—a characteristic well-known in today's culture—is the way station at the end of the road taken by Luther and Calvin and their followers. To be sure, that characteristic which many ascribe to our individualism was well entrenched in the 1830s when French sociologist Alexis de Tocqueville observed our young republic.

> Individualism is a recently coined word to express a new idea. Our fathers only knew about egoism. Individualism is a calm and considered feeling which disposes each citizen to isolate himself from the mass of his fellows and withdraw into the circle of family and friends; with this little society formed to his taste, he gladly leaves the greater society to look after itself. . . . Such folk owe no man anything and hardly expect anything from anybody. They form the habit of thinking of themselves in isolation and imagine that their whole destiny is in their hands.[7]

The statement by Tocqueville describes America today much more accurately than it describes those coming to this continent in the

1600s. And while it was written two hundred years after the Puritans first came to America, it marks a strong departure from the view of the community-oriented settlers who were building the country.

Therein lies the tension presented by the myth of political equality. There is no question that the American culture, like many other cultures, has been one of frequent tensions. The conduct described by Tocqueville is a direct result of the trends created in the American myths of sacrifice and dissent and political equality. Jefferson wrote it and lived it; we carry it to new heights.

As we begin to view ourselves individually, indeed, our focus is more on ourselves and our personal affairs. There is little left for the common good. We isolate ourselves in our own worldview.

7

THE MYTH OF THE SELF-MADE MAN:

Rags to Riches

And I saw that all labor and all achievement spring from man's envy of his neighbor. This too is meaningless, a chasing after the wind.

ECCLESIASTES 4:4

After the murder of the Great Gatsby, F. Scott Fitzgerald's narrator, Nick Carraway, looks through the personal effects of the once-wealthy and idealistic young man whose life had given meaning to the phrase, the American Dream. Carraway comes across a diary in Gatsby's handwriting. Among the writings he finds a daily schedule for work and study, symbolic of the characteristic of discipline. These notations are reminiscent of Benjamin Franklin's *Poor Richard's Almanack*.

The message of the story is that Gatsby, a man who followed the American Dream as projected in the life and thoughts of Benjamin Franklin, did not find happiness with the accomplishment of his dream to rekindle his love affair with his one-time flame, Daisy Fay. Nor did he find success in his endeavors to create a life of leisure and wealth among the elite and the not-so-elite of New York City. Rather, Gatsby's promise-filled life met a tragic and violent end.

In spite of Fitzgerald's comment on the American Dream, accumulating material wealth, typified and given structure in the image of Franklin himself, has become what most Americans see as the greatest offering of the New World. Whether that offering is an actual reality or not is irrelevant. The fact remains that it is accepted as one of the prime myths of the American Dream.

This myth is the heartbeat of America: the myth of the self-made man. (If you just hummed the second part of that couplet: "Today's Chevrolet," you are familiar with one aspect of the American mythology.) This myth was born and raised in the Puritan and Republican myths and blossomed into a myth in its own right, unsurpassed by any others in the nineteenth and twentieth centuries.

BENJAMIN FRANKLIN—SELF-MADE MAN

The most likely person responsible for the birth of this myth—if, indeed, it can be said that any one person was responsible for the birth of this myth—was Benjamin Franklin (1706–1790). Franklin fostered the cultural myth that it is a right of every American to come to his new world and conquer that new world by building a personal empire and by increasing in material wealth.

Professor Bercovitch writes: "That same Puritan myth, differently adapted, encouraged . . . Franklin to record his rise to wealth as a moral vindication of the new nation."[1] Franklin was indeed the prototype of the self-made man.

Inventor, philosopher, diplomat, author, and politician, Franklin was the hero of individualism in America. Born into a family of modest means, he became world-renowned first for his inventions, and later for his diplomatic and political representation of the new nation. Franklin's life, through his publications—*Autobiography* and *Poor Richard's Almanack*—became the model for many Americans. His life became a myth in itself which beckoned men of modest means from all parts of the world to follow in his footsteps along the path to the American Dream.

The *Autobiography* is ostensibly written to his son, telling him how he received the advantages he found in life. It is, of course, a story celebrating his wisdom and craftiness, written in aphorisms and proverbs and designed to set a model for his son and others to follow. Much more than an autobiography, it is a moral code on how to conduct a useful life.

Franklin had an agenda in his writing. The *Autobiography* was "a public relations piece not only for himself but for America, and in developing the hero of his memoirs he created a typical American of the kind he wanted to see settle in this country."[2]

Franklin explains:

> In this Piece [*The Autobiography*] it was my Design to explain and enforce this Doctrine, that vicious Actions are not hurtful because they are forbidden, but forbidden because they are hurtful, the nature of man alone considered: That it was therefore everyone's Interest to be virtuous, who wished to be happy even in this World. And I . . . have endeavored to convince young Persons, that no Qualities were so likely to make a poor Man's Fortune as those of Probity and Integrity.[3]

Perhaps this is advice that should be given in business schools today. One thinks of the slogans, "What's good for General Motors is good for America," or "The business of America is business." Or more recently, one cringes at the character Gecko in the movie *Wall Street*, proclaiming that greed is good for America.

We look with relief back to the advice of our Founding Father, Franklin. Yet we see that even in this passage he sees "Probity and

> *"The most likely person responsible for the birth of this myth—if, indeed, it can be said that any one person was responsible for the birth of this myth—was Benjamin Franklin."*

Integrity" in an individualistic sense. Rather than promoting the greatest good for the greatest number, "Probity and Integrity" are considered a means to make the "poor Man's Fortune." "Probity and Integrity" are seen in their usefulness or utility, as a means to an end and not as an end in themselves.

Probity and integrity are tools with which the man of modest means may advance himself—"make" himself—in the business world. In the eyes of a culture inured to the blatant thievery of Wall Street, these observations seem idealistic. Yet in the embryonic stages of a nation burdened with a hangover from European feudal economic systems, the outward focus on individual advancement over the common good was a substantial shift in worldview.

Just as the *Autobiography* was an argument for a life-style, *Poor Richard's Almanack,* first published in 1733, is more of an instructional manual on life than an almanac. An almanac is designed to give the reader a variety of factual information which the reader may need in day-to-day life. An almanac usually tells the reader about the times of the seasons, the lengths of days, distances between places, definitions for certain words. It is, in short, a storehouse of practical data.

Poor Richard's Almanack, on the other hand, gives us wisdom on how to live. "Early to bed and early to rise, makes a man healthy, wealthy and wise," "A penny saved is a penny earned," and "God helps those who help themselves" are samples of the practical information with which this almanac enlightens its readers. The information is economic in the sense that it is designed to instruct the boy of humble origins in how to become the man of material wealth, after the model of Franklin himself. It is individualistic in the sense that it is aimed at the greatest good for the individual rather than the greatest good for the greatest number.

While Franklin can be said to have started the move towards the pursuit of the self-made man, he cannot be blamed as the author of today's brand of it. In fact, the model of Franklin's life is that of commitment to community, that the end of personal achievement is the common good.

FRANKLIN AND CHRISTIANITY

Franklin was among those who had little argument with the teachings of Jesus Christ. But he did have a bone to pick with those who made up the church of Jesus Christ. Franklin wrote to a friend of the parable in which the man went to heaven and told St. Peter that he should be admitted because he was a Presbyterian.

"What is that?" St. Peter responded.

The man told him and St. Peter, still not understanding the term, said that there were none of those in heaven.

The man in desperation mentioned several different denominations, but St. Peter again said he had never heard of any of those either. Then the man saw his wife through the gate and said, "I'm with her. We're the same religion."

"Oh," St. Peter said. "Why didn't you say you were a Christian in the first place?"[4]

Like Solomon, Franklin instructed through proverbs and parables and wise sayings rather than doctrinal statements. The doctrinal statements of the church were, in Franklin's eyes, of little value to anyone. Straight talk about life would benefit the people in America, and that straight talk centered on Franklin's belief of how we should live.[5]

Shortly before his death, Franklin gave, in a letter to a friend, his creed. He said that he believed in one God who had created the universe and ruled over it. He believed that man's soul was immortal and that there would be rewards and punishments in the afterlife based upon the individual's conduct. Yet he thought that the best service that could be rendered to God was service to fellowman; Franklin was adamant about that tenet of the faith. God wanted us to help our fellowman, to love our neighbors as ourselves.[6]

Franklin admitted to some doubts about the deity of Christ, yet he affirmed Christ's wisdom and morality. Franklin did not want to be pinned down on the question of the historical Jesus but was straightforward in saying that Jesus' system of religion, while of the greatest wisdom ever known, had been corrupted by its practitioners over the years.

The import of Franklin's relationship with the church is that it created, in tandem with the republican myth, the avenue for privatization of religion by further establishing a model in which the new American saw life separate from the church. The individual was privileged to discover a private faith separate from the body of Christ. The schism between religious and secular life, perhaps known in every age, now had a model which legitimized the separation in the growing nation.

This idea of separation, of course, carried over into other areas of life so that each person in subsequent generations, following the model started by Franklin, could walk a path of increasing individualism and isolation from other people and of increasing compartmentalization of life.

THE ECONOMIC BRAND OF INDIVIDUALISM

Franklin's view of economic individualism certainly had room for the development of the common good. Yet beneath the discussion of the public good was a tremendous emphasis on individual advancement. The advancement of the individual seemed to translate to the advancement of the culture at large—"What's good for General Motors is good for America." That philosophy of life was the embryo of the American brand of business.

The American brand of business developed in this country as laissez-faire economics. There was a time in the nineteenth century when the sweatshops in the cities, unregulated by the government or the church or anyone or anything other than avarice, approached the social horrors found in England. The way a citizen made his living was one of the rights accorded him by the Constitution and, according to the myth, he could seek life, liberty, and happiness any way he saw fit. And the free-market economy could not or would not prevent any of the excesses.

But, for many, this is not and was not the view of the early days of American mercantilism. As the industrial revolution grew and changed the growing country, the economic understanding of the country came not from a Dickensian sweatshop, not from an exposé à la Sinclair Lewis, and not from the struggles of nameless, faceless Eastern Europeans or Asians.

The myth of rags to riches, given birth by Franklin, grew to manhood in a clean figure untouched by the sweatshops or the excesses of mercantilism. The myth burst forth from the pen of Horatio Alger (1834–1899), a Unitarian minister who wrote in New York City. Alger's stories of the travels "from rags to riches" introduced not only an idiom to the language but a model for individual advancement for generations to come.

Alger wrote in excess of a hundred novels in which he glamorized the journey to the accumulation of wealth and opened the possibility and hope for every new person who arrived in America. Such books as

Ragged Dick (1867), *Sink or Swim* (1870), and *Tattered Tom* (1871) provided the model for economic individualism for the new nation. The American mythical hero became the young, industrious man who could come to the new world and build an empire for himself with unlimited

---

"The myth of rags to riches, given birth by Franklin, grew to manhood in a clean figure untouched by the sweatshops or the excesses of mercantilism."

---

riches—the new heaven and the new earth came not to the faithful but to the individual who had faith in the American way. The American pilgrim had found his path to the Celestial City paved with dollar signs. By following this path, he attained the status which came to be revered in America: He was a self-made man.

But what was fine in myth and metaphor began to tell a tale of tragedy in practice.

The so-called robber barons were those industrialists who accumulated wealth at all social and human costs. John D. Rockefeller, Sr. (1839–1937), founder and owner of the Standard Oil Company, was sufficiently wealthy that he was able to control the railroads by withholding his business from them if they did not do as he wished. When they became interested in shipping the oil of other companies, he relented on the condition that the railroads charge the companies an extra dime per barrel and pay it to him. As a result of this and other acts of the robber barons, the Interstate Commerce Commission was created to regulate the shipment of oil and other goods in interstate commerce.

Commodore Cornelius Vanderbilt (1794–1877), one of the robber barons of the nineteenth century, was, according to tradition, confronted with a law which hindered his shipping business. A self-made man himself, he had built his vast shipping empire from one ferry boat between New York and Staten Island. When he insisted that he would do as he pleased, regardless of what the law said, his lawyers cautioned restraint. In a huff, Vanderbilt shouted at his lawyers, "What do I have to do with the law? Ain't I got the power?"

THE STRENGTH OF THE MYTH OF THE SELF-MADE MAN

There is no doubt that the rags-to-riches model has been an inspiration to many over the generations. This model, however, is a personal one, an individual one. Not only is it claimed by the individual, it is one which today is rarely thought about in collective terms. When we think about accumulating wealth, we think about it in terms of business, music, athletics—the accumulation for one individual rather than for a group. One notable exception may have been JFK's call for this country to land a man on the moon by the end of the 1960s. That was a call for collective action, but that is not what normally comes to mind when we think of the American Dream.

Through the political documents, through American literature, through economic and religious and political practices, the myth soon became ingrained in American life and flew as a banner for the new-comers to these shores who were seeking wealth and fortune. The explanatory potential of this myth was overwhelming, to the extent that nearly any conduct, however outrageous, could be justified in the name of the American Dream.

The myth had a religious ring to it and appealed to nearly every-one, as if it had the stamp of God on it and was written in the Holy Scripture itself. It filled the bill for the times and provided the rationale for the assault on "the fresh, green breast of the New World."

Howard Hawks' 1940 movie, *Red River*, starring John Wayne, was among the first cinematic comments on the Horatio Alger model of the self-made man. Wayne plays a man who comes to Texas after the War Between the States and stakes a claim to the land "as far as the eye can see" (an interesting play on the covenant with Abraham and a comment on today's interpretation of it). He has no time to build a family or friendships. He is too busy with empire building, too intent on trampling anyone who will get in his way, too occupied by living the American Dream.

He takes on a young cowhand and treats him like a son. As the "son" grows up, he takes over the business. The denouement is reached when Wayne confronts the "son" over a business judgment which protects the lives of the employees at the cost of the accumulation of greater wealth. As they approach a gunfight, Wayne comes to the life-

---

"The explanatory potential of this myth was overwhelming, to the extent that nearly any conduct, however outrageous, could be justified in the name of the American Dream."

---

changing recognition that the empire he spent his life building is not worth the killing of a loved one.

The artistic comment on American life was always directed to someone else. The siren song of riches and power on the American shore is so great that only the bravest and wisest among us are able to resist its sweet music.

I recall talking to a young soldier who had just gotten off active duty. He was lamenting the fact that he and his wife each had to work two jobs to make ends meet. When I asked why they were working those hours, he responded proudly that they needed that much money to make the house payment—a house which was in a very fashionable part of Nashville.

"I decided," he informed me, "that I wasn't going to settle for some little house. I want a mansion. I want the biggest house in the neighborhood. That's why I bought where I did."

Somewhat puzzled that a young veteran would buy a house under those circumstances, I asked what his goals were.

"I want money," he said quite frankly. "And I'll work for it. My goal is to be able to waltz into any car dealership in Nashville and point out the most expensive car and turn to my accountant and say 'Write a check for it.'"

"Have you considered the effects that might have on your marriage and on any family you may wish to have?"

"All that will be taken care of when it comes," he assured me.

"You may be building your house on sand," I suggested.

"Doesn't make any difference," he shrugged. "My goal is to have money. Nothing else matters."

Over the years we have lost the Puritan view that work is for the common good and have accepted a distorted view of the Franklin doctrine which dictates to the very fiber of our culture that work is for personal advancement.

The additon of the myth of the self-made man encouraged the shift of the worldview from the common good to the advancement of the individual. The focus, of course, has tremendous drawing power and can result in great personal rewards. But the logical extension of the shift from the common good to unfettered individualism is a crisis of definition at the core of any community.

8

THE MYTH OF INDIVIDUALISM I:

The Search for the Soul

There is one spectacle grander than the sea, and that is the sky; there is one spectacle grander than the sky, that is the interior of the soul.

VICTOR HUGO, *Les Miserables*

A popular tune of the 1960s and 1970s sings of the good life and then, in a stifled cry, asks, "Is this all there is?" The singer has seen the best the American material life has to offer, yet concludes, like the writer of Ecclesiastes, that all is vanity, that pursuing material things in this life is chasing after the wind.

The response to the era of the robber barons, in some circles, created another tension in the American worldview—the questioning of the soul. Is this all there is? Is making and accumulating wealth the sole purpose for man's existence on this earth? These are among the questions which caused the American in the nineteenth century to look into the inner reaches of the soul.

The resulting myth was the search for meaning in life, the search for the soul of the American pioneer. The quest for material wealth certainly did not fall by the wayside. Indeed, it has remained at the forefront as the prime focus of many Americans to this day. Yet, that material abundance was not shared with all and, while satisfying a few, left many in search of another truth in life, a truth found inside the person, in the soul of the new American. The American Dream could be defined not only in material acquisition but in understanding and celebrating the soul.

Economic materialism is a pervasive factor in our cultural beliefs. While this country likes to consider itself concerned with the value of human life, we have all seen the individuals and corporate entities who are more concerned with material items than with the welfare of others. And we have all read the literature lamenting that situation.

The tension of the value of property versus the value of the person arose early in the history of this nation. In the early days of this country, in most states, the criminal codes dictated greater penalties for certain property crimes than crimes of violence against the person. In Tennessee, for example, voluntary manslaughter, often simply defined as the taking of life in the heat of passion, carried a lesser penalty than grand larceny (stealing property over the value of fifty dollars) or simple robbery (taking property from the person of another by threat without using a deadly weapon). It is difficult to argue that our early state governments were greatly concerned with the value of human life when life was devalued compared to property.

As the American worldview concentrated more and more on individual and material acquisition, there were those who followed that concentration in pursuit of the spiritual truths of life. In looking inward, they were adding to the body of American myths which increasingly isolated the individual from the culture around him. This path toward individual isolation would result in a nation which has come to find great difficulty in achieving community in any sector. On the road to finding the soul, the search led the seekers down a path of unending individualism toward the eventual end of destruction of community in the American culture. The myth of individualism bids us to find the "self" before we find anything else.

THE TRANSCENDENTALISTS

The leader of the departure from the growing materialistic view of the economic tradition was Ralph Waldo Emerson (1803–1882), a Harvard-

educated Unitarian minister, often called the Father of Transcendental-
ism in America. A man of poor health, Emerson stepped down from the
pulpit at age twenty-nine and toured Europe, where he met and be-
friended the poets Samuel Taylor Coleridge and William Wordsworth
as well as the essayist Thomas Carlysle, who was to be a lifelong friend.[1]

**"The response to the era of the robber barons,
in some circles, created another tension in the
American worldview—the questioning of the
soul. Is this all there is?"**

Emerson believed that the soul transcends material things, that life
is much more than what you can see or feel. "The one thing in the
world which is of active value," he wrote, "is the soul."

He closed his essay, "Self-reliance," with these lines:

A political victory, a rise of rents, the recovery of your sick or the
return of your absent friend, or some other favorable event raises your
spirits, and you think good days are preparing for you. Do not believe
it. *Nothing can bring you peace but yourself.* Nothing can bring you
peace but the triumph of principles. (emphasis added)

Emerson made a lasting impact on fellow Americans Walt Whitman, Henry David Thoreau, and William James, as well as British author Matthew Arnold and German philosopher Friedrich Nietzsche. As
an author and lecturer, Emerson's views were rich with the images of
nature and naturalism. He called for expression and action on the part
of individual persons. His 1837 lectures at Harvard, entitled "The
American Scholar," were called by Oliver Wendell Holmes, the "intellectual Declaration of Independence."

The Transcendentalists, many of whom were Unitarian ministers,
followed Emerson and believed that the spirit had left the church and
had been substituted by material views. The church must surge ahead,
they thought, and give the congregations a new vision of spirituality.
The spirit was real; material things were only shadows of that reality.

WALT WHITMAN

The search for the soul was greatly advanced by the life and works of American poet Walt Whitman (1819–1892). Born in New York, Whitman began his adult life as a newspaper reporter and, at age nineteen, he published, edited, and delivered his own newspaper on Long Island.

His first volume of poems, *Leaves of Grass,* was published in 1855 and underwent nine more printings during his lifetime. Whitman's poems and his newspaper writing showed that he was a socially active man and that his interests were more in the people with whom he interacted, the lives he crossed in his activities, and the expressions of humanity that teemed in the cities. Unlike others of his generation, Whitman cared less about how to advance the individual than about how to recognize the individuality in the individual.

Whitman's emphasis on sensuality and spirituality is expressed in the first three words of the poem, "Song of Myself." "I celebrate myself," Whitman begins, and this is the key to Whitman's life.

For Whitman, success in life was learning, experiencing, and living. Life was measured in the soul rather than the wallet. Whitman's influence upon the next generations was tremendous. His impact upon the development of the American worldview is unlimited.

Whitman viewed America as a land of ideas, the land of "the American idea . . . the great Idea, the idea of perfect and free individuals." Whitman wrote, "The chief reason for being the United States of America is to bring about the common good will of all mankind, the solidarity of the world." "The common good will" was distinct from the common good sought by the Puritans and the individual rights sought by the republicans. "The common good will" was the opportunity of each individual to find his new world within himself and to conquer that new world by the full understanding and expression of the soul.

Free individuals were Whitman's view of the American Dream. The Puritan myth and the myth of restoration and the new beginning were differently adapted to the circumstances and isolated within the soul. Whitman called for Americans to lead themselves on an exodus from the world of materialism to the conquest of the promised land which would be found within themselves.

NATHANIEL HAWTHORNE

The dark side of the American worldview began to appear in the arts of the nineteenth century, for example, in the works of Nathaniel Hawthorne. In his novel, *The Scarlet Letter*, the heroine, Hester Prynne, is caught in adultery and required by the village leaders to wear a scarlet "A" on her chest.

As a heroine, Hester Prynne is, in Professor Bercovitch's words, "Hawthorne's 'living sermon' against the 'haughty and carnal' Mrs. Hutchinson, who 'could find no peace in this chosen land.'" Comparing Hester to the biblical Esther, Bercovitch writes:

> As her name implies, she is the "hidden one" who emerges as the star of a new age. Christologically, the "A" she wears expands from "Adulteress" to "angelic." Historically, as the "A" for America. It leads from the Puritan utopia to that brighter period when the country will fulfill its "high and glorious destiny."[2]

The theme of the persecution of Hester Prynne becomes the theme of the persecution of the pure goals and intentions of America. The purity of America, according to Hawthorne, has been adulterated by the intolerance of the institutional church, by the new American view of individualism, and by rejection of the values of the New World. It is a call to the primordial sense that America was pure in the beginning. America, so Hawthorne thought, had to transcend the adulteration and reach the potential of the promised land—a potential found not only in nature but also in the heart.

HERMAN MELVILLE

The reflections of the darker side of the American worldview also appear in the classic, *Moby Dick*, a complex novel which investigates, among other things, religion and individualism. Captain Ahab is the symbol of the new American individual, restrained by nothing except that mission to conquer for himself and himself alone all that the New World has to offer—from the "dumb brute" of nature to the white purity of God.[3] Ahab's maniacal crusade is representative of the singularly

American view of its mission to conquer all that was out there to be conquered.

The imagery and dialogue of the novel stress that the biblical mandate to have dominion and stewardship over the earth has turned to a wild flight of singular and obsessive proportions. Melville suggests that our commitment to the common good based on biblical principles has been distorted into a "survival of the fittest" free-for-all on the pristine pastures of the New World.

THE STRENGTH OF THE MYTH OF INDIVIDUALISM

It is not difficult to sense in these writings the rejection of the materialistic and the search for the soul of the individual and the pure soul of America. This myth, like the others, was based upon the Puritan myth but was developed over changing times in a context which yearned for new answers. This myth of individualism started down a path which took it to a destination far beyond the soul. As America met the challenges of the twentieth century, the transcendentalist view of spirituality in the church gradually changed colors when placed on the background of European philosophy and existentialist alienation.

The search for the soul was no longer a myth of man seeking harmony in the perfection of the new world of the heart but was transformed into a myth of isolation, alienation, and relativism in a new world unconnected to God or country or honor. Francis Schaeffer called this shift in the views of truth the most dangerous thing facing the church in the twentieth century. The American Dream, according to this myth, was found in the exclusive mission of each of us to find a sense of perfection in the conquest of the new world of meaninglessness in life. Nearly a century after the transcendentalists searched for a new spirituality, the "Lost Generation"—a phrase coined by author Gertrude Stein for the American expatriates living in Paris in the 1920s—denied that spirituality and searched for the meaning of self.

The myths which make up the American Dream have indeed been differently adapted to meet a changing culture. New York City in the 1990s is not the Long Island which, in Fitzgerald's words, once "flowered for Dutch sailors' eyes—a fresh, green breast of the New World." Things have changed, and we change with them. The myths which reflect the beliefs of our culture change in response to the changing culture. All of American mythology seems to have dovetailed into the myth of individualism. The model provided by Franklin in *Poor Richard's Almanack* is a far cry from the model represented by Captain Ahab in *Moby Dick* or the old man in *The Old Man and the Sea* or Gecko in *Wall Street*.

"Nearly a century after the transcendentalists searched for a new spirituality, the 'Lost Generation'—a phrase coined by author Gertrude Stein for the American expatriates living in Paris in the 1920s—denied that spirituality and searched for the meaning of self."

But alive and well among the myths is the original theme: uniqueness, exclusive mission, and conquest. The language may be much more subtle. It may be hidden in advertisements in glossy magazines or in six-figure television commercials on sporting events or in the steamy pages of romance novels, but the language is still there. The stories change and the themes drift slightly with them. Yet the farther these stories and themes stray from their original emphasis on community, the darker the stories are. *Moby Dick* sounded the alarm a century and a half ago. The farther the stories and themes stray from a dependence upon God and venture into the search for a sound reliance upon man, the greater the sense of alienation and angst. The farther these stories and themes stray from their original context in the New World, the dimmer the hope that we shall ever find perfection in the New Jerusalem.

THE CRISIS AHEAD

The American Dream has come a long way and so has the nation. The Dream has undergone great contextual changes and therein lies the crisis ahead. The metamorphoses in the myths from a nation of people who were dedicated to the common good to a nation of people who are self-seekers has sent this nation into the worst crisis of its history. The model before us is not one in which we help our fellow man but one in which we shout, "Am I my brother's keeper?" as we dodge personal responsibility on the pathway to the new world of material accumulation and unbridled self-adulation.

No longer do we know our heritage. The pathway to individualism is a pathway in which we burn our bridges behind us.

We would do well to recall the counsel of Moses:

> When the LORD your God brings you into the land he swore to your fathers, to Abraham, Isaac and Jacob, to give you—a land with large, flourishing cities you did not build, houses filled with all kinds of good things you did not provide, wells you did not dig, and vineyards and olive groves you did not plant—then when you eat and are satisfied, be careful that you do not forget the LORD, who brought you out of Egypt, out of the land of slavery. Fear the LORD your God, serve him only and take your oaths in his name. Do not follow other gods, the gods of the peoples around you. (Deuteronomy 6:10–14)

9

THE MYTH OF INDIVIDUALISM II:

The Individual in Crisis

See to it that no one takes you captive through hollow and deceptive philosophy, which depends on human tradition and the basic principles of this world rather than on Christ.

COLOSSIANS 2:8

As we discuss the Transcendentalists and their contribution to the myths of the American Dream, we think also of philosophy and philosophers and ask why we discuss it at all. How does it affect us today? What is the application for us in the modern world? After all, we've come a long way since the time of the Puritans and the Transcendentalists and even the robber barons.

Why do we care at all about the myths and philosophies of the last century? That's a question that many a college freshman has asked, usually in a state of perplexity somewhere between Plato and Diogenes. What good is it anyway? Why should we sit around and contemplate whether the chair we are sitting on is really a chair? Why should we ask if something really exists? We often feel like Samuel Butler who wrote that all philosophies, if you ride them home, are nonsense; but some are greater nonsense than others. If I can see it or feel it or touch it, the college freshman laments, I know it's there.

The simple answer for our college freshman is: We study philosophy because we do it, because we all live out our philosophies of life whether we can articulate them or not. We all act out our myths. Philosophy, shining through the prism of our daily lives, is the theoretical aspect of our mythical structures, the mortar which holds the mythical bricks of our worldview. When the mortar or the bricks fail, the wall comes down.

The college freshman scratches the back of his head and mutters that the simple answer sounds a whole lot like the hocus-pocus that he's read from Kant or Schleiermacher or, for that matter, Will Rogers or Leo Durocher.

THE CRISIS OF THE INDIVIDUAL

The result of the search for the soul and the growth of unrestrained individualism is the loss of relationship to the past, to our foundations, and to the myths which have given meaning and purpose to our lives. The salient American vision is lost in a blur of individual myopia. Individualism is no longer the unifying American drama but a drama which divides and alienates and pits neighbor in competition with neighbor.

This trend has raged unchecked as the American has continued to look inward to himself as the ultimate purpose for life. The more he looks inward, the less he can see outward. And the less he can see outward, the more vulnerable is the society in which he lives.

John Steinbeck, in the role of narrator in the novel *East of Eden*, asks the questions, "What do I believe in? What must I fight for and what must I fight against?"

In the same passage he answers those questions in terms of individual creativity: "Once the miracle of creation has taken place, the group can build and extend it, but the group never invents anything. The preciousness [creativity] lies in the lonely mind of a man."

After reciting the threat of the group to destroy the individual, as he sees it, he continues:

And this I believe: that the free, exploring mind of the individual human is *the most valuable thing in the world*. And this I would fight for: the freedom of the *mind to take any direction it wishes, undirected*. And this I must fight against: any idea, religion, or government which limits or destroys the individual. This is what I am and what I am about. I can understand why a system built on a pattern must destroy the free mind, for this is one thing which can by inspection destroy such a system. Surely, I can understand this, and I hate it and I will fight against it to preserve the one thing that separates us from the uncreative beasts. (emphasis added)[1]

Steinbeck's worldview as expressed in this passage is one of antagonism to the group commitment. He rejects the Puritan call to commit to the common good and the republican call to support a culture of laws, not of individual men. The myths of our worldview have evolved

> **"The salient American vision is lost in a blur of individual myopia. . . . The more he looks inward, the less he can see outward. And the less he can see outward, the more vulnerable is the society in which he lives."**

through the short history of our country from those myths which supported Winthrop's biblical worldview—we must consider ourselves all members of the same body—to those which supported Steinbeck's existential worldview—he will fight every effort to do so.

Winthrop saw God in the universe and engaged in a covenant with Him. Steinbeck saw only the free, exploring mind of the individual human being, resisting and rebelling against the needs, the aspirations, and the exploring minds of his fellow human beings, who likewise wished to take any direction, undirected. Steinbeck would fight any person who allowed his undirected freedom to cross the path of Steinbeck's own undirected freedom. For Steinbeck, the highest priority of humanity was to explore without restraint or inspection, and the highest value was the individual expression of self.

Steinbeck called this freedom. Others might suggest that it tends toward chaos. The crisis of the individual is at the heart of the tension between the two.

INDIVIDUALISM—THE METAMORPHOSIS OF THE AMERICAN MYTH

How do the myths of our forefathers apply to our lives today?

The myths still live but in an unrecognizable form. These myths have been gutted by certain philosophies which have caused a metamorphosis in the American worldview. The result of the metamorphosis is the loss of our historical perspectives. The creature which crawled out of the cocoon is unchecked individualism. The myths, models, and metaphors of this individualism defy the checks and balances of the original myths and manifest themselves in simple, popular philosophical slogans which exalt the individual over the common good.

We have become a nation of individuals who have placed themselves above the good of the community and often see the community as a gathering of individuals who are the objects of our efforts to be "winners" in life. Those other individuals are the promised land which must be conquered by the individual "winner."

Many of today's students would not recognize the works of the German philosophers Georg Hegel (1770–1831) and Friedrich Nietzsche (1844–1900), or the novels of the American Nobel Prize-winner Ernest Hemingway (1899–1961). Yet these men have left a legacy which has had a great impact on the myths of the American Dream.

How do Nietzsche and Hemingway fit into all this? They were both influenced by the American search for the soul, by Emerson and Whitman, and by the backlash to a cultural milieu in which material goods were exalted over the individual.

Nietzsche's philosophical outlook was somewhat complex to say the least. He, along with Russian novelist Ivan Turgenev, professed a philosophy called *nihilism*—simply stated, the rejection of tradition, morality, authority, and the social order which held these things as sacred. "One interpretation of existence has been overthrown," Nietzsche wrote of religion, "but since it was held *the* interpretation, it seems no meaning is left in existence." In the vacuum left by the absence of God, Nietzsche philosophized, there was nothing.

Nietzsche added a twist to this thought. Rather than accept the despair which naturally arises from these thoughts—the thought that nothing has any meaning in this world, that there is no hope of anything meaningful in this life—Nietzsche promulgated the idea of the superman and, through its cultural distortions, the super-race. The rugged individualist would rise above the hopelessness and rule the world. The will to power, by this myth, was the greatest of man's endeavors.

Hemingway took the philosophy of Turgenev and Nietzsche and portrayed it in literature. His characters reflected the thought that if nothing (Hemingway used the Spanish term *nada* for the despair caused by the meaninglessness of life, his brand of nihilism) had meaning in life, then man could only adhere to his own code, a code of rugged machoism in which men asked no quarter and gave none. No man was an island in the stream. Each person is rushed along by the current, meaningless in this world, the "truth" being the ultimate opponent, death.

The Old Man and the Sea is a Hemingway classic about man against nature and the futility of life and love. All of Hemingway's characters had an honor about their code. The goal of life was to live up to the code of machoistic individualism so that the character could accept the unexplained tragedies of life—Jake Barnes' inability to have Lady Brett (*The Sun Also Rises*), the death of Catherine Barkley (*A Farewell to Arms*), the death of Thomas Hudson (*Islands in the Stream*), and the crossing of the river and the entering of the trees to meet the only truth in life, death itself. The code was modeled on the life of Hemingway, a life which exalted selfish interest over any other concern.

The search for the soul in a godless universe derailed the American Dream. The individual was no longer guided by a set of cultural myths which defined the individual in the context of the community. The myths spawned in this context drove the individual on an exodus led not by God but by his own will, into a promised land filled with insufficient conquests to satisfy the individual lust.

OTHER CONCERN
SELFISH INTEREST

CATALYST FOR THE CRISIS

The First World War changed our culture most rapidly and radically. In American classrooms, this war is often overshadowed by the Second World War. We think of the First World War as light-years away. In fact, surveys show that most American high school students do not even know the century in which this war was fought.

But this war provided the incubator for the nihilism and the despair found in Hemingway and the arts of this century. The war, with its death and destruction far beyond that known or seen before by man, changed the way Americans and Europeans looked at the world. The optimism prevalent in the country, including the church, that man was basically good and only occasionally given to doing evil was vastly altered by the Great War.

The thoughts of Hegel, Nietzsche, and other German philosophers were only whispers confined to academicians and philosophers before the First World War. A sense of community was still abroad in the land, and most people paid lip service to the idea that there was a transcendent good which applied to all of us in the community. For many people, the war exploded the myth of the American brand of romanticism and hastened the way for a popular but distorted view of the search for the soul.

No longer was war a business of gentlemen. No longer could it be considered "good"; the horror of war came home from the front. In the wake of the war came a somber view of the world, a nihilism which blew away the "celebration of self" and substituted a dark and morbid wonder about self. This view is expressed in Dalton Trumbo's novel, *Johnny Got His Gun*, a pessimistic antiwar novel aimed at exploding the cultural myths of small American towns in the World War I era.

The message is that unchecked individualism, with its natural and foreseeable consequences, destroys our culture. The American Dream was being viewed in the realms of philosophy and the arts by the cynical eye of the European and American philosophers. The artists and writers of the "Lost Generation" painted a portrait of our culture from the eyes of those who had seen an unheard-of callousness, from the hearts of those who grieved.

God, as they knew Him, was "blown to bits"; all that they had trusted by trusting in God was torn asunder by the savagery of the war. For the people experiencing that war, the conduct of mankind did not add up to the Christian expectations held in their culture.

The result is the emergence of a human being who is guided not by the standards of the community but by the emerging myth of individualism. The highest calling in life for this human being is to live at the direction of his unchecked will, a life without any rules. It is free-falling in the abyss.

A CRISIS OF PASSAGE

Independence and *individualism* are not synonymous terms. *Independence* can be healthy. Independence is necessary for children to grow and develop; it prepares them to leave the nest and assume their responsibilities. And it battles the peer pressure and conformity of the world which results from the focus upon individualism. A required ingredient in ethical conduct, independence can lead to contentment and fulfillment in life.

But *individualism* is another thing. We must look at the logical results of our myths of individualism. For many individuals today, particularly among the young, the contents of the myth of the American Dream belong to another era, lost and long forgotten. The pursuit of the promised land still exists, but the purpose of the pursuit is buried in a history no longer considered relevant.

The breakdown in education, in families, in business, in life-styles, in our culture at large has left an America without a coherent vision of purpose and without a unifying drama in the culture. The myths have been differently adapted into an extinction of meaning and the redefinition of mission. The pilgrim to this country was chosen by God to

"The breakdown in education, in families, in business, in life-styles, in our culture at large has left an America without a coherent vision of purpose and without a unifying drama in the culture."

conquer the promised land; the nineteenth-century American was chosen to conquer the promised land; the twentieth-century American was chosen to conquer; and, the twenty-first-century American is to conquer at his beck and call. The loss of purpose occasioned by the meta-morphosis of our myths has each person in crisis.

According to Francis Schaeffer, the ideas of philosophy trickle down through art into music and finally into the general culture where the ideas, though changed, affect us in many ways. Schaeffer says that the philosophies of the Enlightenment were expanded by German phi-losopher Immanuel Kant (1724–1804), possibly the most significant philosopher of that time. These philosophies were then adapted loosely by Georg Hegel, then adapted by Christian existentialist Soren Kierkegaard (1813–1855), and eventually settled into a secular and reli-gious existentialism.

Schaeffer says that during this journey those thoughts crossed what he calls "the line of despair"—the line at which thought switches from the absolutes of good and evil to the synthesis of relativism. Beneath that line there are no absolutes of good and evil, no good which is always good and no antithesis which is always bad. There is no God which is always good but only a deceptive god who is now here and now there, a slippery god, a god of convenience to be called upon when we know that he will tell us the things we want to hear, a god of our liking and our creation, shaped and molded in our images in response to the whims of a fickle culture. Meaning is lost. Purpose is lost. It all dies in the relative struggle among individuals.

Schaeffer adds: "So this change in the concept [the change in world view from the absolutes of God to the relativism of the Enlightenment] of the way we come to knowledge and truth is the most crucial prob-lem, as I understand it, facing Christianity today."[2]

There is an old saying that he who knows nothing beyond the brackets of his birth and his death is an orphan. As we lose contact with the myths which have formed our worldview, we lose the wisdom which has guided society for thousands of years.

In the book, *The Power of Myth*, Bill Moyers discusses with Joseph Campbell the death of the myths which guide the conduct of our cul-ture. Campbell says:

Greek and Latin and biblical literature used to be a part of everyone's education. Now, when these were dropped, a whole tradition of Occi-dental mythological information was lost. It used to be that these sto-ries were in the minds of people. When the story is in your mind, then you see its relevance to something happening in your own life. It gives you perspective on what's happening to you. With the loss of that, we have really lost something because we don't have a comparable literature to take its place. The bits of information from ancient times, which have to do with themes that have supported human life, built civilizations, and informed religion over the millennia, have to do with deep inner problems, inner mysteries, inner thresholds of passage, and if you don't know what the guidesigns are on the way, you have to work it out yourself.[3]

Moyers: "Where do kids growing up in the city—on 125th and Broadway, [in New York City] for example—where do these kids get their myths today?"

Campbell: "They make it up themselves. This is why we have graffiti all over the city. These kids have their own gangs and their own initiations and their own morality, and they're doing the best they can. They are dangerous because these [myths] are not the laws of our civilization."

Moyers: "Rollo May says there is so much violence in American society today because there are no more great myths to help young men and women relate to the world or to understand that world beyond what is seen."

Campbell: "Yes . . ." [4]

Historically, rites of passage mark the maturing of persons. Young children are known for their selfishness. Rites of passage mark the maturing of the child in age and knowledge and in growth of understanding of the world. The purpose of that growth is to enable the individual to live in the community called the human race. But our culture is in reverse.

THE CRISIS OF THE TEAM PLAYER

A result of the crisis of the individual is the loss of identity in the community. In our individualism and its isolation, we have a tendency to snicker at those who are willing to give of themselves to the betterment of the community, to sacrifice their good for the common good.

Public service, for example, was once considered an honorable profession. The *New York Times* recently reported that only one of three hundred sixty-five seniors in the class of 1989 at Yale University are interested in a federal Civil Service career; the Foreign Service and the Intelligence communities were once a haven for Ivy Leaguers. The same report indicates that only 16 percent of those who were graduated from Harvard's JFK School of Government in the past ten years are now in government service.[5] The biblical directive that we are all members of one body has drowned in a "God helps those who help themselves" mentality.

The fact is that today our culture places a much higher degree of worth upon people who elevate themselves. For all our talk about team players, people who give to the common good are not among our role models. In labor-management relations, teamwork is something attributed to the Japanese. Americans are too busy thinking about raising wages through strikes or in scuttling a company into bankruptcy for great personal profit, after the model of Frank Lorenzo and Eastern Airlines. As negative as those examples are to most of us, we still look to the individual as the builder of our society.

Yet we are now a country which in the latter quarter of the twentieth century is seeing new firsts—the first FBI agent convicted of espionage for the Soviets, the first CIA officer defecting to the Soviet Union and fatally compromising agents loyal to the U.S., the Marine Guards at the U.S. embassy in Moscow cavorting with Soviet KGB agents, and legions of military members and government employees convicted of espionage, embezzlement, and petty thievery.

But before we judge and condemn the wrongdoers, we must look at a culture in which our myths and models cry out that we only go around once in life, that we must grab all the gusto we can, that the only true thing in life is our relationship to ourselves. C. S. Lewis once wrote that if loyalty is mocked in a culture, why should we be shocked by treason? If community is mocked in our culture, why should we be shocked by treason and theft and selfishness?

> For several centuries, we have been embarked on a great effort to increase our freedom, wealth and power. For over a hundred years, a large part of the American people, the middle class, has imagined that the virtual meaning of life lies in the acquisition of ever-increasing

status, income, and authority, from which genuine freedom is supposed to come. Our achievements have been enormous. They permit us the aspiration to become a genuinely humane society in a genuinely decent world, and provide many of the means to attain that aspiration. *Yet we seem to be hovering on the very brink of disaster, not only from international conflict but from the internal incoherence of our own society.* (emphasis added)[6]

THE GREAT IRONY

The great irony of our quest for individualism is that the result is not a nation of rugged individualists who continually improve things within the society by building and improving and looking out for one another. Our quest for individualism results in an unconscious conformity. The prevalent view of history as somehow irrelevant strips us of our identity and eventually of our independence. If our culture disregards the myths of our past, it does not mean that there are no myths to which we conform our conduct. Professor Bloom writes:

> Actually openness results in American conformism. Out there in the rest of the world is a drab diversity that teaches only that values are relative, whereas here we can create all the life-styles we want. Our openness means we do not need others. *Thus what was advertised as a great opening is a great closing.* No longer is there a hope that there are great wise men in other places and times who can reveal that truth about life. . . . Gone is the real historical sense of a Machiavelli who wrested a few hours from each busy day in which "to don regal and courtly garments, enter the courts of the ancients and speak with them." (emphasis added)[7]

Gone are those who draw the wisdom for their conduct by examining and communing with the wisdom of the ages. Rather, wisdom often originates with the spirit of the age, the whim of culture.

Bloom saw it in our decade. Alexis de Tocqueville saw it a century and a half ago. Individualism was strangely compatible with conformism.

> He [Tocqueville] described the American insistence that one always rely on one's own judgment, rather than on received authority, in forming one's opinions and that one stand by one's own opinions. . . . But, as Tocqueville observed, when one can no longer rely on tradi-

tion or authority, *one inevitably looks to others for confirmation of one's judgments.* Refusal to accept established opinion and anxious conformity to the opinions of one's peers turn out to be two sides of the same coin. (emphasis added)[8]

Professor Sacvan Bercovitch wrote: "The same Puritan myth, differently adapted, encouraged . . . Horatio Alger to extol conformity as an act of supreme individualism."[9] That is why the subtle power of peer pressure and the myth of individualism go hand in hand and are seemingly irresistible. The relative value of individualism is that we know no absolute standards and, therefore, we look to the whim of the culture to find our standards. "Conformity as an act of extreme individualism"— these words are absolutely haunting to Americans who are interested in individual rights.

Vance Packard, in his 1957 book, *The Hidden Persuaders*, says that excepting those behind the Iron Curtain, Americans are the most manipulated people in the world. The bombardment from the media in the secular world more than anything else guides our conduct and our thoughts. Packard writes,

> Large-scale efforts are being made, often with impressive success, to channel our unthinking habits, our purchasing decisions, and our thought processes by the use of insights gleaned from psychiatry and the social sciences. Whether we are thought of as "consumers" or "citizens," the hidden persuaders are at work trying to invade the privacy of our minds.[10]

Without a set of absolute standards to guide us, without a set of myths to teach us about those standards, we are guided by the instant myths created by television today and gone tomorrow.

The great irony is that the more individualistic we see ourselves, the more we lose our relationship to the past and the more we conform to the present. As a result, instead of a nation of rugged individualists, we have a nation of weak conformists ready to join any group that will fill the gap of lost independence.

The danger is well stated by William R. Inge, Dean of St. Paul's Cathedral, who wrote that there are many spirits of the age and if we marry the spirit of our generation, we will be a widow in the next generation.[11]

As we seek to find our independence in an age which has lost touch with its past and the traditions which make us independent, we

"Our quest for individualism results in an unconscious conformity. The prevalent view of history as somehow irrelevant strips us of our identity and eventually of our independence."

will find that there are many groups which profess independence yet demand conformity. Groups come and go. She who finds her security and identity in a group of this generation will be lonely in the next generation.

POLITICALLY   CITIZENS/VOTERS
ECONOMICALLY   PRODUCERS—MACHINES
                CONSUMERS—ANIMALS

10

THE MYTH OF RELATIVISM:

The Culture in Crisis

This is the verdict: Light has come into this world, but men loved darkness instead of light because their deeds were evil.

JOHN 3:19

Some years ago I read a testimony in a Christian publication which stuck in my mind. The story related the experience of a young woman from the Midwest who went to college in the late sixties. Perhaps this struck me because I went to college in the late sixties, also. At any rate, she moved into a dormitory and learned that some people were smoking marijuana on her floor. In an effort to be tolerant, she said nothing although she did not like her roommate using marijuana in their room.[1]

"Don't be old-fashioned," the roommate complained.

She met a young man, a senior, who owned a nice sports car and she "fell" for him. On the first date, he asked her to his apartment and she politely declined. "Why not?" he asked.

She shrugged. "Ladies just shouldn't do that."

After several dates, he asked her again and she agreed. He became agitated when she refused to go any farther than the living room.

"Why not?" he asked.

She replied that she was a Christian and that she should not do that. He smiled condescendingly and muttered, "Oh, one of those."

He did not call her for a while, and she saw him with another girl in his sports car. When she asked him why he did not call her anymore, he said, "Because you're too old-fashioned."

Some time later, he called her again, and this time she was excited about their date. But when it came time to go farther than the living room, she again refused.

"Explain to me why you won't go," he said.

She thought. "Because of my religion."

"You don't really believe that stuff?"

"Yes, I do," she insisted.

"Then explain to me what it is that will not permit you to do this."

All this was new to her. In the cornfields of the Midwest, she did not encounter these things. After a good deal of thought, she was unable to express in satisfactory terms her objection to drinking, drugs, and extramarital sex. Far away from home geographically and mentally, she was unable to explain why she could not be "free" of all that "superstition."

Twenty years later, she still regrets her inability to express her faith and her beliefs in a systematic way which would have persuaded her boyfriend, rather than being persuaded by his "new" views of life.

What happened to her values? Or, more importantly, what happened to the values which we all presumably held in common? They were nowhere to be seen.

I am baffled by those questions because I shared a similar set of circumstances in which the academic environment constantly disparaged the political and social views held by the majority of Americans in the 1960s. Likewise, I was unable to articulate specifically the political or social creed which brought me to that campus. However, the myths of the American culture were deeply ingrained in my "faith" so that it took a while before I began to wonder if they were, indeed, still shared as common beliefs in our culture.

Carl F. H. Henry writes:

Our generation is lost to the truth of God, to the reality of divine revelation, to the content of God's will, to the power of His redemption, and to the authority of His Word. For this loss it is paying dearly in a swift relapse into paganism. The savages are stirring again; you can hear them rumbling and rustling in the tempo of our times.[2]

How did we come to this loss? The many influences of individualism, relativism, and pragmatism in the American culture in the past fifty years have resulted in a loss of cultural perspective on the foundations of our ethics both in Scripture and in the previous developments of our culture. The crisis in culture arises from the seduction, indeed, the rape, of the American mythology by the myth of relativism. The result of relativism is a culture with no roots, which is no culture at all.

ANTITHESIS—RELATIVISM AS MYTH

Francis Schaeffer laments the loss of the idea that there is an antithesis in this world: that there has been a force of good and that force of good is God, and that there is a force of evil and that evil is the antithesis or opposite of God. Both are absolutes. The Judeo-Christian view of history has always been that God is unchangeable and that history is the recording of the unchangeable God's works in the linear chronology of man's stay on this planet.

The prevalent and underlying thought of relativism is the Hegelian view, which has as its main point the concept that history has evolved through a series of syntheses. There is a thesis in any given time or epoch, and for every thesis there is an opposite, an antithesis. But the thesis and the antithesis are not absolutes. The tension is resolved by

---

"The result of relativism is a culture with no roots, which is no culture at all."

---

combining the thesis and the antithesis into a synthesis which then becomes a new thesis. The new thesis then has an antithesis and so on. This, very simplistically, is the Hegelian view of history.

If the Hegelian view is the ultimate truth, then the view that God is the thesis and evil is the antithesis means that God then combines with evil to form a new thesis, or, indeed, a new and different god.

The worldview which arises from the Hegelian view is that all things are relative, that all things change as history changes, that all things derive their meaning from the circumstances about them, and that nothing—not even God—is unchanging or absolute. And if nothing, including God, is absolute, then nothing, including God, is true. Therefore, the "truths" of today do not help in our search for knowledge. They only hinder because they, too, will change.

Professor Bloom writes:

> Values are not discovered by reason, and it is fruitless to seek them, to find the truth or the good life. The quest begun by Odysseus and continued over three millennia has come to an end with the observation that there is nothing to seek. This alleged fact was announced by Nietzsche just over a century ago when he said, "God is dead." *Good and evil now for the first time appeared as values, of which there have been a thousand and one, none rationally or objectively preferable to any other.* . . . For Nietzsche this was an unparalleled catastrophe; it meant the decomposition of culture and the loss of human aspiration. (emphasis added)[3]

This change in view has expanded the metamorphosis of the cultural myths and the emerging worldview. That a culture in which individualism is among the most prized myths should come into crisis with relativism should be no surprise. Individualism and relativism are not, by any means, mutually exclusive for they take on many of the same characteristics as they creep through our society.

Relativism elevates man to the level that he and he alone is the measure of the universe. What "is," is what he says "is." What is important is what strikes his fancy. Relativism cuts us off from our neighbors, our communities, our families. Most people today know more about the president or a professional athlete or a rock musician than about their neighbors. Many people see the face of the president in the news more often than they see the faces of their children. Such is the result of the emerging myths of relativism.

RELATIVISM—THE METAMORPHOSIS OF CULTURE

There have been a number of books in the eighties which have decried the influence of relativism and pragmatism upon our culture. One of the foremost is E. D. Hirsch's book, *Cultural Literacy*.[4] Hirsch lays the loss of our common pool of shared cultural knowledge, the information which makes our culture cohesive, at the foot of John Dewey and the pervasive nature of his philosophies of pragmatism. Simply stated, pragmatism is a philosophy in which ideas have no intrinsic worth but are useful only if they achieve desired results. Thus, truth is found, not in ideas, but in that which "works." This philosophy emphasizes the means to the end. If it works, do it. The truth, then, is redefined as the means which obtains the ends. Those means which apply in one situation may not apply in another. Therefore, the truth is not absolute but situational or relative.

Among the things Dewey believed was the proposition that students should be taught the skills of how to gain knowledge rather than the knowledge itself. The result is a generation of students who may know the methodology of matters but who have lost the knowledge which makes the culture distinctive. By failing to learn the information which makes our culture distinctive, students and an entire generation have lost touch with their past. They are not rooted in the myths of the American Dream but have defaulted to a relativism in values which is crippling our culture.

Hirsch supplies the illustration of his father, an executive in a large corporation. He liked to write memoranda to the executive staff, and in the memoranda, he liked to use Shakespearean references to make his points. Over the course of his career, his references became less and less effective because the executive staff understood less and less of the meaning of the Shakespearean imagery. The phenomenon he observed, according to Hirsch, was the rise of a generation of MBAs who knew something about business but nothing about Shakespeare—a generation of the culturally illiterate running the economy of America.

So what? So what if businessmen know nothing about Shakespeare? The problem is not Shakespeare. The problem is a lack of knowledge of the principles of culture in those who are in charge of the operation of a vital part of the culture. In other words, they have book learning but no common sense. They have learned how to read the book, but they have not learned how to apply what it says to real life. Now, Shakespeare may not equate to common sense, but lack of the knowledge of the principles which drive our culture does.

A lack of cultural literacy not only denies the individual an understanding of human nature (for lack of a better term), but it also prohibits effective communication among the members of the culture. In a business, failure to communicate adequately means the failure of the business. In a culture, the failure to communicate adequately means the failure of the culture.

Our culture has not accepted relativism unknowingly. Bloom tells the story of a discussion he had with a psychology professor who made the grandiose statement that his job was to clean the students' minds of all "prejudices."

> He knocked them down [the students' "prejudices"] like tenpins. I began to wonder what he replaced those prejudices with. He did not seem to have much idea what the opposite of a prejudice might be. He reminded me of the little boy who gravely informed me that there is no Santa Claus, who wanted me to bathe in the brilliant light of truth. Did this professor know what those prejudices meant for students and what effect being deprived of them would have? . . . My informant about Santa Claus was just showing off, proving his superiority to me. Had he not created the Santa Claus that had to be there in order to be refuted?[5]

This has been the experience of many university and seminary students in this country. For many professors, today's prejudices are any of the belief systems held by students—that is, any of the belief systems which are not identical to theirs. Some prejudices are okay; others are not. Certainly, Professor Bloom's colleague would not wish to dispel such a prejudice as one prevalent in today's universities: Truth is relative, or any of the corollaries which proliferate like academic rabbits and are engaged in their version of survival of the fittest.

In this respect, it may be fortunate that the universities are designed so that students only spend four years there. Fortunately, many students do not attend universities for the purpose of learning. The thoughts and ambitions of their professors, as well as much of what the professors say, never enter their minds.

In the now-famous beginning to his book, possibly the most-used quote of the decade, Bloom says, "There is one thing a professor can be absolutely sure of: almost every student entering the university believes, or

---

"The problem is a lack of knowledge of the principles of culture in those who are in charge of the operation of a vital part of the culture. In other words, they have book learning but no common sense."

---

says he believes, that truth is relative. If this belief is put to the test, one can count on the students' reaction: they will be uncomprehending."[6] As the quote suggests, the belief is broad-based, yet it is not strongly held. It is not held as a result of scholarly inquiry and rigorous cross-examination, rather it is learned as a myth of our culture. Relativism has become our culture's way of explaining the world around it—everything is relative; what you believe is fine for you, but don't tread on me.

The metamorphosis of our worldview will result in the formation of new myths to fill the void of the old. Those myths and stories are founded in relativism and broadcast into our culture so that our conduct is now being guided by a set of standards which have never been our own and which have not been approved, voted upon, or adopted by anything resembling a public consensus. If we begin to build our guide signs and work out our answers to life's questions based on the view of life supplied by our cultural media, can we possibly hope for a humane society in which the values of our Constitution, the Declaration of Independence, and our other political documents—the values developed in Western civilization in the centuries after the Protestant Reformation—will be intact?

Relativism found expression in England in a 1967 interview with Charlie Watts of the British rock group, the Rolling Stones. Watts said, "I'm against any form of organized thought. I'm against . . . organized religion like the church. I don't see how you can organize ten million minds to believe one thing."[7] "I'm against any form of organized thought!"—there are no truths to be found in organized thought or, indeed, anywhere.

The shame of that statement is not only its content but also its context. That statement comes from a British youth whose father's generation rallied behind Winston Churchill and a thousand years of Anglo-Saxon heritage. They believed most valiantly and fervently in one thing: the preservation of that heritage and tradition through the fight to stem fascism in Western Europe and around the world. Watts's blind statement dismissed that effort just three and a half decades after Churchill pronounced: "If the British Empire shall last a thousand years, men will say, 'This was their finest hour.'" That finest hour passed quickly.

The question is: What did Watts know about the organized mind? He did not have to face the Luftwaffe or the buzz bombs. He did not see the Battle of Britain. He did not know the courage of the Royal Air Force, those few to whom so many owed so much. He did not understand the deep meaning of the fingers raised to form a "V" which Churchill flashed as a sign of defiance. English tradition says that during the Hundred Years War the French would amputate the first two fingers on the right hand of the captured English bowmen so that the bowmen could not fight again. When Churchill raised his fingers in the sign of a "V," he was sending a message of courage and defiance from the British people, just as British warriors had done since the Hundred Years War.

If Watts's cultural education was such that he did not understand or care for that part of the British heritage, then it is no wonder that he considers no allegiance to anyone but himself.

In America, our culture is already well down the path to a fragmentation which will spell the failure of the culture as we know it. We are cocooned like so many moths in our relativistic beliefs and care nothing for the beliefs of others. The relativism in our culture does not permit dialogue, only dissent; permits no objective standards, only subjective lives searching for an elusive meaning. We are no longer pilgrims searching for a new beginning in our promised land. We have been metamorphosed into a state of somnambulism in which we travel through life with our eyes half open, drawn by a vague flame, a candle which we think has freed us from our cocoon. Such is the danger of relativism.

THE ENEMY OF RELATIVISM

The enemy of relativism and of those who espouse relativism is, of course, absolutism—the belief that there are absolutes, like God or good or evil, in the world. These absolutes do not change over time or with circumstance; they remain constant.

Bloom continues:

> The danger they [the students in our culture] have been taught to fear from absolutism is not error but intolerance. Relativism is necessary to openness; and this is the virtue, the only virtue, which all primary education for more than fifty years has dedicated itself to inculcating. Openness—and the relativism that makes it the only plausible stance in the face of various claims to truth and various ways of life and kinds of human beings—is the great insight of our times. *The true believer is the real danger.* The study of history and of culture teaches that all the world was mad in the past; men have always thought they were right, and that led to wars, persecutions, slavery, xenophobia, racism, and chauvinism. *The point is not to correct the mistakes and really be right; rather it is not to think you are right at all.* (emphasis added)[8]

These are not the children of the brave new world but the "elite" students, Bloom says, entering the top ten or fifteen universities in the

> *"The relativism in our culture does not permit dialogue, only dissent; permits no objective standards, only subjective lives searching for an elusive meaning."*

country today. These are not the children of communism, products of Marxist mind-control, the robots of the totalitarian society which we feared a couple of generations ago, but American children coming out of high schools which are the best our society has to offer.

On a recent television special featuring education in America, Barbara Walters found that most high school students she surveyed thought

the Holocaust was a Jewish holiday and were unable to locate the
United States on a world map. She concluded, "Today's high school
students live in a world of misplaced values. They are becoming a generation of undisciplined cultural barbarians."[9] They are cultural barbarians because they have not learned and thus do not understand the
myths, beliefs, and absolutes that hold our culture together.

Malcolm Muggeridge suggests that Christendom has not been an
innocent bystander but has, by its failure in leadership and its adherence to social and intellectual liberalism, contributed to the decline of
our culture.

> Previous civilizations have been overthrown from without by the in-
> cursion of barbarian hordes. Christendom has dreamed up its own dis-
> solution in the minds of its own intellectual elite. Our barbarians are
> home products, indoctrinated at public expense, urged on by the
> media systematically, stage by stage, dismantling Christendom, depre-
> ciating and deprecating all its values. The whole structure is now tum-
> bling down, dethroning God, undermining all its certainties.[10]

No, he is not talking about Europe. Yes, he is talking about the
United States. He is speaking in the context of Alexander
Solzhenitsyn's address at Harvard University in which he derided the
West for a lack of courage in spiritual and moral matters.[11] Nobel Prize-
winner Solzhenitsyn is a man who has seen a culture, the Soviet Union,
with the barbarians in command.

The enemy the barbarians must overcome is the millennia of the
Judeo-Christian heritage, which represents the absolutes of our culture.
As long as the absolutes remain, the walls against relativism will not
come down.

RELATIVISM IN BUSINESS

What has happened to the absolutes in this culture? Are we able any
longer to agree on a code of morality by which we should all live?

Time magazine recently carried a cover article concerning ethics in
this country. The article was bemoaning the fact that honesty and integrity seem to have failed in every sector of American life: graft in the
Defense Department; scandal on Wall Street; chicanery in Congress;

and on and on. What seems to be the problem? The problem lies in the lack of a basis by which we govern our conduct.

Relativism has neutralized the guiding factors of the mythology of the American culture and formed in its place a mythology in which all is permissible. The myth of the self-made man, without its context within the standards of the other myths of the American Dream, becomes avarice unchained. While we are trying our best to be tolerant, we find that there are others, like Gecko in *Wall Street*, who contend that greed is good for America. On the basis of our cultural faith in relativism, we can only be tolerant and agree. The problem is that a whole generation of Americans in universities today has agreed.

The question is the one Professor Bloom asked: With what do we fill the gap left after the "prejudices" are dispelled? Once we have stripped our educational processes of our cultural values, what is left? Do we question whether any of these cultural values are in fact universal, that is, values held in this culture as well as all others?

Charles Colson wrote in the October 1989 edition of his ministry newsletter, *Jubilee*, that the question of ethics crept up at Harvard University recently. John Shad, the former chairman of the Securities and Exchange Commission, donated thirty-five million dollars to Harvard Business School to establish an ethics department. In response, Harvard president Derek Bok wrote that ethics courses today seek not to convey a set of moral truths but try to encourage students to think carefully about complex moral issues.

Colson laments the fact that our society deplores scandals in government and in business but rejects the moral basis for an ethical code which would avoid them. Is there any wonder that we find no ethical or moral code in American business? Is it any wonder that the decline in American business is one of the chief economic problems facing this nation as we stand on the threshold of the twenty-first century?

RELATIVISM IN THE ACADEMIC COMMUNITY

At a social gathering recently, Bloom's book was mentioned as an interesting comment on American education. The first suggestion raised, that we are not in touch with our traditions, brought from a young assistant professor in a local college (who had not read the book) the immediate response that we must not be bound by the chains of the past. Certainly his statement is true—we do not wish to be enslaved by the past.

But this professor, without inquiry into the meaning of tradition or how we are not in touch with it, dismissed tradition as "enslaving"—no dialogue, no 'academic interchange, simply the relativistic dismissal of tradition as an important factor in our lives and our quests to find the meaning of man's sojourn on this planet. This was the metamorphosis of the myth of sacrifice and dissent, cross-pollinated with the myth of relativism, which allows a person whose vocation is academic inquiry to dismiss summarily the strong views of another academician.

Professor Bloom's comments have, indeed, drawn strong reaction from many quarters in the academic world. As with many myths in our culture, the myth of relativism has strong proponents. However, contrary to the tolerance purportedly promoted by relativism, those proponents will not permit free dialogue on the issues.

This sort of relativism—the dispelling of the so-called prejudices of the past, those absolutes which were at the same time the embodiment and the embryo of all evil—prejudges without rational investigation the beliefs of those who would engage in dialogue and point to something as elementary as tradition. The practice of relativism, then, produces the opposite of its preaching.

George Will, a columnist for the *Washington Post*, wrote in the November 7, 1989, edition that there have been efforts by many universities to control speech and thought by limiting discussion of issues to certain nonsensitive areas. Those nonsensitive areas exclude, as at the University of Michigan, speech giving offense on the basis of race, ethnicity, religion, national origin, sex, sexual orientation, creed, ancestry, age, marital status, handicap, or Vietnam-era veteran status (this university regulation was ruled unconstitutional by a federal court).

The University of Connecticut, according to Will's article, prohibits "inappropriately directed laughter" on its campus. Somehow, that would not have washed back in the sixties. In fact, the myth of sacrifice and dissent was based upon the courage of many men and women who voiced opinions concerning the thoughts and beliefs of others. The republican myth was built upon two centuries of investigation and dialogue, the Reformation and the Enlightenment; during both opinions were strongly expressed on the shortfalls of others in a variety of areas.

"The practice of relativism, then, produces the opposite of its preaching."

In discussing educational reforms, the president of Cornell University stated that the universities must give more attention to the moral well-being and instruction of students. He was immediately shouted down by jeers of "Whose morality?" "Who will do the teaching?"

Colson writes concerning that incident:

> In an earlier time, the obvious answer would have been to point to 2300 years of accumulated moral wisdom, or to a rationally defensible natural law, or to a moral law revealed by God in the Judeo-Christian scriptures. Today, however, few educators, or any other leaders who shape public attitudes, have the audacity to challenge the prevailing assumption that there is no morally binding objective source of authority or truth above the individual.[12]

If I am the measure of all things, if all that exists is what I see and feel and touch, then the wisdom of the ages is of no use to me and is no greater than my own values. The writings of the ancients (those who lived before my birth) are only babblings of DWEM—Dead White European Men—the epithet used by those who protested mandatory studies in Western civilization at Stanford University. Relativism reduces Plato, Aristotle, Kant, and the authors on the required "Western Civ" reading list at Stanford to objects of scorn and hatred.

RELATIVISM IN LAW

Nowhere is the impact of relativism so marked as in the field of law. The road to relativism was paved by Oliver Wendell Holmes, Jr., and his book, *The Common Law*.[13] Holmes, a Justice of the United States Supreme Court, wrote that there should be no other influence on the law than the rule of *stare decisis*, the Anglo-American proposition of case law. A court must look to previously decided cases for propositions of law to decide the case before it. While that does not necessarily sound too bad, the impact of that theory did not arrive on the scene until much later.

Supreme Court Justice Fredrick Vinson phrased it this way: "Nothing is more certain in modern society than the principle that there are no absolutes."[14] It is often pointed out that Mr. Justice Vinson states that proposition as an absolute, thus disproving his own hypothesis. Be that as it may, the result of this trend in law is what Francis Schaeffer terms *sociological law*, that is, "law which has no fixed base but law in which a group of people decides what is sociologically good for the society at the given moment; and what they arbitrarily decide becomes law."[15]

In the decade between *Abingdon School District v. Schempp* (1963), the school prayer case, and *Roe v. Wade* (1973), the abortion case, Holmes's views of a neutral—that is, free of any values—legal base ran amok in American jurisprudence. As recently as 1954, Justice William O. Douglas, a civil libertarian in his own right, refused, in *Zorach v. Clausen*, to "find in the Constitution a requirement that the government show a callous indifference to religious groups. That would be preferring those who believe in no religion over those who do believe."[16]

In *Roe v. Wade*, the right to life, one of the inalienable rights guaranteed by the Constitution and the republican myths upon which this country was founded, was to play second fiddle to the right to privacy, a right which had to be "interpreted" into existence by the Supreme Court itself. For those who have viewed the case from the legal perspective, it is a stunning case. As Richard John Neuhaus wrote: "For the first time . . . it was explicitly stated that it is possible to address these issues of ultimate importance without any reference to the Judeo-Christian tradition. . . . For the first time in American jurisprudence, the Supreme Court explicitly excluded philosophy, ethics, and religion as factors in its deliberations."[17]

Can there be law without the underlying standards upon which the law is founded? The answer to that question is no. The underlying standards of the law in the American courts are the standards of the various myths of relativism. Relativism in the law, of course, turns law into the tool of the powerful, not necessarily the rich but the group who has the ear of the judge. The standards become questions of social interpretation and situational need rather than a stable foundation upon which just and recognizable laws are established.

For example, if we apply the University of Michigan regulation forbidding statements which may be considered offensive by certain groups in the culture, we have destroyed the First Amendment provision concerning free speech, one of the bulwarks of the republican myth.

The logical extension of this in the field of law is that we will be guided not by a set of laws but by the whim of those with the loudest voices, those who can say what the law ought to mean. We become not a nation of laws but a nation of persons seeking conformity to a certain standard accepted by those in control of the means of communication within the culture.

Constitutional lawyer William Bentley Ball wrote:

> I propose that secularism militates against religious liberty, and indeed against personal freedoms generally, for two reasons: first, the familiar fact that secularism does not recognize the existence of the "higher law"; second, because, that being so, secularism tends toward decisions based upon the pragmatic public policy of the moment and inevitably tends to resist the submitting of those policies to the "higher" criteria of a constitution.[18]

Even now, several chapters of the American Civil Liberties Union, once the self-proclaimed protector of free speech, have endorsed regulations which would censor speech based upon the content of the speech. In a 15 July 1990, *New York Times* News Service article, Neil A. Lewis wrote that the ACLU is undergoing "new efforts to rethink the First Amendment." Lewis quoted a professor of law at Whittier Law School and former president of the California ACLU chapter: "The ideal is that everybody should have a chance to speak and everybody should be listened to. But racism, for example, has proven intransigent, and we live in a real world, not an idealized marketplace of ideas." So much for the impassioned arguments of previous generations that the campus is the free marketplace of ideas.

Therefore, we assume that in the real world, some speech—the speech which fits this professor's definition of racism—should be censored. We ask the old question: Who determines what speech should be censored in the "real world"? The answer from the ACLU seems to be, in the cases of the government universities like the University of Michigan, whatever political or social agenda happens to be in vogue. And the circle comes back to the standard of what they, the government censors, do not like or agree with.

We all may agree that "hate speech" should be disallowed in some circumstances. But we all do not agree on what should be classified as hate speech. Some Christian groups and some feminist groups contend that certain sexually oriented materials should be banned because those materials are obscene and devalue human life and trample on human dignity. The ACLU and the universities have stood firm in their objection to any effort to remove obscenity and the basest forms of sexploitation from the print and electronic media. Yet is not obscenity, as it devalues human life and exploits human dignity, "hate speech" in its rankest form? As the feminists turn up the heat on raunchy pornography, will the defenders in the universities and in the ACLU continue in their defense of the dissemination of that material under the First Amendment? Or will their relative values be adjusted because they believe in the feminist cause and will they "rethink the First Amendment?"

RELATIVISM IN SCIENCE

What is the threat posed by relativism? There are many. The threat to Christianity is, of course, set out by Schaeffer. If there are no absolutes, there is no absolute God. There are only relative gods, and those gods can be anything we want them to be. If there are no laws upon which we can rely, we cannot rely upon the law. If there are no stable institutions in which we can put our faith, how can we have faith in our institutions? If the majority of the people lost faith in the institutions of this country, how can the country survive?

But relativism threatens another area of our culture more than it does Christianity. Relativism is a threat to technology. One of the results of the metamorphosis of the myths in our society is the idolatrous view of science and technology. They have become our gods, able to explain all, able to save all. Yet they are fallible and limited. And their practitioners, for the most part, do not portray them as other than what they are; neither is at odds with Christianity.

The nineteenth-century view of the feud between science and theology was fanned by a news media that cannot live without such feuds and by state school systems that must reduce all issues to the lowest possible level if they are to teach at all. Beneath this surface, science is not a major controversy in theology today. Neither theologians nor scientists contend that their discipline is something that it is not. Each sees its parameters.

But both are at odds with relativism. Science and technology require an environment which is not ruled by chance or by natural selectivity or by relativity. Science and technology thrive on absolute laws and stable rules.

> *"The nineteenth-century view of the feud between science and theology was fanned by a news media that cannot live without such feuds and by state school systems that must reduce all issues to the lowest possible level if they are to teach at all."*

Surely, those who espouse relativism will quickly point out that philosophical relativism does not deny that there are natural absolutes, that is, that there are laws of nature which permit science to function. They merely deny any transcendent absolute. But that answer is just too convenient.

Relativism and science are on a collision course that will lead this culture to a radical realignment of how we view "truth" in our culture.

RELATIVISM IN ATHLETICS

Nowhere is relativism less attractive than in athletics. Once a common denominator among children designed to teach teamwork, sportsmanship, and fellowship, athletics has become the most visible area in which commitment to the common good has been forsaken for selfish ambition. From disputes over contracts which bring millions of dollars to individuals to the use of steroids to the ridiculous overcoaching in peewee leagues, sports is not serving the function of assisting young boys and girls in physical, educational, and spiritual development but offers only glimpses of exercises in selfishness and deceit.

Where is sportsmanship? If we applied the standards of sportsmanship today that were expected thirty years ago, a football game would be paralyzed by unsportsmanlike conduct penalties—all of them justifiable. We would not be able to watch a tennis match on television because all the John McEnroe clones would have forfeited.

Sports without sportsmanship is an American phenomenon and a reversal of centuries of sportsmanlike tradition in the fellowship of athletic competition. Today we see taunting and swaggering and gyrating. We see every team, no matter what their record, holding up a finger and chanting, "We're number one!" We see replays of the hardest hits; we see debates over the calls of the officials; we hear mindless drivel from commentators. All of this is designed to take the team out of sports and introduce self-worship.

On the lecture circuit, wide receiver Chris Collingsworth tells that he began his professional career with the Cincinnati Bengals under the legendary coach Paul Brown. When he scored his first touchdown, he spiked the ball, did a little dance, and hot-dogged off the field. Coach Brown considered that unsportsmanlike conduct. When he got to the sideline Coach Brown motioned for him to come over. "Collingsworth," he said, "next time you score a touchdown, act like you've been there before." Sports no longer educates our students on how to act like they've been there before.

The fact is that, unlike the playing fields of Eton, American sports fields no longer develop young men and women for the game of life. Instead, they teach young men and women that any type of conduct is tolerable as long as it helps you advance in the sport.

One of John McEnroe's opponents said that you had to admire his athletic ability, but you did not have to respect him as a person. Sports was not originated to develop athletic abilities as much as it was to prepare the athlete for life and to foster respect of one person for another.

I DON'T MIND AND YOU DON'T MATTER

Many do not share Nietzsche's fear that this view of the world without God was an "unparalleled catastrophe which meant the decomposition of culture and the loss of human aspiration."[19] They have covered over

---

"When we hit the ground at the bottom of that abyss, when death takes us and there is nothing after life, I have no reason or motivation to be concerned with anything but myself. In the 1990s paraphrase of the old 'mind-over-matter' idea, I don't mind and you don't matter."

---

the seriousness of Nietzsche's claim and looked only upon the surface. There is no scholarly inquiry here, no rigorous cross-examination, nothing but an inward view of the world—mankind studying himself in his mirror

As Professor Bloom puts it,

> In short, Nietzsche [in lamenting the death of God] with the utmost gravity told modern man that he was free-falling in the abyss of nihilism [if he lived without God]. Perhaps after having lived through this terrible experience, drunk it to the dregs, people might hope for a fresh era of value creation, the emergence of new gods.[20]

Free-falling in the abyss of nihilism may be what attracts those who are content only to view themselves, for free-falling in the abyss is what man does when he sees the world as man-centered. If we are all free-falling for eternity or if our existence ends when we hit the ground, then there is no reason for me to be concerned about anything but me. What happens to you has no effect on me, indeed, makes no difference to me at all. When we hit the ground at the bottom of that abyss, when death takes us and there is nothing after life, I have no reason or motivation to be concerned with anything but myself. In the 1990s paraphrase of the old "mind-over-matter" idea, I don't mind and you don't matter. Love is a vanity, wealth a chasing after the wind. And that is a long distance from the myths of a country which began with a sense of community.

But the challenging point is that after swallowing the sweet wine of relativism, the threat of free-falling in the abyss of nihilism is not all it's cracked up to be. In fact, the adventure might give some relief from the isolation of our individualism; it might be "a new value creation . . . a new emergence of new gods." This free-falling might provide us with something that we cannot find in the myth of individualism: some perverse sense of community, some sense of others who will shout "bravo" when we rail against the community.

American critic Leslie Fiedler writes:

> God has been abolished by the media pundits and other promoters of our new demythologized divinity. We continue to insist that change is progress, self-indulgence is freedom, and novelty is originality. In these circumstances it's difficult to avoid the conclusion that Western man has decided to abolish himself, creating his own boredom out of his own affluence, his own vulnerability out of his own strength, his own impotence out of his own erotomania, himself blowing the trumpet that brings the walls of his own city tumbling down.[21]

But what happens when the myths and stories of our culture are no longer there? Or when the answer that the stories give us is that there is no truth or meaning or significance; that all is relative?

Charley Reese, a columnist for the *Orlando Sentinel*, has written:

> Abandoning one's faith does not mean becoming a person with no faith. Rare is the human being whose brain can stare into the abyss of an empty meaningless universe and retain its sanity. What happens is that people pick or create other religions.
>
> This is what accounts for the religious-like behavior we see in a variety of causes ranging from communism to animal rights to libertarianism to environmentalism. People, desperate for meaning in their lives, take secular issues and convert them into religions. Thus, they become adamant, evangelical, hostile to dissenters, immune to reason, (their beliefs are matters of faith, not logic). In a word, zealots. Their priests are psychologists and social scientists.[22]

CULTURE UNITES
CIVILIZATION PULLS APART

We find in our culture that the stories upon which our nation was built have lost their concrete foundation, and the stories which have appeared in their stead have tended to drive us apart rather than unite us as a culture. Like individualism, the myth of relativism drives us to tribalism in which each of us seeks identity in a variety of aimless tribes—a tribalism in which the underlying ethics are summed up, not as a love of God and love of neighbor, but as a selfish slogan: I don't mind and you don't matter.

CONCLUSION

This is the crisis facing the culture as it heads into the twenty-first century. As our culture is transformed (or fails, depending upon your perspective), we must not again fall syncretistically into the camp of culture and choose one side over the other. We must not default like a computer to the one who speaks the loudest. We must hold tight to the gospel as universal and insist that it speaks to all generations and all cultures. We must see the pictures painted in Scripture and apply them to our culture. It is a challenge to the church to supply the transforming myth that will guide the future.

I am reminded of the short story about the aftermath of World War III. A family of survivors of a nuclear holocaust search the ruins of the world for other survivors. Unable to find anyone, they begin again, like Noah and his family. After a long time, they come upon one elderly man ravaged by the effects of the nuclear blasts. He tries his best to say something but is unable to speak. Finally, in a low, raspy voice, he says, "Let me tell you the gospel."

At the end of our culture, should some of us weather the storm of relativism, will there be a survivor who will whisper, "Let me tell you the gospel"?

11

THE MYTH OF THE CHRISTIAN NATION:

The Congregation in Crisis

And therefore, let us learn not to think of him [Jesus] otherwise than what he himself teaches, and not to assign to him a character different from what he has received from the Father.

JOHN CALVIN, *Harmony of the Gospels*

Listen to the rhetoric of these inaugural speeches:

George Washington: It would be peculiarly improper to omit in this first official act my fervent supplications to that Almighty Being who rules over the universe, who presides in the councils of nations, and whose providential aids can supply every defect, that His benediction may consecrate to the liberties and happiness of the people of the United States a Government instituted by themselves. . . .

Abraham Lincoln: Fondly do we hope, and fervently do we pray, that this mighty scourge of war may speedily pass away. Yet, if God wills that it continue until all wealth piled up by the bondsman's two hundred and fifty years of unrequited toil shall be sunk, . . . as was said three thousand years ago, so still it must be said, the judgments of the Lord are true and righteous altogether.

John F. Kennedy: I have sworn before you and Almighty God the same solemn oath our forebears prescribed nearly a century and three quarters ago. . . . And yet the same revolutionary beliefs for which our forebears fought are still at issue around the globe—the belief that the rights of man come not from the generosity of the state but from the hand of God. . . . With a good conscience our only sure reward, with history the final judge of our deeds, let us go forth to lead the land we love, asking His blessing and His help, but knowing that here on earth God's work must truly be our own.

As Americans that rhetoric makes our hearts glow. Even as Christians, we stand up straighter when we hear those glorious words. But what are they saying to us? If we scratch the surface of the words, who are we exalting? As we interpret these words, we are exalting America and "the American way of life." In the Christian context, is that good or bad? In the Christian context, have we built our own Tower of Babel so that we are wed to political and social issues under the guise of our Christianity when those issues have little or nothing to do with the teachings of Jesus Christ and the church?

Each of us comes into the church carrying a certain amount of cultural baggage. If we recognize it, that is not particularly bad; then we can do something about it. But the question arises: Just how far do we go in incorporating the mythical views of the culture into our faith in God and God's truth?

The myths of individualism and relativism, in one form or another, have become the cultural baggage for many of the people in this country. Most Americans have a worldview comprised of the combined myths which have been prevalent in this country. Very few adopt the cultural views of Nietzsche or Hemingway, but those views will metamorphose our own understanding of the American myths. The resultant worldview retains the vestiges of the original American myths as they have been transformed by individualism and relativism.

The American myths, as they have evolved, attack one of the primary foundations of the Christian faith: the commitment to community. When the American carries the prevalent worldview into the church, he or she wants to adapt the church view to his or her worldview. The members of the congregation often see the Christian faith through the lenses of the American myths. The result in most American congregations is the worship of an American faith which is not Christianity but a perverted and diluted version of the Christian faith.

The member in the pew is often without a firm foundation in the faith, like the person who has little faith or knowledge but goes from one relativistic view to another, often without understanding what he

---

"The 'god of the civil religion' is the god of the American Dream."

---

or she is doing. The epistle of James describes such a person as double-minded "because he . . . is like a wave of the sea, blown and tossed by the wind" (James 1:6).

At the National Prayer Breakfast in 1973, Senator Mark Hatfield said:

> Let us beware of the real danger of misplaced allegiance, if not outright idolatry, to the extent we fail to distinguish between the god of an American civil religion and the God who reveals Himself in the Holy Scriptures and in Jesus Christ.
>
> If we as leaders appeal to the god of civil religion, our faith is in a small and exclusive deity, a loyal spiritual Advisor to power and prestige, a Defender of only the American nation, the object of a national folk religion devoid of moral content. But if we pray to the biblical God of justice and righteousness, we fall under God's judgment for calling upon His name, but failing to obey His commands.[1]

This counsel should be taken to heart not only by Christians but by all Americans. The "god of the civil religion" is the god of the American Dream.

Martin Lloyd-Jones writes: "The man who thinks he is godly because he talks about God and says he believes in God and goes to a place of worship occasionally but is really living for certain earthly things—how great is that man's darkness."[2]

128 AN AMERICAN VISION

THE AMERICAN RELIGION

When we combine the Christian faith with the American Dream, the Christian faith takes on all the characteristics of the American myths and loses the distinctiveness of the teachings of Jesus Christ. The values of America as expressed in the myths are substituted for the wisdom of Christian living as set out in Scripture.

In the last two decades, a number of scholars have applied the term *civil religion* to the American context. The civil religion is the worldview of the culture dressed in the garb of religion. In the United States, it is the American Dream disguised in the camouflage of the Christian faith—the American religion.

Robert L. Linder and Richard V. Pierard define *civil religion* as:

[T]he use of consensus religious sentiments, concepts and symbols by the state—either directly or indirectly—for its own political purposes. These purposes may be noble or debased depending upon the type of civil religion and the historical context. *It involves mixing traditional religion with national life until it is impossible to distinguish between the two.* . . . It usually leads to a blurring of religion and patriotism and of religious values with national values. In the case of American civil religion it is a rather *elaborate matrix of beliefs and practices born of the nation's historic experience and constituting the only real religion of millions of its citizens.* (emphasis added)[3]

While Linder and Pierard caution that not everyone agrees on that definition, there is a widespread acceptance of the phenomenon by historians, sociologists, political scientists, and theologians as an existent reality in our culture.

The above definition is an accurate working definition, but the American religion is broader than the context of individual-state relations and occurs in the context of the relationship of the individual to the culture as well as the state. It dictates not only the individual's worldview but his actions in pursuit of that worldview.

Will Herberg defines *civil religion* as follows:

It is an organic structure of ideas, values, and beliefs that constitutes a faith common to Americans as Americans, and is genuinely operative in their lives; . . . It is the American religion, undergirding national life and overarching American society . . . And it is a civil religion in

CORPORATION FOR ECONOMIC

WORLDVIEW

ACTION IN PURSUIT OF THAT WORLDVIEW

the strictest sense of the term, for in it, national life is apotheosized, national values are religionized, national heroes are divinized, national experience is experienced as "Heilgeschicte," a redemptive history.[4]

These two definitions point out the parameters of the American religion, the basis of which is the American myths and the beliefs which flow out of them.

Sociologist Robert N. Bellah has argued during the last twenty years that America finds moral and spiritual meaning in its civil religion.

Behind the civil religion at every point lie biblical archetypes: Exodus, chosen people, promised land, new Jerusalem, sacrificial death and re-birth. But it is also genuinely American and genuinely new. It has its own prophets and martyrs, its own sacred events and sacred places, its own solemn rituals and symbols.[5]

These, of course, are the same themes which comprise the foundation of the American Dream. The American religion is the exercise of the culture differently adapting the American Dream to the present generation and committing itself to it as a religion.

This is not new to culture nor to the Christian faith. Early empires had civil religions and early cultures adapted the Christian faith.

Malcolm Muggeridge writes:

Christendom, however, is something quite different from Christianity, being the administrative or power structure, based on the Christian religion and constructed by men. . . . The founder of Christianity was, of course, Christ. The founder of Christendom I suppose could be named as the Emperor Constantine. . . . Christendom began when Constantine, as an act of policy, decided to tolerate, indeed, positively favour the church, uniting it to the state by the closest possible ties.[6]

Tracing the history of the Christian church and its propensity to "soak up culture like a sponge," Jacques Ellul points out that it is not the Christian faith that is faltering in our world but Christendom. Christendom, which Ellul calls *Christianism*, has been devoured by cultural myths. He writes of the history of the church with sarcasm and sadness:

If unity cannot be attained [between the church and the Roman Empire] by the destruction of everything external, by the expansion of a pure Christianity, perhaps a combination and unification can be achieved by the *accommodation of Christianity and that which resists it.* This is the great program which Christianity first adopted in relation to Greek philosophy. But that is only one example. . . . Now we find something that far exceeds those attempts. Scandinavian legends, German Christmas trees, the festival of light, and the meditations of Arab mystics, all find an entry into Christianity. Everything is considered. No truth or beauty or religion cannot be integrated into Christianity. Our task is not to delay or annul but contrariwise to produce unity with everything that can be of service. Christianity adopts everything and *the process has never ceased.* (emphasis added)[7]

The problem arises, as Calvin pointed out, when we assign to Jesus a character different from that which He received from God. In the derision of Jesus during the passion, the Roman soldiers dressed Him in purple as the king of the Jews. They were using Jesus to mock the Jewish insurrectionists of the day. Halford Luccock writes that "this indignity has been inflicted upon him again and again. More than once has he been . . . clad in costumes that do not fit his personality, with the result that the man who walks before us has been so completely disguised as to be unrecognizable."[8]

When we place Jesus in the garb of the American mythology, we are repeating the mockery inflicted upon Him during the Passion week. That is the problem with the American religion—it renders the Christian faith unrecognizable. *+ UNDERSTANDING*

HAS THE AMERICAN RELIGION SPOILED OUR FAITH?

William Gladstone, the British prime minister, once said, "There is one proposition which the experience of life burns into my soul; it is this, that a man should beware of letting his religion spoil his morality. In a thousand ways, some great, some small, but all subtle, we are daily tempted to that great sin."[9] In our lives, we must be just as diligent not to let our American religion spoil our morality as we are to avoid allowing the culture of another country dictate how we conduct our daily lives.

The soul of the American church reveals a severe case of schizophrenia, created by the tensions in loyalty to community versus loyalty to self, in loyalty to God versus loyalty to the myths of the nation. The crisis in the congregation is that what is "genuinely operative in our lives," to borrow Herberg's phrase, and in our church is built upon the traditions of the nation rather than on the revelation of Jesus Christ.

An easy test for each of us is: When confronted with the daily issues of life, when stabbed by the annoyances of work or family or neighbors, when faced with the nagging of the bottom line of our checkbooks, where do we find our wisdom to deal with life's daily issues? When you are behind the wheel of a car and another vehicle cuts into your lane of traffic, what pops into your mind? When an alarmist program on any of several social issues presents a bleak view, what is your reaction? Fear? Distrust? Revenge? Anger? Or do you look to the sovereignty of God and know that His hand is upon the course of the world?

The answers, of course, reveal the myths which drive our conduct. Plato once said, "What is honored in a country will be cultivated there." Likewise, what is honored in a person will be cultivated in his daily life.

What's the problem? Has not the American Dream served us well so far? We would all have to answer that, in some respects, it has served many of us well. Yet in many respects it has been a cruel taskmaster.

"Plato once said, 'What is honored in a country will be cultivated there.' Likewise, what is honored in a person will be cultivated in his daily life."

We often hear the lament that many individuals are left out. The fact is that all are left out by the reality of the lack of spiritual substance of the American Dream. And that is the crucial distinction. As a dream, maybe it has served well. As a reality, it, like everything else mortal, is severely flawed because it leaves out the Christian faith.

As a result, the Christian church in the United States has little influence when considering the numbers of those involved in church life. *Christianity Today* summarized the situation in these words at the end of 1979:

Sixty-nine million Americans profess personal faith in Jesus Christ. Sixty-seven percent of Americans today are church members. A recent Gallup study determined that forty-four percent of the public attend church frequently, and forty-five million Americans of fourteen years and older described themselves as "highly religious." Why then has this great army of Christian soldiers not been more successful in beating back the forces of evil? This is American futurologist Tom Sine's explanation: "We have been remarkably effective at diluting his [Christ's] extremist teaching and truncating his radical gospel. That explains why we can have a nation of 200 million people, 60 million of whom profess to be Christian, and yet make such an embarrassingly little difference in the morality of our society."[10]

What has happened in this country to the faith which led a band of Judean fishermen to take the gospel around the world; to the faith which led a group of European dissidents to strike out of the Old World in search of religious freedom in the New World?

There is a tradition of the church that depicts St. Thomas Aquinas on a visit to Pope Innocent II. The Pope was in the process of counting a large quantity of money. Referring to the passage concerning the healing of the beggar by Peter in Acts 3, the Pope chuckled and said, "You see, Thomas, the church can no longer say, 'Silver and gold have I none.'"

"True, holy father," St. Thomas replied. "And neither can she now say, 'Arise and walk.'"

The American church, as it counts its many blessings, has lost its greatest blessing—the ability to look at the miserable and spiritually bankrupt in the congregation and say, "Arise and walk."

The American religion has spoiled our morality.

THE AMERICAN DREAM IN THE CHRISTIAN CHURCH

The congregation member who sits in the pew two or three Sundays a month must sit in the pew of the culture every day of the month. Reinforced almost by the minute are the symbols of America's greatness and the American "way of life." He or she is bombarded by the secular world with constant messages that the meaning of life is found in the material life of our culture.

The new member or the immature Christian or the stagnant Christian faces the confrontation when he or she enters the church and asks: what is in this for me? This is not to say that the search is illegitimate. The challenge to the church in the next century is to help the individual climb the wall and escape from the bonds of cultural individualism to the promises of eternal community.

Yet the mind-set in the American church is most often individualistic, built upon the myths of the culture. The member in the pew has at the foundation of his worldview the uniqueness-mission-conquest

> *"The challenge to the church in the next century is to help the individual climb the wall and escape from the bonds of cultural individualism to the promises of eternal community."*

game plan. The member aims that game plan at the church community in an effort to adapt the church to the self rather than the self to the church. As a result, the congregation becomes a gathering of individuals rather than a fellowship of believers arising from this unique community. Sadly, the member does not break through the cultural facade of the church to the questions posed by the Christian faith to each member of our culture.

Jesus warns us that we cannot serve both God and mammon. We cannot serve both the Christian faith and our cultural myths. We cannot worship God and follow the insatiable lusts our myths place before us under the rubric "success." Martin Lloyd-Jones writes: "Both demand our entire allegiance, and therefore they cannot be mixed. But man in sin and in his supposed cleverness sees two things at one and the same time; and he glories in his double vision."[11]

As we look at the American myths, we can see that each is adapted individualistically by the member and by the congregation so that the member can retain his or her position in the culture. The myths are adapted for comfort as well as for personal use.

Myth of Our Christian Origins

The myth of our Christian origins declares that the United States is a nation founded by Christians, and thus we should continue to conduct ourselves much as those Christians did, theologically, at least. This argument is heard most often among conservative wings of politically conservative congregations, among people who equate the welfare of the nation with the welfare of the Christian faith, as if the two were somehow dependent upon each other. What is good for America, it seems, is good for the church. While it is true that the Judeo-Christian heritage has had a great impact upon the growth of Western civilization, it is not true that the fortunes of the Christian faith are dependent on the fortunes of the United States. We often confuse the role of the United States in the world with the redemptive work of God. We often think that it is America's role to bring history down the path to an end of our liking. Our history seems to be synonymous with the history of God working in the history of the world.

The equation of the Christian faith with the interests of the world and the nation is one of the greatest dangers of the American religion. This equation explains why the decline in America's prestige at home and abroad is disconcerting to most American Christians. Just as the decline of the British Empire in the twentieth century spelled the decline of Christianity to British Christians, American Christians see the decline of American prestige abroad and the American culture at home as the decline of Christianity and the church. The failure of one, it seems, is the failure of the other. As a result, we have seen in the past two decades a strong alliance between Christian groups and conservative political causes, often to the detriment of the church.

In the conservative wings of the church, those who try to maintain and retain "Puritan theology" are often maintaining and retaining historic cultural norms. Those who argue vociferously for certain cultural norms as being biblical must closely examine themselves and their positions to ensure that they are defending their religious convictions and not their cultural convictions. If we tie the two together, as the Romans or the Greeks tied their civil religion to the welfare of their state, there is cause for concern. We generally tie the two together to advance our personal political outlook rather than the cause of the church or the goal of maturing in the Christian faith. That is why members who are conservative politically are often conservative theologically, assuming that they have not substituted politics for faith altogether.

But if we remember that the church is of the kingdom of God and not equivalent to the kingdom of man, our concerns for the faith are allayed. The Christian faith is strengthened when we recognize that God is in control of the kingdom of God, and He does not have to rely upon man or his kingdom. He is not a political puppet of the American government any more than He was the puppet of the Greeks or the Romans or anyone else.

Myth of Restoration and the New Beginning

In most instances, we are all entitled to a second chance. That's what we all believe. We are entitled to a second chance. The other guy may not be, but the myth goes deep in our culture, and we continually look for a second chance when the first one does not turn out to our liking.

This view, however, collides with commitment, particularly in the church. How easy it is to pick up and start in a new church if this one does not satisfy us, if this one does not uplift us, if this one does not encourage us. How easy it is to pick our churches by our own criteria so that they meet our needs rather than viewing the church as the body of Christ in which we are to commit to participation and encouragement of our brothers and sisters.

In Presbyterian churches, an elder is a spiritual leader of the church who is elected by the congregation and ordained for life. He takes certain vows before God with the view that his service is of lifetime tenure. Recently, an elder in our denomination became dissatisfied with the preacher in his church. Rather, his wife became very dissatisfied with the content of the preacher's sermons and began a campaign against the young preacher. The elder himself was silent about the matter. But the decision came when the governing body of the church received a letter stating that the elder and his family had become members of the Baptist church down the street. No inquiry, no reference to vows, no confrontation in accordance with Matthew 18, no commitment to the body of Christ. They "just up and left."

The personalizing of the myth of restoration and the new beginning allow us to "just up and leave" at the time of our choosing. And it happens not only in the church where a variety of factors block fellowship and commitment to the body, but it happens also in businesses where one partner or one employee may run out on the others, and it is happening in the home where resolution of familial difficulties is often found in the new beginning.

As a result, we lose the meaning of fellowship and community in the church, and we lose the meaning of God's promise of the real restoration and new beginning.

Myth of Sacrifice and Dissent

How easy it is to leave the warm fuzzies of the faith and step over the fence to demand "my rights" through the myth of sacrifice and dissent. This myth so permeates our culture and our church that it has rendered the concept of church community and discipline meaningless. By church discipline, I mean the method of instruction as well as correction with the view toward guiding and helping people in their individual Christian walks. The term in vogue is *accountability*. The whole idea of discipline in any form, instruction as well as correction, is anathema to many of the strains of individualism and much of the American church. The individual involved in the discipline can very easily leave one church building, like the elder mentioned above, and go down the street to the next without any thought of loyalty or faith or anything else. He can dismiss his perceived problem and find a "new beginning." Without commitment, sacrifice is not uncomfortable and dissent is not unpleasant. Discipline in the church is much the same as discipline in, say, any fraternal organization. It's my life and I don't have to share it with anyone. If I don't like it, I leave.

In Collinsville, Oklahoma, a woman who was having an affair was counseled by the elders of her church. After a period of counseling, she refused to quit the affair and was compelled to withdraw from the fellowship of the church. An announcement was made to that effect before the congregation. In a libel suit against the elders, a jury awarded her $390,000. One juror said: "I don't see what right the church has to tell people how to live." Her lawyer said: "It doesn't matter if she was fornicating up and down the street. It doesn't give [the church] the right to stick their noses in."[12]

The Collinsville case is the end of the pike begun by Roger Williams and the dissidents in early America. Deep within the American Dream is the myth that permits people to dissent to the extent that legitimate instruction and correction is often cause for dissent and departure. This is an un-Christian attitude but very American, and it is in the fiber of the American church.

As a result, we find ourselves circling the wagons in our Christian enclaves. We do it both in time—Christian life is reserved for Sunday morning—and space—we live our Christian life at the church. The fact is that we have diluted the Christian faith to the extent that it is often nothing more than a number of splinter groups which argue for or against one cultural point or another. Franklin wrote two hundred years ago that he believed in the Deity but that he saw a number of "religions" around him "more or less mix'd with other articles, which, without any tendency to inspire, promote or confirm morality, serv'd principally to divide us, and make us unfriendly to one another."[13] By *religions* he meant denominations. Things have not improved in two hundred years.

Myth of Political Equality

The myth of political equality is a fundamental problem in the structure of the church. Christians often act in the political process as if they were any other political group. And with that attitude they present themselves to the public as simply another one-shot political lobby.

There is a great debate in the evangelical church about the role of the church in the political process. Many are advocating an active role not only in the political process but in the legal system to counter what is seen as a secular attack on the church and on Christian values. Those who are proposing this counterattack are Christians just as sincere as those who think that Christians must be very careful in the political and legal arenas lest they show a witness which is hateful and strident.

Christian political influence has been felt in our country from Blue Laws to prohibition. But it is only influence. Political power is the end sought by political groups. By definition, political groups are formed to impose their will upon others and to do so by the lawful manipulation of the political process. Historically, power politics and Christian witness have not mixed well. (I am not talking about speaking out as Christians and as citizens. I am talking about legal coercion.)

Nowhere does the political tradition in America (as displayed in the republican myth) strike so hard as in the battle over abortion. The shame is that there are elements on both sides shouting epithets at each other, refusing to listen and to dialogue. That is the American myth, but it reflects poorly on Jesus Christ when it is done in His name.

A friend of mine in his late thirties was recently married to a young woman he had known for nearly a year. My friend, who shall go by the name Sam, is a cultural Christian. Like many Southerners, he is very familiar with the doctrines and the lingo of the Southern church. Like many Southerners, his upbringing has hardened him to any efforts to look sincerely at the gospel. Sam married at a time when he was evaluating the course of his life and thinking again about the church.

Sam approached me one day and said, "I don't know what you think about abortion but my wife is an employee of an abortion clinic." The opposition to abortion in the Jackson, Mississippi, area was being led very stridently by several Christian groups, so I knew the conversation was going downhill in a hurry.

Sam was very calm. "Let me tell you what I see of the Christian church. They spit in my face and my wife's face, they call me baby-killer, they march in front of my house, my house I tell you, not the abortion clinic. They throw human feces on my porch." He reflected for a moment. "I have a hard time with that."

I could not say that I blamed him. I have no problem with the goals and intentions of the pro-life groups active in political confrontations. But I believe categorically that stridency is not a Christian characteristic; it is an American characteristic. Those assembled before Pilate shouted, "Give us Barabbas" because Barabbas was the embodiment of what they were looking for in the "king of the Jews." He was a popular hero who reflected the popular mind of the time. His tactics were violent, but they were what the culture wanted. That is why his contrast to Jesus is so remarkable. The people of Jerusalem sought the way of the culture rather than the way of Jesus and the prophets.

The civil rights movement is the counterargument. The early movement was peaceful, but it became very strident as it moved into the late sixties and early seventies. To use the civil rights movement as precedent is to call upon the American tradition rather than the Chris-

---

"I have no problem with the goals and intentions of the pro-life groups active in political confrontations. But I believe categorically that stridency is not a Christian characteristic; it is an American characteristic."

---

tian tradition. We betray the faith when we reach out and grab the methods of the world. No doubt the methods used in the civil rights movement worked in some areas. Yet over the years, they were perverted, and now, even when applied in secular circles, they are often counterproductive.

Relying upon secular tactics rather than Christian practices is a sellout of the Christian faith to an American myth.

Myth of the Self-Made Man

The myth of the self-made man has become the bedrock of the American religion. Little needs to be said about the power of money in the culture or money in the church. The fact that Christians forsake the faith for the dollar is evident in every congregation.

Ray Kroc, the founder of MacDonald's hamburger chain, purportedly said that his priorities in life were God, his family, and his business. And when he arrived at the office on Monday morning, they were reversed.

Whether or not Ray Kroc meant that is irrelevant. That attitude, seen in different forms in other areas of life, is as American as baseball or apple pie.

The *Jackson Clarion-Ledger*, in its June 30, 1990, edition, carried an Associated Press article which stated that two hundred thousand children between the ages of ten and fourteen are taking anabolic steroids given by teachers and parents in order to enhance their athletic prowess. Cable

News Network places the number at two hundred fifty thousand. Maybe if the parents and coaches worked as hard at developing the character and spiritual life of these kids as they do boosting their own egos by giving them drugs, the children would be better off.

When the myth seeps into the church and the member in the pew sees the church's message as honoring the self-made man, the Christian faith is tainted and is packaged as the American religion.

Myth of the Search for the American Soul

Like the myth of sacrifice and dissent, the myth of the search for the American soul has contributed greatly to the compartmentalization and privatization of the Christian faith in America. Christians bring the American views of individualism into the pews with them so that they act and think individualistically rather than collectively, as members of the same body. Thinking individualistically makes it very easy to turn on your brother in order to enforce your perceived rights. Thinking individualistically makes it very easy to pursue your comfort at the expense of your brothers and sisters in the church. Thinking individualistically makes it very easy to use Christianity to support individualistic life-styles of many descriptions.

In his now-famous interview, Robert Bellah was told by an interviewee named Sheila, "who has received a good deal of therapy," that she believed in God. "I'm not a religious fanatic. I can't remember the last time I went to church. My faith has carried me a long way. It is Sheilaism. Just my own little voice."[14]

The American myth has infiltrated the church so that many members, ludicrous as it may sound, search their souls for that "little voice" to send them on their way each day. That voice may be emotion, lust, will, illness, or a dozen other things. The crime is that it has come into the church and is accepted and called the voice of God.

Myths of Individualism and Relativism

The privatization of the faith has been helped, of course, by the myths of individualism and relativism. These American myths have been the sacred stones upon which the temple of the American god has been created.

In speaking of the civil religion, Linder and Pierard state that it has changed in the nineteenth and twentieth centuries.

> The evangelical consensus became the Protestant Establishment, the chosen nation theme now smacked of superiority and condescension, the mission of American democracy turned into strident nationalism and the philosophy of progress transformed into blatant materialism. In the process civil religion became more and more an expression of *American tribal ethnocentrism.* (emphasis added)[15]

Tribalism will increase in the nineties as the American culture becomes more acrid and fragmented. Consequently, tribalism is carried unwittingly into the congregations. American Christianity risks becoming yet another tribe in the American tribal ethnocentrism.

Ironically, in the context of the church, the evolving myths of individualism and relativism, the most antithetical to the Christian faith, do not weaken the American religion but strengthen it by making it more insular. Relativism and its prophets have thrown out the Bible as the infallible standard of faith and practice. Without standards for our experience, belief, and ethics, we are in a moral free-for-all. Therefore, it is easier for the member in the pew to latch on to an Americanism which gives some sense of permanence without being committed to something specifically identifiable. These myths have made the church attractive to many people because the people see in the church and its teachings an affirmation of the American Dream.

Charles Colson describes one radical instance which occurred in New York City at the Episcopal cathedral of St. John the Divine. The worshipers at St. John the Divine today enter a sanctuary adorned with a Jewish menorah, Muslim prayer rugs, Shinto vases, and a "Christa," a crucifix with a female Christ. "Sermons" have been preached from the pulpit by such diverse "preachers" as Jesse Jackson, Norman Mailer, several rabbis, imams, Buddhists, atheist scientists, and politicians running for office.

The dean of the cathedral justifies this "worship" by stating, "This cathedral is a place for birth Episcopalians like me who feel constricted by the notion of excluding others. What happens here—the Sufi dances, the Buddhist prayers—are serious spiritual experiences. We make God a Minnie Mouse in stature when we say these experiences profane a Christian church."[16]

142

AN AMERICAN VISION

The myths of relativism are alive and well in this church in New York City. Each tribe in our culture has some representation in the worship services. Perhaps they think it is a greater sin to offend a tribe in our culture than it is to offend God by syncretistic services elevating man to the same level as God.

But these churches are the ones which get the publicity, and they are the extreme. There are many, many American churches of all denominations in which the myths of the American Dream are just as pervasive. However, the myths are accepted because they are easier to swallow.

When English commentator Alistair Cooke heard the G. K. Chesterton quote that America is a nation with the soul of a church, he supposedly retorted, "She also has the soul of a whorehouse."

THE DANGERS OF THE AMERICAN RELIGION

The Apostle Paul wrote to his son in the faith, Timothy: "For the time will come when men will not put up with sound doctrine. Instead, to suit their own desires, they will gather around them a great number of teachers to say what their itching ears want to hear. They will turn their ears away from the truth and turn aside to myths" (2 Timothy 4:3–4).

What happens when we come to a church which has differently adapted the American myths as its foundational propositions? What happens in a church which professes to follow the teachings of Jesus Christ yet has genuinely operative in its beliefs the individualism and relativism prevalent in the American religion? What happens when a person seeking the Christian faith follows a model of uniqueness, exclusive mission, and conquest rather than a model of love for God, love for neighbor, and love for enemy? There are several items to consider in these questions.

First, the member in the pew comes to the church on Sunday morning seeking some answer from God concerning the tensions of our culture. However, when he hears and sees the god of our culture preached from the pulpit, whether it be in St. John's in New York City or in the mainline denominations on Main Street or in the fundamentalist churches around the country, he is duped into thinking that the word he receives is somehow from the Word of God.

The member in the pew may hear from the god of the American religion who is invoked to manipulate support for a wide range of causes. The Vietnam War, abortion on demand, the battle against AIDS, all lay their claims at the altar of the American religion. Once tied to a tenet of the American religion, the issue has the sanction of the sacred and becomes *American* so that it cannot be defeated with any degree of rational thought or logic. In the American religion, the pulpit itself becomes not the proclamation point of the Word of God but the dispenser of American mythology.

Second, as a result of seeing the practice of the American religion, we break with the faith which professes the teachings of Jesus Christ. Leo Tolstoy, author of *War and Peace*, wrote in his book *Confessions*:

> My break with faith occurred in me as it did and still does among people of our social and cultural type. As I see it, in most cases, it happens like this: People live as everyone lives, but they all live according to principles that not only have nothing to do with the teachings of faith, but for the most part, are contrary to them. The teachings of faith have no place in life and never come into play in the relations among people; they simply play no role in living life itself. The teachings of faith are left in some other realm, separated from life and independent of it. If one should encounter them, then it is only as some superficial phenomenon that has no connection with life.

The teachings of the Christian faith then are left to some other realm. The member in the pew then defines *life* according to the faith of the American religion. Congregation members find themselves in the

> "In the American religion, the pulpit itself becomes not the proclamation point of the Word of God but the dispenser of American mythology."

American culture, just as Christians found themselves in the Roman culture, the Greek culture, the British culture, or any other culture. Faith in life in the culture creates the same pressures for conformity, the same demands for contribution to the welfare of the culture, and the same distortions of the view of the people in the pew. Therein lies the danger of the American religion. We live as everyone lives, according to the principles of life guided by American myths. The teachings of the faith never come into play. The teachings of Jesus Christ are "separated from life and independent of it."

Third, as a result of the separation from the faith, the American myths fill in where faith has been shoved aside. In the model of conquest, health-and-wealth theology thrives. God becomes the enabler of the conquest to satisfy our earthly desires. "Name it, claim it, and frame it" becomes the prayer. This occurs not only in the pursuit of wealth and happiness, as expressed by some of the televangelists, but it occurs in all of our endeavors. Whatever our promised land, the god of the American religion is there to ensure the victory—not the victory for Christ but our victory, the victory for our thought or our side or our religion.

Dietrich Bonhoeffer wrote: "That was the fatal mistake [the failure to recognize the extraordinary calling of Jesus to love of God and neighbor and enemy] of the false Protestant ethic which diluted Christian love into patriotism, loyalty to friends, and industriousness, which in short, perverted the better righteousness into *justitia civilis*. Not in such terms as these does Jesus speak."[17]

The pursuit of the faith of love is replaced by a faith which is competitive, tribalistic, and self-seeking. In the mainline denominations, the cry from the top levels of the hierarchy may not be for individual happiness and success at the congregational level. But the cry is made in the spirit of conquest. Their view is to be forced upon the "unbelievers" in the pews so that the denomination will reflect the view from the top. The denomination then becomes the sword of conquest for certain hierarchical ideas and views. The love taught by Jesus, the love for enemy, is relegated to the back of the bus so that we may get on with the conquest.

Fourth, the member in the pew begins to adapt his conduct to the tenets of the American myths rather than the Christian faith. One example of this phenomenon occurs in the American family. In the black inner cities, the phenomenon of one-parent families has been examined frequently. The father leaves the family or was never there in the first place. The child grows up without a male role model and is lost in his effort to find meaning in life. William Raspberry, in his August 28, 1990, syndicated column suggests that this is the reason for the substitution of machoism for manliness—a substitution that is destroying a generation of children in the inner city.

But what about the two-parent families, particularly the Christian two-parent families? What about the absentee father or the absentee mother syndrome in the Christian family? The business world seems to swallow fathers and mothers just as quickly as the inner city.

"My work is the most important thing in life" becomes the banner of the worn-out individualists seeking their own identity. "If I didn't work this hard," the husband says when his wife asks for companionship for herself and the children, "you couldn't have the nice things that you do." "God wants me to work this hard to support the family" becomes the rationale of the American religion. The result is the same as in the inner city: the child grows up without a father or mother—a new definition of American orphan.

Fifth, the Christian faith becomes the justification for conduct in the business arena. The flames of this phenomenon are fanned by the myths of the self-made man and the search for the soul. Business becomes the extension of self. The American businessman, or in many instances the American businesswoman, has the feeling that he or she is called to a certain profession or business. He/she has a mission to

> **"'My work is the most important thing in life' becomes the banner of the worn-out individualists seeking their own identity."**

succeed by worldly standards at that business. And the conquest is on. Because the business becomes a question of identity, it is easy to put everything else subordinate in priority to the business. Ego grows; loyalty goes. The business begins to swallow all the hours, and the family disintegrates. The success of the business is personal, individualistic success—a success recognized by the world. Identity, well-being, self-esteem, all ride on the success of the business.

The person can enter the church, contribute to the church, hear applause for the business, and enjoy the facade of the Christian businessman. But he may never hear a sermon which teaches him that his efforts are misguided.

These are not the hybrids of American business who have perverted the honest earning of a dollar into the personal quest for the Holy Grail. These are not the ego-equals-empire eccentrics who grace the ethical wasteland of American business. These are not the empire-building megalomaniacs, like Donald Trump, Ted Turner, Michael Milken, or Ivan Boesky.

These are men and women who identify themselves as Christians yet who substitute the American Dream for the Christian faith and justify their actions by saying that the Bible dictates that they must find the blessings of God in health and wealth. It is reflected in the lawyer who works ten, twelve, fourteen hours a day to pump up his ego and then rationalizes by saying that God has given him the blessing of making a good life for his family. It is reflected in the accountant who can walk out on his wife and children by saying that they are interfering with his business and justify it by saying that God does not want him to be miserable. It is reflected in the seminary professor who can bury himself in his work so that he rarely participates in the lives of his children or his wife. It is reflected in the doctor who cannot understand why his wife leaves him after he has ignored her and the children for ten years and then rationalizes it by saying that God has called him to help the sick and needy. It is reflected in the young man who describes his dreams to be very wealthy and then adds: I can cite you authority in the Scripture for it. Of course, he never does.

That is the danger of the American religion. The Christian faith provides the facade, but the American myths drive the train. The stamp of approval of the American tribal god is upon it.

G. K. Chesterton wrote that Christianity has not been tried and found wanting, it has been found difficult and not tried at all.

CONCLUSION

The American Dream can be a cruel master, seducing us and then letting us down. It can lead us to a dead end; it can make us hate ourselves and those around us. The pursuit of the Dream rests on the themes of uniqueness, mission, and conquest; therefore, it encourages anger and combativeness, and can become all-consuming. Consequently, we focus on ourselves and pit our tension against our families, neighbors, and faith itself. These characteristics are the opposite of the Christian faith.

The crying shame is that we pass on to our children the American Dream in the guise of the Christian faith. Our legacy to our children is angry, combative, and consuming. When they observe worship in the dead churches, we teach them that it is okay to conduct our worship that way since the real importance is in the marketplace. When they wonder why they cannot develop close friendships which are not manipulative but are loving and serving, we say it is okay, because the real importance is in competition and in advancement.

A child in our congregation, when asked what God had done in his life or what God could do in his life, shrugged and said, "I guess He could make me rich." That child's god is the god of his parents, the god of the American religion. Only by the grace of God will he know anything of the God of the universe.

The primary role of the church is to teach the gospel to the member in the pew. The success of the church today, as always, is measured by the extent it equips the members in the pew to question and cross-examine the cultural myths based upon the foundation of scriptural principles. Jesus found fault with the Pharisees for following the traditions of their religion rather than following the revelation of God in Scripture. "You have let go of the commands of God and are holding on to the traditions of men. . . . You have a fine way of setting aside the commands of God in order to observe your own traditions! . . . Thus you nullify the word of God by your tradition that you have handed down. And you do many things like that" (Mark 7:8–13).

All too often, the member in the pew finds that the myths and traditions of the American Dream have nullified the tenets of the Christian faith. The American Dream has diluted the teachings of Jesus and truncated the gospel. The result is the American religion—a civil religion which is espoused by millions of Americans in and out of the church. Christianity has not been tried and found wanting; it has been found difficult and not tried at all.

It has been found difficult and, therefore, misunderstood and opposed by those who profess the cultural faith. Martin Lloyd-Jones writes:

> I have often been told by converts that they get much more opposition from supposedly Christian people than they do from the man of the world outside, who is often glad to see them changed and wants to know something about it. Formal Christianity is often the greatest enemy of the pure faith.[18]

But what should Christians do? Or, rather, what should those do who attend church, who are looking for answers to the larger questions of life, and/or who are looking for an alternative to the American mythology?

The next chapters discuss some of the answers provided by the Christian faith.

PART 2

A CHRISTIAN VISION

12

AMERICANS AND THE CHRISTIAN FAITH

Americans are drifting away from spiritual values as they become richer. . . . sooner or later, we will have to go back to our fundamental values, back to God, the truth, the truth which is in God. . . . We look to America, and we expect from you a spiritual richness to meet the aspirations of the 20th century.

LECH WALESA

Before we shift gears away from the impact of the myths of the American Dream upon our culture and to the quest of the Christian faith, we should recognize one point. As we examine our cultural vision, we must recognize that never before in history has a culture survived after it has forsaken its religious foundations and after it has debunked its moral code. The United States will not be the first.

On the other hand, this is not the first declining culture in which the church has found itself. Historically, the faith has thrived in adverse cultural circumstances but has slumbered in prosperity. This holds true even though the Christian faith is not completely separate from our culture. The faith is a path of life which is different from what we have come to know in America. The Christian faith, which was in the fabric of the lives of early Americans, is now lost in much of the modern American life-style. Its remnant is evident in America yet the heart of the Christian faith has been devoured by the myths of the American

151

Dream. That is a primary tension in our culture—the struggle between the myths of the secular culture and the foundation of the culture in the Judeo-Christian heritage.

The Christian faith counters the prevalent American life-style by calling us back to the wisdom of the ages while bidding us to cling to our culture. It calls us to a spiritual life in a material world, yet it challenges and pierces the precepts of modern America. It calls us to our roots in America, yet it spurs us to address and overcome the obstacles of the future. The Christian faith is not the opponent of American life-style, for it cannot be separated from American life. It is the conscience of American life calling us back from our self-perceived uniqueness, from our self-perceived autonomous missions, and from our conquests over our fellow human beings and over the environment. As Americans and as Christians, we must understand the world in both visions. *CHRISTIANS / AMERICANS*

THE CHARACTERISTICS OF THE FAITH

By *faith,* in this context, I mean the act of being a Christian in the United States as we enter the twenty-first century. I am not trying to define *faith.* Rather, I am speaking of our experience, who we are and who we have been as human beings on this planet and in this country; our beliefs, how we think in the context of the American myths; and our ethics, how we behave when confronted by our culture. These, of course, appear as three items but are, in fact, one. Our intellect, our will, and our emotions are three items. They cannot be completely separated but are each in us. Likewise, our experience, our beliefs, and our ethics are three items which cannot be completely separated but are in each of us. The Christian faith is the integration of the three so that we may live on this earth in a certain way. The three are integral to life and belong together. The three comprise the biblical meaning of "heart." The Christian faith is a faith of the heart.

So, I am not speaking of fideism, or faith as opposed to belief, or faith as mysticism, or faith as anything else other than that which guides our experience, our belief, and our conduct. Christian faith is not a religion in the sense that it prescribes our daily conduct in legal terms. Rather, it is the practice of a life in relationship with Jesus Christ. The

HEART   EMOTIONS — OUR EXPERIENCE
*   INTELLECT — HOW WE THINK*
*   WILL — OUR ETHICS*

Christian faith provides the individual, heartfelt answer to the question: Who is Jesus Christ? That individual answer reflects the faith in each of our hearts, and that is the essence of being a follower of Jesus Christ.

With that in mind, I would like to address some of the attributes of faith in the American context.

1. Faith Is Not a Substitute for Culture

As we discuss faith in the context of experience, beliefs, and ethics, it is apparent that our faith is something that is practiced rather than defined, much like the practice of law or of medicine. It cannot be separated from our lives or our living. Faith is something we do each day, a way we look at the world, a way we act toward each other. Some might call it a Christian worldview, but it is broader than that because it cannot be separated from what we learn as Americans. Christians, indeed, have double vision since the world is seen through an American set of lenses and through a Christian set of lenses.

How can that be? How can an individual be both since the myths of the American Dream are not the tenets of the Christian faith? Granted, it's not easy. That's why living as a Christian in the United States, or anywhere else, takes practice. The Christian faith is a call for

> **"Our faith is something that is practiced rather than defined, much like the practice of law or of medicine. It cannot be separated from our lives or our living."**

each man and woman to view the world from both perspectives: that of American and that of Christian. But the Christian must be able to tell the difference. The call is not to reject the American culture but be in it as a contributing member, to find success not in the worldly way but in the way Christ has taught—by loving and serving. The Christian faith is a faith which requires one to think about life, to examine the philosophies of life, and to arrive at the truth of life. It takes time, inquiry, and priority. It is not easy.

I am reminded of a story Arthur Gordon, an editor for *Guideposts* magazine, told about his young and ambitious days when he left Georgia, convinced he was going to be a great writer and take a position with a magazine in New York City.[1] When he received one rejection slip after another, his dream of succeeding as a writer seemed to be floating out the window.

Through his business, he had an appointment with T. J. Watson, the president of International Business Machines. After lunch, Watson asked Gordon what he really wanted to do in life. Gordon confessed to him the disappointments he had in writing. "Every time I submit something to an editor it is rejected."

Watson gave him some advice. "Go back and look at all your failures. Find the mistakes you've made and learn from them. Success is on the far side of failure. Success only comes after we have learned the many lessons of repeated failure."

Likewise, faith in the sense of living as a follower of Jesus Christ comes on the far side of culture and comes only after we have learned the many lessons of living in the culture.

What are the lessons our culture teaches? They are many and I have not, by a long shot, learned most or even many of them. So it may be somewhat presumptuous of me, a relatively young man, chronologically and in the faith, to set out on a discussion of faith for Christians. I consider myself to be in Gordon's position rather than Watson's. I consider myself to be learning from my failures in the American culture.

As faith is not a substitute for culture, culture is not a substitute for faith. That applies both to the so-called fundamentalists who, in many instances, preach a cultural religion in the name of the gospel. And it applies to those who are at the opposite pole from the fundamentalists and who preach a social message in the name of the gospel. The governing board of the National Council of Churches, for example, passed a resolution at its May 1990 meeting, which condemned the upcoming celebration of the five hundredth anniversary of Columbus's landing in the western hemisphere. The resolution alleged that Columbus's landing launched a legacy of "invasion, genocide, slavery, 'ecocide,' and exploitation of the wealth of the land."[2] While there are instances in the history of Western civilization in which those terms might arguably be applied, these words are hardly conciliatory. Rather, they are strident and lead to schism and rejection of the cultural growth in this hemisphere. They distort the Christian message in a manner far worse than any of the fundamentalist groups.

The cultural factors which impact us have impacted many generations before us. The mingling of church and state, of faith and religion, of God and mammon, has distorted the tide of Christianity throughout the ages. Granted, we in America have been unable to interrupt that pattern significantly, but that does not change our call to follow Christ or to live in the manner He would have for us.

In his discussion of Martin Luther, German theologian Dietrich Bonhoeffer wrote, "No, Luther had to leave the cloister and go back to the world, not because the world in itself was good and holy, but because the cloister was only a part of the world. . . . The only way to follow Jesus was to live in the world."[3]

Likewise, the position from which elements of the church, both conservative and liberal, reject our culture is only a part of the culture. We are in it whether we like it or not.

Our success in living in the world is on the far side of our culture. As we travel through this world, we must remember that we will not reach the far side of our culture until we reach the far side of life. Nevertheless, we must continue to travel.

2. Faith Is Not Absolute; God Is

The philosopher Arthur Schopenhauer said that every man takes the limits of his vision to be the limits of the world. Likewise, every generation takes the limits of its culture to be the limits of reality. Each generation formulates its own truth based upon the beliefs of that generation.

As we have discussed in the first part of this book, our faith is not exempt from our worldview but is based on it. Therefore, our faith is relative. There is no way we can avoid it. Our faith is relative in at least four ways.[4]

First, our faith is limited by the knowledge that we possess. None of us has complete knowledge of the world. We know only a small portion of what is to be known. Any answer we give on any subject is limited by what we know at a certain point in history. Such is the limitation of finite man. What we know about certain things today is much more than what people knew in, say, the fifth century. But it is much less than what people will know in, say, the twenty-fifth century.

If a person in the fifteenth century argued that the world was flat, he was not unusual. That was what his culture taught him. His knowledge was limited but accepted. If we argue today that the world is flat, we are foolish. Yet we argue things today that will seem foolish six centuries from now. We must recognize that. Yet we must act on what we know, recognizing that our philosophies of life and our views of the world are based on that imperfect, incomplete body of knowledge.

Second, our faith never remains constant. No person at any time has complete faith in God. In the human condition, we straddle that fence between faith and doubt. At times we lean heavily on our faith. At other times we chuck our faith out the window in order to latch on to some whim of the world. Our faith here on earth fluctuates constantly on a continuum just short of absolute faith all the way down to absolute rejection.

The Texas Driver's Handbook has a drawing that helps illustrate the fact that the faster the pace of our lives, the less perspective we have on things and the less our faith comes into play. When not moving, the driver enjoys a field of vision of one hundred eighty degrees or more. At twenty miles per hour, the field of vision is reduced by approximately two-thirds. At forty miles per hour, the field of vision is further reduced by two-fifths. At sixty miles per hour, the field of vision is barely wider than the beams of the headlights.

Likewise, our views and decisions of the world are based in part on how fast we are traveling in life. When things are good and going fast, our faith may be less than when we are standing still.

Third, our faith is limited by our time and place in history. The twentieth-century Christian church should not be expected to respond to culture in the same way as the martyrs of the first three centuries. Americans should not respond to their culture in the same way as, say, Romanians respond to theirs. Times and places change and are different, calling for different responses. Our backgrounds and our worldviews are different. We hear things differently. And those things we hear and see shape our view of ourselves. Remembering that any description of the Christian faith is an interpretation of that faith, our interpretations are dependent upon our positions in time and space.

Fourth, faith depends on the relationships we bring to the circumstances of life. Consequently, it is important to recognize that faith is not simply based upon our experience, but our beliefs and our ethics as well. The thoughts and values expressed in daily life are relative if not relativistic. They depend on our relationships to people and things.

There is a story of a Maine farmer who was approached by a man in a business suit. The man asked how much the farmer thought his prize Jersey bull was worth. The farmer studied the man, thought for a moment, and said, "Are you the tax assessor or did you just hit him with your car?"

Likewise, our faith is tested by relationships to other beings, to reason, to life, to all things around us. We give our answers to the questions of life and faith based upon our changing relationships. The Christian faith as practiced is relative, based upon the preceding considerations, and not relativistic.

I do not want to make more of this simple observation than is required. This is simply the other side of the coin of the cultural worldview. I mention this to point out that we often differ in our interpretations of world events, personal relationships, or Bible passages. Our differences are most often caused by the differences in our worldviews, because our worldviews are relative. Therefore, we should be very reluctant to be dogmatic about our views on world events, personal relationships, or Bible passages. A Chinese person is not likely to view the world the same way as an American. That does not, however, mean that we forsake our own views. On the contrary, we must examine our views and hold them dearly when we are convinced, after rigorous cross-examination, that we are right. But we must be hesitant to compel our neighbor to agree with our worldview.

I know a seminary professor who liked to say that there is only one meaning in any given Bible passage. If you disagree with someone on the interpretation of that Bible passage, there are three possibilities: first, you are right and the other person is wrong; second, the other person is right and you are wrong; third, and most likely, you are both wrong.

Niebuhr writes: "To make our decisions in faith is to make them in view of the fact that no single man or group or historical time is the church; but that there is a church of faith in which we do our partial, relative work and on which we count."[5]

As Christians, we affirm that God is absolute but we must recognize that human beings are not. When a human gives the answer, it is relative. Human beings may interpret the Word of God or the will of God, but it is only an interpretation. A human being falls far short of the glory of God and, in his finiteness, cannot understand the infinity of God. As a result, the things that we show to the world as Christianity are things which reflect only our understanding and only a partial faith in Jesus as Lord.

3. Faith Is Not Created to Answer Our Perceived Needs

It has been said that if God did not exist, mankind would have to create Him. But the meaning of the Christian faith is in Jesus Christ and not in response to our perceived needs. We can only understand this when we realize that we are unable to know Jesus totally, just as we are unable to understand Scripture fully. Calvin often said, "The finite cannot comprehend the infinite."

The radical nature of faith is that it does not fit neatly into our worldview. In fact, faith runs counter to our efforts to classify and systematize our culture and thereby seek and maintain order. Jesus was born in a manger, hardly the place for a king. He had no army or wealth or power; indeed, He did not seek them. He was submissive to God yet not rebellious to the civil authorities. He was humiliated when He could have overcome; He was humble when we might have expected arrogance; He was weak when He had at His fingertips immense strength; He died when He could have lived.

The fact is that the Christian faith, at its base, is radical to our thinking and foreign to our very nature. The faith is not convenient nor is it easy.

French historian Jacques Ellul demonstrates five areas in which the Christian faith is contrary to the nature of humanity.[6] The first is in the nature of grace. Grace, that is, God's gift to humanity which is not based on merit but is a unilateral act on the part of God, is unacceptable to human beings. Deep in our hearts, we refuse to believe that we are unable on our own to work our way into heaven, that we are without merit and we cannot depend upon ourselves but must depend upon a God who is much greater than we are.

We may give lip service to this idea, but deep down inside we are not willing to degrade ourselves to that level. It's just not us. We spend most of our resources building ourselves and our culture to reflect our own excellence.

> "As Christians, we affirm that God is absolute but we must recognize that human beings are not. When a human gives the answer, it is relative. Human beings may interpret the Word of God or the will of God, but it is only an interpretation."

Second, the image of God as Father, like the idea of the necessity of grace, is intolerable to modern man. The metaphor of father suggests kindness and love and warmth, the relationship that most children seek with a father. Yet, in reality, that relationship is never perfect and is often less than perfect. Fathers are often those with whom children compete: they compete for the parent's affection, for his time, for his love. In *Oedipus Rex*, the father is the enemy who is killed in the end. Ellul suggests that psychiatry is not fabricating the tensions which develop between fathers and children. Those tensions, according to Ellul, make us reject the view that God, if He is really God, is a Father.

But, Ellul argues, the image of the Father is an accommodation of language to human beings; we have taken the inherent struggle of father and son and applied it to God. Scripture contradicts our cultural views of ourselves and our worth when it portrays God as a loving Father. It strikes through our cozy view and shows us a God who is far beyond the images we can create for Him. Jesus used the term *Father* as an image. Human beings supplied the analogy and the limitations that go along with it.

Third, the faith is in a Christ who is weak in the political sense. This strikes at the heart of culture, order, and the American worldview. Christ is not the American self-made, rags-to-riches man. In America, weakness in anything is not a favored trait. Americans are not likely to turn the other cheek and will find varieties of explanations why weakness does not apply to them or their circumstances. We cannot conceive of Vince Lombardi saying, "Weakness is not everything. It's the only thing."

The tenet of our faith that life centers on service and submission, however defined, is foreign to the heart of humanity. Little else need be said. Culture builds our worldly and fleshly pride and power. Faith strikes it down.

Fourth, our culture builds on the idea of freedom. But faith announces a freedom incomprehensible to human beings—a freedom unacceptable to humanity because it is built on permanent self-control and love of neighbor. "What people want when they talk about freedom," Ellul writes, "is not being subject to others, being able to have their own dreams or go where they want to go. Hardly more. They definitely do not want to have to take charge of their own lives and be responsible for what they do."

Freedom often means comfort and security—that's what the culture teaches. But faith does not promise comfort and security; it calls for love, submission, and service. It calls for a freedom which breaks our bondage to all that is created by culture. It calls us into a relationship to the only free thing in the universe—God. That's just not us.

Fifth, faith calls us to the beatitudes. We spiritualize them; we deny them; we dismiss them as unattainable. And therein lies the problem. Culture would have us seek our own place, give us the pride of achieving certain goals, allow us the assurance that we are worthy in our own merit. Yet, the beatitudes are a description of the Christian who lives a life of faith.[7] They may be standards which cannot be reached by natural human beings, but that does not excuse us from the effort to conform to them.

Our pride does not allow us to give more than lip service to the beatitudes. In our very nature, we cannot follow them, for we seek power, not an endless and unattainable effort to be meek. We know that the meek do not inherit the earth. Not in our lifetimes! In our hearts, the American religion helps us reconcile the beatitudes to our conduct. Faith requires us to reconcile our conduct to the beatitudes.

These are just five areas in which the Christian faith is unpalatable to the human condition. I am not talking about unbelievers. I am talk-

ing about those in our churches who profess to be followers of Christ—
all of us. We balk at the incorporation of the Christian faith into our
experience, our beliefs, and our ethics because we see the kingdom of
God tearing down our kingdoms. We often forsake faith and turn to our
worldview, which helps us help ourselves, which helps us conform to
the "truths" we have found in our worldview—the "truths" which elevate us over our neighbor.

The Christian faith was not created to meet our needs.

4. Faith Is Not a Set of Rules or Rituals

When we speak of religion, we often think of heaven, and then we
think of hypocrisy and rules. Hard pews on Sunday mornings come to
mind and people trying to be on their best behavior. But the Christian
faith has little to do with that. It is divorced from the church buildings
and the rules and the rituals. While the Bible may prescribe certain
methods for the worship of God, it also prohibits the building of institutions and rituals for the purpose of working our way to perfection.

John Calvin wrote that there are four kinds of men: first, those few
who worship God sincerely from the heart, and second, those few who
openly express a contempt of God. These two kinds of men are a minority. Third, there are those who do not reject God but are basically
profane people—more along the lines of agnosticism. Fourth, there are
those who are "religious":

> The ungodliness of many is after a sort shrouded under ceremonies,
> and the feigned profession of the worship of God. So that in all ages
> there have been certain worshippers of God who have worshiped him
> like *stage-players, whose holiness* did wholly *consist in gestures and vain
> pomps.* In Paul's time, even as at this day, a peculiar study of godliness
> was to be found in a few, whose religion, though it were impure, and
> their heart feigned, deceitful and double, yet are they counted after a
> sort religious, in respect to their zeal. But hereby appears what ac-
> count we may make of *bare religion, which drives headlong,* through un-
> advised heat, the professors thereof, *to resist the kingdom of God and to
> oppress his glory.* (emphasis added)[8]

Religion, as Calvin defined it here, was the oppressor of the faith.
Those whose hearts were empty yet who followed a set of rules which
they believed to be the faith were the enemies of the faith.

"The real trouble," wrote Dietrich Bonhoeffer, "is that the pure Word of Jesus has been overlaid with so much human ballast—burdensome rules and regulations, false hopes and consolations—that it has become extremely difficult to make a genuine decision for Christ."[9]

The Christian faith is not founded upon nor bound by the understandings of man. Bonhoeffer wrote, "Jesus invites all those that labour and are heavy-laden, and nothing could be so contrary to our best intentions, and so fatal to our proclamation, as to drive men away from him by forcing upon them man-made dogmas. If we did so, we should make the love of Jesus Christ a laughing-stock to Christians and pagans alike."[10]

The duty of the church and the duty of every Christian is to recognize the cultural myths as an influence separate from the Christian faith. This duty includes the examination and analysis of the American myths and the American religion and the comparison of those tenets to the tenets of the Christian faith. This duty is to avoid building structures and institutions which prescribe rules for admission.

The Christian faith is not a new set of laws for modern man nor is it a set of rituals which will make us holy.

5. Faith Does Not Create an Identity Group

In our culture, with the rise of alienation and loss of individual identity, some seek Christendom in order to find an identity here on earth. Many expect the faith to instruct them on earthly political and social views. Group identity serves to focus my vision upon myself, so that I can identify myself with a recognizable group in our culture. In so doing, I can identify with that group's perceived worth, values, and prominence. In America, individuals are constantly classified by race, sex, etc., as if that made a difference to the individual's character, reliability, or integrity.

The trial of Mayor Marion Barry in Washington, D.C., reflects the consequences of group identity. Barry, videotaped by government agents while in the act of using cocaine, was indicted in a twelve-count indictment for, among other things, possession of cocaine and lying to a grand jury when he denied using or possessing cocaine. From the beginning, racism was alleged by the mayor and his lawyers and denied, of course, by the government. The mayor, tried by a predominantly black jury, was found guilty of one misdemeanor, not guilty of another, and a hung jury on all other counts. A carnival atmosphere reigned in Washington for the entire period of trial preparation and trial. T-shirts were sold, videos shown, accusations made. Based on all the circumstances, we must conclude that the hung jury resulted from the identity of the jurors with Barry on the issue of race.

An analogy can and has been drawn by white and black commentators to white juries in the South in and before the civil rights movement acquitting white defendants who had victimized black citizens. Carl Rowan, syndicated columnist of the *Washington Post,* wrote in his August 16, 1990, column (just days after the verdict and mistrial) that the calls for "racial solidarity" were thick in and out of the courtroom, just as they were subtly present in many courtrooms before the civil rights movement. Rowan concludes that the same principle stands in the Barry trial—group identification by race is more important than commitment to principles like justice, truth, and honor.

While it is true that we are members of the body of Christ, faith is personal in that it is the experience, the belief, and the ethics of each individual. Each person is made in the image of God. We are not made in groups nor are we dealt with by God in groups. In Christ there is neither Jew nor Greek, slave nor free.

The Apostle Paul wrote shortly before he was executed by the Romans: "And of this gospel I was appointed a herald and an apostle and a teacher. That is why I am suffering as I am. Yet I am not ashamed, because I know whom I have believed, and am convinced that he is able to guard what I have entrusted to him for that day" (2 Timothy 1:11–12).

Paul found his truth, not in finding himself, but in finding God. Faith is looking away from the frailty of human identity and looking toward the identity we find that God has given us as human beings.

6. Faith Applies to Unbelievers as Well as Believers

These characteristics of faith apply to the faith of unbelievers as well as believers both inside and outside the church. The human condition being what it is, each person has faith in something: Christ, the church, the government, self, Allah, the culture. G. K. Chesterton once said that it is widely supposed that when man no longer believes in God, he believes in nothing. The truth is that when he no longer believes in God, he will believe in anything.

The human condition being what it is, not all of those inside the church live in the practice of the Christian faith. God's grace being what it is, some outside the church provide better examples of the practice of the faith than Christians do.

Because the American culture offers the hope of such vast physical comfort, the American myths are a constant lure away from the faith, and the faith is in constant battle with the fleshly desires of the myths. Our American vision distorts and blurs our vision of the faith.

THE OPTIONS

What shall we do?

In view of these relativities, Niebuhr sees three alternatives taken by mankind.[11] First, people become nihilists and affirm materialism. A heavy dose of this has entered the philosophies of the nineteenth and twentieth centuries. Skepticism has reigned; existentialism has flourished; despair and despondency have resulted. Nearly all Americans will at some time suffer serious depression. We no longer know the practice of the happy, contented life. Greater pleasures entice us. Our culture may promise a panoply of earthly delights but it wreaks havoc on the spiritual side. Yet we never reach that garden of earthly delights which the American culture and myths daily promise.

Second, mankind can flee to the authority of some relative position, substituting that relativity for the absolutes of God. Cultural mythologies like the American Dream set forth the absolutes of a culture and substitute them for the absolutes of God. A church, state, philosophy, or value becomes absolute, and the individual has developed another religion to meet the needs found in the relativities of culture. In the decline of Christendom in America and in Europe, a variety of religions and philosophies have filled the vacuum. But each is simply an absolutizing of the relative, just as Christendom was an absolutizing of the relativities of the cultures which created Christendom to displace the Christian faith. Marxism has often been called a Christian heresy. The New Age movement is simply a warmed-over version of the Eastern religions. All provide an inspiring but empty substitute for the real thing.

Third, mankind can practice the Christian faith with a view that human beings are relative and live only a short period on this earth, but God is absolute and eternal. In this perspective, people live with the

> *"American myths are a constant lure away from the faith, and the faith is in constant battle with the fleshly desires of the myths. Our American vision distorts and blurs our vision of the faith."*

faith in God as the giver of absolutes. But he or she will recognize and accept that while the views taken in the world are important to life and living, they are limited to the time and space and circumstances of the beholder. Individual human beings will recognize that the interpretation of the hearer is just that—an interpretation. Finite man sees the world through a glass darkly in hope and prayer that someday he will see it face-to-face.

All of us on this earth face these three options as we look out at a hostile environment and seek some assurance that we have a comfortable place in the universe.

AMERICANS AND THE INCENTIVES OF THE CHRISTIAN FAITH

If we recognize that the Christian faith is not what the culture believes it to be, that it is not found in Christendom, that it does not offer what the American Dream will offer in terms of material comfort and pleasure, then what are the incentives to practice the Christian faith?[12]

1. The Certainty of Judgment

A first incentive is the solemn certainty of judgment. Philosophers from Plato to Kant have argued that man must meet the Judgment Day: a day of rewards and punishments meted out by a Supreme Being. Surely few in our culture live today as if this is a real possibility. The philosophies of existentialism in the twentieth century have taken much of the sting out of the threat of the Judgment Day. People in our time act as if they do not believe that there will be such a day. Or else they do not care because they are too busy getting what they can out of the present moment to worry about the future.

The Apostle Paul wrote that those in the church should not be deceived by the teachings of the day, and there were as many then as there are now. We are taught that we have a choice over what we do with our bodies, as if our selfish choices were paramount to any other considerations—a modern-day perversion of Gnosticism. We are taught in the New Age religions that god is in us and we can become god over time—an old song sung to a new tune. Inside the church many are preaching universalism, the belief that God will save all people from the final judgment. That is clearly compatible with the views of our culture as a whole.

William Ellery Channing once wrote that immortality is the glorious discovery of Christianity. In other words, when we reach the glory that God has promised, we will overcome all doubt in immortal life.

Of one thing we can be certain: we will all find out in the end. Each of us must die, and each of us will then find out if that is the end or if there is something more.

It calls to mind Pascal's wager. Blaise Pascal (1623–1662), one of the foremost mathematicians, scientists, and theologians in Western intellectual history, put forth in his classic work, *Pensees*, the proposition that God exists, or He does not. Then he proposed a wager. He said that the risk of placing one's faith in God was very small in the event that God did not exist. If God did not exist, the gambler loses nothing but will simply return to the earth. But the risk of rejection of God is tremendous. If God does exist and one does not put faith in Him, the gambler loses eternal life and happiness and gains eternal reprobation. Based upon the possible outcomes, Pascal suggested, it is a small step to practice the Christian faith.[13]

2. The Practice of Love for Others

A second incentive is virtually unheard of outside the Christian faith. Christians are called to live as the fruit of the light. Jesus said that the greatest commandment was to love your God and to love your neighbor as yourself. In America at the end of the twentieth century we say: Preposterous! More than that, we simply ignore it. But as we have discussed, those who first came to this continent took this commandment seriously and many of them practiced it as a cardinal rule of the Christian faith.

Granted, times have changed. In the development of this country we have swallowed a heavy dose of "me-firstism" and a disregard for the welfare of others. Oh, we may give to a few charities and go to an awards banquet for some do-good outfit, but we keep that mere sentimentality in its place and do not let it interfere with our own pursuits. Sometimes, we may get a good feeling from helping someone else. In fact, it has become vogue for professional entertainers to give charity concerts to raise money for the farmers or the famine, if the price and the publicity are right. But in the Christian church charity has been done for centuries. Today, the Catholic charities do that work every day. Large percentages of church budgets go to benevolences, all without the fanfare of self-praise.

Service to your neighbor was and is a way of life. We can always find a personal benefit. Looking out for others keeps you from self-pity and dwelling upon the perceived miseries of life. Helping others does make you feel better. But the Christian faith holds as a tenet that the way to find your life is to lose it for others, and your neighbor benefits. Practicing the Christian faith is a practice of love for others, plain and simple. It is giving to others rather than taking.

Paul gives us some practical applications in his letter to the Ephesians. He says that in dealing with each other we should not lie to each other or lose our tempers with each other. We should treat each other honestly, without slander or bitterness or lewdness. If we found those qualities in a caring neighbor, we would have found a friend. There are few things less attractive than lying, foul-temperedness, dishonesty, cynicism, and lewdness among young people.

If we exhibited those positive qualities in the context of love for our fellow human being, we would make life a lot more pleasant for our families, our neighbors, and our fellow employees. In the Christian faith, one is called to forget about self and to help others. Naive? In America, it may be considered naive, but it is principled. And if it is contrary to what our culture says, well, much of faith is.

3. The Nature of Wisdom

A third incentive to practice the Christian faith is the nature of wisdom. The body of literature known as Wisdom Literature specifies some of the general ways to find the happy life. In the Ancient Near East, Wisdom Literature was found in the books of Proverbs, Psalms, Ecclesiastes, as well as in the writings of nearly every civilization. Wisdom Literature was often traded, and as a result, some of the Wisdom Literature of the Ancient Near East outside of Israel appears in the Bible. Wisdom is wisdom, then and now.

The Wisdom Literature had a very definite message: To stay healthy, wealthy, and wise in this world, keep your nose clean and stay away from wicked people. Successful living was found in fairness, self-control, pleasant speech, and neighborliness. Much of the same tone is seen in Franklin's proverbs in *Poor Richard's Almanack* and the *Autobiography*. Some might say it is common sense living.

The practice of the Christian faith is a life of wisdom which begins with focus upon God and the welfare of family, neighborhoods, and children. Our culture whines: Who says that is the best way to live? Yet we are learning painstakingly in our culture what the ancients knew centuries ago. For the culture to survive, there must be certain behavioral norms. For the culture to thrive, there must be a certain morality. Those who say, "Whose morality?" are merely ducking the issue. One of the great problems in America as we face the twenty-first century is that our social norms, those perpetuated in our mythological structures, have, through individualism and relativism, fallen into disuse. As a result, our social structure is disintegrating faster from our cultural illiteracy and intellectual obstinacy than it would from the bombs of all of our enemies and perceived enemies combined. The result is the moral as well as physical decay of our inner cities, the skyrocketing violent crime rate, and the degradation of human dignity through abortion, obscenity, racism, homelessness, and educational bankruptcy.

One of the main tenets of the Wisdom Literature was that we pass the wisdom along to the next generation. Syndicated columnist William Raspberry of the *Washington Post* writes in his August 10, 1990, column that the disintegrating social norms have placed many of our children at great risk. He cites approvingly a report done by former assistant Secretary of Health, Chester Finn, a faculty member at

Vanderbilt University. The report has as its theme, according to Raspberry, that the "awful things which happen to the American

---

**"We are learning painstakingly in our culture
what the ancients knew centuries ago."**

'underclass' are less a result of inadequate government intervention than of their own disastrous behavior." Finn concludes:

> We must steel ourselves to speak the truth in public places about social norms that we know to be good for children and about the malign consequences of deviating from those norms. . . . [For example], with rare exceptions, two-parent families are good for children, one-parent families are bad, zero-parent families are horrible. . . . Children fare better in some circumstances than in others, and no decent society will remain silent when it comes to pointing out which circumstances are which.

The Wisdom Literature tells us which circumstances are which.

The Christian faith, as expressed in the Wisdom Literature of the Old and New Testaments, has given us the social norms by which this country, in the Judeo-Christian heritage, has created a "decent" society. We are learning that the abandonment of those norms gives us the hostile streets of Washington, D.C., New York City, and New Orleans. And the hostility in those streets is flooding over into the rural streets and byways of our nation.

4. A Life of Spiritual Happiness

A fourth incentive is that the practice of the Christian faith leads us to a life of spiritual happiness, joy, and peace. There are very few among us who would argue that we are not seeking in this world a life of happiness, joy, and peace for ourselves and our loved ones. Indeed, the entire advertising industry is built on the yearning of each of us for happiness, joy, and peace. There are very few products advertised which are guaranteed by their advertisers to make you sad or angry. Each of us has that yearning in our souls for peace with ourselves and our environments.

In Ephesians 5:18, Paul writes that we should not get drunk on wine but be filled with the Spirit. Then he follows in verses 19 through 21 with five participles used as imperatives.[14] One offsets the other; for example, getting drunk on wine is contrasted with the benefits of living with the Holy Spirit of God. When one is drunk on wine, one tends to become depressed, uninhibited, and more self-centered than usual. Drunkenness tends to lessen one's relationship to those around him or her. But the Holy Spirit heightens the relationship to those in the community.

Paul says to live in fellowship by addressing each other with psalms and hymns, worship God with all your heart, live a life of gratitude for what God has done, and submit to one another in all areas of life out of reverence for Christ. If the Christian community could only do that, it would be an irresistible witness in a world which is filled with the symptoms of intoxication on wine and material things. If each of us would do that, we would find the life of happiness and joy and peace we are seeking.

But the great irony of our culture as it approaches the twenty-first century is that we are simply unable to find that sense of happiness and joy and peace in the pursuit of self. The irony is made greater because in our search for freedom, we have discarded the pursuit of godliness, which our forefathers knew to be the key to a joyful life. We have substituted for the life of godliness a cultural search-and-destroy mission with self as both the prize of victory and the body to count as the trophy.

One of the great rock-and-roll singers of the 1950s and 1960s was a young man named Sam Cook who had the rare artistic ability to convey mood with his music. But Sam Cook, a man with a tormented soul, died at age thirty-five at the hands of a irate husband who found him with his wife in a Chicago hotel.

He sang a song which turned out to have autobiographical overtones. One of the verses went something like this: "Come on, let the good times roll." It's an upbeat tune, light and quick, but the voice of pathos and despair chills the "good times."

Sam Cook's problem was that he tried to soothe his soul with external things. But he was unable to do it: not with enough musical talent for a hundred people; not with all the money he ever dreamed of; not with alcohol or drugs or other men's wives. I can't; you can't; Sam Cook couldn't; nor can the American church.

William Barclay once observed,

[T]he person who Jesus could do nothing for is the person who thinks himself so good that he does not need anything done for him; and the one person for whom Jesus can do everything is the person who is a sinner and knows it and who longs in his heart for a cure. To have no sense of need is to have erected a barrier between us and Jesus; to have a sense of need is to possess the passport to his presence.[15]

Our sense of need for happiness and joy and peace is the passport to His presence, but our insistence upon doing it our way is the barrier to the very things for which we yearn.

5. The Increase in Morality

A fifth incentive is the increase in morality in the community. No, I am not talking about moralism, and I am not contradicting what I said earlier about rules and rituals. I am talking here about our conduct toward our neighbor. Even in the early church, this was an attraction of the Christian faith.

And nowhere was it more attractive than to women and children. In the early church, this was among the strongest of the defenses of the faith. Women and children are the big losers when the culture turns to immorality, when pornography and obscenity are pervasive, when violence is ubiquitous, when selfishness is rampant, when families and cities deteriorate, and when the social and religious structures are bankrupt.

The Christian faith was the foremost blessing of God for women and children as they became, possibly for the first time in history, recognized as persons made in the image of God. In the Christian church, the dignity of human life has always been an attraction to women, children, and minorities, particularly slaves.

But there has always been that element that supports the moralism of the American way of life and attacks the morality of the Christian faith as being in opposition to it. Now, they may be correct in the assumption that the Christian faith and the American religion are not one and the same and, in fact, on many tenets are not in accord with each other. But those who attack the Christian faith most often attack it on the grounds of selfish moralism in an effort to require others to conform to their view of morality. To the charge that the Christian faith improves the morals of a given culture, the faith must plead guilty.

6. Hope and Restoration

A sixth incentive is much like the flip side of the coin of the fourth and fifth incentives. The Christian faith is the faith of hope and restoration.

When looking at the Christian faith, we must recognize that the alternative, the American Dream as it has been perverted by the American myths, is bankrupt. U.S. News and World Report published an essay recently on the moral bankruptcy of American cities. It is a bleak and hopeless view of life in the cesspool of America.

According to U.S. News, in New York City, there are 830,000 people on welfare, 500,000 drug abusers (in some neighborhoods as many as one out of four people are intravenous drug abusers), and a huge homosexual population which makes New York City "the AIDS capital of America." Each year 10,000 "crack babies" are born. Every day 366 cars are stolen and 200,000 people annually jump the turnstyles to get into the subway free. In 1989, there were 93, 387 robberies, up from 8,757 in 1952. And during the summer of 1990, random violence and murder claimed the lives of four small children in one week.[16]

The result of the American Dream, as it has been perverted in America, is the mass destruction in the cities, a contagious destruction which is spreading to the rural areas. The lack of moral purpose, the attacks on ethical structures, and the popular philosophies abroad in the culture have left America a moral and spiritual wasteland. As we look today in the news and in the popular cultural expressions, we see alienation, anger, hatred, spite, illness, hopelessness, and a variety of social ills which are prevalent to an extent unknown in history. And as we focus upon our governmental capabilities to remedy the situation, there is little reason for hope. And nothing is more devastating in this world than hopelessness.

Hopelessness has a tremendous impact upon the individual also. A friend of mine entered a large Washington, D. C., hospital some time ago. After he was checked in, a woman whom he described as looking more like a social worker than a nurse visited him and began asking questions. She was writing the answers on a clipboard. She said that they liked to get to know the new arrivals in this cancer ward. How had he gotten to the hospital, she asked. He said his wife had driven him. What was the last thing they talked about? Who were his friends and when was the last time he saw them? When was the last time he went to church?

"The lack of moral purpose, the attacks on ethical structures, and the popular philosophies abroad in the culture have left America a moral and spiritual wasteland."

"I'm a grown man," he said. "I know this isn't a social visit. What do you really want?"

She responded frankly. "Very few people walk off this ward. Most of them die here. The ones who walk out of here have strong families, strong friendships, and strong faith. They have the hope to get out of here. Those who don't have hope, don't get out."

My friend not only had the hope, he had the faith, and he was one of the few who walked out. He died some time later after a recurrence of his cancer, but he died as one who had fallen asleep in Christ and not as one ignorant of death or who grieved like the rest of men who have no hope. He was a strong, brave man, and his strength, courage, and hope came from his faith in Jesus Christ.

The Christian faith is the light of hope in the world, first for the individual, then for the culture. The prophet Isaiah wrote:

> The LORD will guide you always;
>> he will satisfy your needs in a sun-scorched land
>> and will strengthen your frame.
> You will be like a well-watered garden,
>> like a spring whose waters never fail.
> Your people will rebuild the ancient ruins
>> and will raise up the age-old foundations;
> you will be called Repairer of Broken Walls,
>> Restorer of Streets with Dwellings.
>
> (Isaiah 58:11–12)

The hope of the world, even for the inner cities, is still Jesus Christ. The hope of the world, even for the cancer-ridden, is still in the atonement for sin made by a Jewish man two thousand years ago. The hope of the world, even for the alienated and disillusioned and despondent, is the restoring power of God in Jesus Christ.

7. Liberty and Individual Freedom

A seventh incentive is the liberty and individual freedom found in the faith. Dietrich Bonhoeffer wrote,

> When the Bible speaks of following Jesus, it is proclaiming a discipleship which will liberate mankind from all man-made dogmas, from every burden and oppression, from every anxiety and torture which afflicts the conscience. If they follow Jesus, men escape from the hard yoke of their own laws, and submit to the kindly yoke of Jesus Christ.[17]

The Apostle Paul is often called the apostle of Christian liberty. He was a man who could find liberty while wrapped in chains, whose soul could smile when his body was beaten, whose heart could rejoice when his muscles were starved. He writes of a liberty found in the faith for all who follow Christ: men and women, slave and free, Jew and Gentile. It was a radical statement back then and is a radical statement today.

At the end of this century, Americans are still looking for the freedom to fulfill the myths which have guided this country, to find that promised land and conquer it for themselves. The failure to do so—the failure to reach the perfection that is depicted on television day and night, the failure to find life, liberty, and happiness—leaves us in a rut. Our culture dictates our experience, our beliefs, and our ethics. It leaves us in chains, beaten and starved by the failure to meet the expectations thrust upon us daily. The German term is *angst:* a malaise, a feeling of despair.

In the so-called sixties generation, the yearning for liberty from cultural bondage drove many to drugs and alcohol, to utopian communes and small, peaceful farms, to mountaintops and Pacific islands, to sex and EST, to rejection of all the values of the culture in the hope of finding the one value which would provide the meaning of life. Unfortunately, it was not where we were told it was.

As we approach the twenty-first century, that yearning is still active and is directed toward many of the same things: sex, drugs, alcohol. But it has reentered the bondage of the cultural myths and searches for fulfillment in the acquisition of material goods, in the search for the soul, and in a dozen cults and religions which promise the conquest of our personal promised lands. It feeds upon itself. As we conduct a land rush toward our promised land, we beg those around us to show us how to do it. Our mission to the promised land becomes just another set of rules and regulations prescribed by the gurus of Madison Avenue, another set of chains bound with personal greed. In Bercovitch's view: The mark of extreme individualism is absolute conformity. The search leads not out of the chains and into the light of freedom but deeper into the darkness of the dungeons.

Paul was beyond all that. He found his freedom in Christ. His was a freedom that was not demanding but loving; not strident but self-controlled; not arrogant or ambitious but submissive and serving. He found a freedom and peace sought by every human being but alien to our cultured ways. He found joy and happiness and peace in a relationship with God.

We learn the message that we cannot reach the promised land under our own schemes—the message Paul sent to the churches in the first century. We are told, like generations before us, that we will find liberty, not in the laws of the culture, but in the grace of God.

CONCLUSION

How do we know all this is true? By God's grace, by recognizing that God has promised it to us. We recognize that we are created by God, yet through our own free will we have rebelled against Him and have become alienated from Him. We recognize that God loves us and sent His only-begotten Son to redeem us so that we may dwell with Him for eternity. The Bible tells us this. Our faith is by the work of God through His Holy Spirit.

We either believe it, or we don't. He has also told us the secret to living in this world until that day comes. Again, we either believe it, or we don't.

But believing is not enough. There are many who claim to believe it, to have a cognitive understanding of it, but conduct themselves as if they did not. Faith is more than mere belief. Faith is just as much our experience and our ethics. God has called us to that faith. We either hear Him, or we do not.

With this look at faith in the American context, the question arises concerning the practice of our faith. How do we live as Christians in the American culture as it stumbles into the twenty-first century? God gives us His grace to live in the coming century just as He has given His grace to live in each of the past centuries.

His grace comes to us in three ways: through His Word, through the sacraments, and through prayer. These are called *the means of grace* and are defined as "those institutions which God has ordained to be the ordinary channels of grace, i.e., of the supernatural influences of the Holy Spirit, to the souls of men."[18]

We follow His grace and receive His grace in faith. It is grace because it sets us free from the cultural myths and pressures and permits us to walk our independent paths through this world. It is grace because it shatters the cultural myths, not only ours but the myths of mankind since the beginning. It is grace because it allows us to live our lives in joy, happiness, and peace in a way that one unfamiliar with the faith cannot comprehend.

The grace of God comes to us in His Word. The Word of God pierces the cultural veil over our lives and beckons us to Christian liberty. The Word of God is the Gibraltar by which all human endeavor must pass. The Word of God shows us that the myths of our day are not the operative myths for a life of joy, happiness, and peace. We are not the chosen few; we are not unique, other than in the image of God, either collectively or individually, in the terms our cultural myths put forth. Our self-perception of uniqueness is pierced by Scripture.

Second, the sacraments are God's grace to us because they provide an antidote for the myths of our culture. They call us away from the conformity which individualism demands of us and set us on a path of independence in which we can journey through our lives as unique beings made by God. The sacraments show that individualism and independence are different terms and describe different ways of life. The sacraments pierce the cultural myths that we are on an exclusive mission in our lives to conquer the promised lands. The sacraments call us to holiness and community and away from selfish ambition and vain conceit.

Third, prayer is the relationship to God that provides significance and security in our lives. It is God's grace to us through interaction with the Holy Spirit. Prayer takes the conquest out of our cultural myths by showing us that God is in command and that we are sojourners in this world, reliant upon His strength and not our own. That is a great gift.

We either believe it, or we don't.

The warning in Jesus' parable of the two sons is just as appropriate today as it was then.

> "What do you think? There was a man who had two sons. He went to the first and said, 'Son, go and work today in the vineyard.' 'I will not,' he answered, but later he changed his mind and went. Then the father went to the other son and said the same thing. He answered, 'I will, sir,' but he did not go. Which of the two did what his father wanted?"

> "The first," they answered.

> Jesus said to them, "I tell you the truth, the tax collectors and the prostitutes are entering the kingdom of God ahead of you." (Matthew 21:28–31)

In the next three chapters, these three means of grace shall be discussed in relation to American life and the American Dream.

AMERICANS AND THE WORD

It is impossible to enslave mentally and socially a Bible-reading people. The principles of the Bible are the groundwork of human freedom.

HORACE GREELEY

In the past two centuries, the Bible has been criticized by those in universities and seminaries who are given the opportunity to speak without confrontation by those of different views, without rigorous cross-examination, or without close review of what others in their community say. They have captive audiences in their small communities. But their influence has crept outside those communities into the communities at large. Their influence is pervasive.

The so-called higher critics (none of their names are known outside seminary walls) have prejudiced the American public against the Bible as a part of our cultural education. Their attacks, whether in good faith or not, have served to remove the Bible from the classroom, from the family dining table, and from the bedside stand. Americans do not read the Bible as much as they did formerly. We have in our culture replaced the wisdom of the ages with the political and social slogans of the moguls of Madison Avenue and the gurus of the television networks.

Before I sound too strident, I confess that I am among them. I grew up in this nation inculcated with the American Dream but not seeing or hearing a Bible in the home, in the school, and very rarely in the

Presbyterian church. I was easy game for the professors. No one had to convince me that the Bible "wasn't true" (whatever that means). I knew without even having to read it. Now, my antagonism against the Bible might have been because it described a manner of living at odds with the one I learned as I grew up in this culture. That anyone would assert that "success" was not in material acquisition was astounding to me; turning the other cheek was for sissies. But all the same, as a young man, I was convinced deep down (which, at that age, is just beneath surface level) that it wasn't "true."

Fortunately, people grow and are not bound by the attitudes and arrogance of their youth. I had done what Ted Koppel spoke of in his commencement address at Duke University:

> In the place of Truth, we have discovered facts; for moral absolutes we have substituted moral ambiguity. We now communicate with everyone . . . and say absolutely nothing. We have reconstructed the Tower of Babel and it is a television antenna. A thousand voices producing a daily parody of democracy, in which everyone's opinion is afforded equal weight, regardless of substance or merit.[1]

I was surely guilty. I was among the many who did not know the place of Truth. Moral absolutes? In my college education, I never heard the phrase used. I heard a thousand voices and none of them had meaning, yet all had equal weight, regardless of merit. But I find now that there are several reasons why I was wrong in my assessment that neither I, nor anyone else in modern society, needed to be familiar with the Bible.

WHAT DOES THE BIBLE DO FOR US?

What does the Bible do for us? How is it God's grace to us? The Bible is God's grace to us in that "it is the power of the Holy Spirit as a divine person acting with and by the truth as in His sovereign pleasure He sees fit."[2] For the power of salvation and sanctification, the Bible rests upon the work of the Holy Spirit. That is a form of special grace.

In addition, there is the moral power of the Scripture, which is given in common grace to all who read it. Scripture speaks to universal contexts in many ways. Many things have changed since the days of the Old and New Testaments, yet many things about human beings remain the same. The Bible speaks to those universal yearnings of mankind, and it speaks to them with a universal truth. The basic concerns confronting people two or three thousand years ago confront people today.

"Moral absolutes? In my college education, I never heard the phrase used. I heard a thousand voices and none of them had meaning, yet all had equal weight, regardless of merit."

We are concerned with love and our loved ones; we are concerned with our families and our livelihoods; we seek security and significance in our lives; we search for identity and purpose in life. Scripture is the Word of God and the grace of God to us on those topics in all generations.

The Bible pierces the cultural myths and particularly the mythical tenet of uniqueness. The adaptation of our cultural myths to ourselves has given today's American a sense of uniqueness—a confused focus on the self that ironically clashes with the despondency of alienation and facelessness found in our mass culture. In piercing this cultural tenet, the Bible confronts our self-perceived uniqueness and returns us to the uniqueness we find in our relationship to God.

This chapter will discuss several ways in which God's Word is His grace to us. In doing so, I would like to work within a loose framework from the least important to the most important, recognizing that the overall priority of God's Word is the revelation of grace and salvation to us.

Communication in the Culture

There is a breakdown in our country, a breakdown in communication, but more importantly, a breakdown in understanding. The irony is that we now have a greater capability to communicate than ever before. We have a greater capability to educate than ever before. And yet we are bombarded with triviality and boorishness on television. We are shocked into responselessness in "art," and we are disgusted into deafness in the schools, both in secondary and higher education. We are numbed by failure on all these fronts and lured into lethargy by the increasing arrogance of those whose jobs are partly the cause of the failure.

But the breakdown in communication is more pervasive than simply our capabilities. It is more than snoozing while a teacher or professor or pastor drones on. It is more than escapism in the absurdity of cable television. As E. D. Hirsch has pointed out in his book, *Cultural Literacy*, we are simply unable to understand at the fundamental level of understanding the symbols we use when we communicate with each other. As a result, our symbols—our words and our pictures—must be more base, more outrageous, more shrill, and more voluminous to convey the same meaning.[3]

Why is that? Well, there are a variety of reasons. But one is that we no longer have a pool of common knowledge. We argue over whether the study of Western civilization is necessary to education in these times. We relegate the authors and the classics of our culture to the dustbin as irrelevant and wonder why the education system is in a shambles from top to bottom.

Western civilization is founded upon the Judeo-Christian heritage, and the Judeo-Christian heritage is founded upon the Bible.

If we are unfamiliar with the symbols in the Bible, with the basic concepts, with the figures and stories, words and phrases, we are severely limited in our capability to communicate in our culture.

Without a knowledge of the foundation, we lose the capability to convey the deeper meanings of life in our culture. Nobel Prize-winner Albert Camus, an existentialist by philosophy and an atheist by religion, wrote of his native France in the novel, *The Plague*. Yet Camus was unable to describe France in the twentieth century without using the imagery of the Roman Catholic church. A picture of France without the Roman Catholic church is not a true picture of France. Camus, as an artist, recognized that fact.

The American Nobel Prize-winner William Faulkner has been called a Christian humanist (so was John Calvin). He, like Camus, is unable to describe his native Mississippi without describing Christianity, or at least the Mississippi expressions of organized religion. His symbolism is tremendous. Without an understanding of the Bible, the underlying currents of such classics as *The Sound and the Fury, Light in August,* and *Fable* are lost.

American literature is teeming with biblical imagery. If we do not understand it, we lose an important window of communication in our culture. Ernest Hemingway's first novel was entitled *The Sun Also Rises.* Presumably he did not select that title at random. Hemingway was biblically literate and knew the meaning of the words. If you do not know the context of that title, you lose an important insight into the meaning of Hemingway's view of the world. Knowing that the title comes from Ecclesiastes gives you a better insight into the themes of the book. The same is true of Hemingway's *The Garden of Eden,* a book posthumously published, and many other works of American literature.

In our daily use of the American vernacular, biblical imagery abounds. We speak of "an eye for an eye," "turn the other cheek," "walk another mile," "the kiss of death," "a David and Goliath matchup," "spare the rod and spoil the child," "the spirit is willing but the flesh is

---

"American literature is teeming with biblical imagery. If we do not understand it, we lose an important window of communication in our culture."

---

weak," "the prodigal son," "the good Samaritan," "walk on water," "bear your cross," "the patience of Job," "a little birdie told me," "cast your bread upon the water," a woman as "Jezebel," "the handwriting on the wall," and literally dozens of other idioms in our language which come from Scripture. Literate people in America, indeed, all over the world, know the meanings and communicative richness of these phrases and idioms and use them to communicate the deepest meanings of life. Each of the idioms loses its communicative richness if the receiver is unfamiliar with its context in Scripture.

Without the common pool of knowledge which has been available to all previous generations, our ability to communicate the meaningful themes of life is inhibited. As a result, in much of our cultural communication, we are unable to convey meaning above the base level of the emotional.

Insight into History and Tradition

Plato said that the unexamined life is a life not worth living. A second way the study of the Bible impacts our culture is the knowledge and insight it gives into our history and traditions. We, as Christians, have an obligation to ask questions about our history and our traditions. Our obligation is to seek the truth in our culture and in our universe, to listen for the truth—not someone else's version of the truth, but the ultimate truth about the meaning and purpose of life.

Do we seek anymore? Do we ever wonder where people learn the things they believe? How many people do you know who can articulate and defend a personal worldview?

The Pharisees, Herodians, and Sadducees often came to Jesus with questions about life, but the questions were designed to trap Him. They already had their answers to the questions; they didn't want to learn. They wanted to trap Him. Often our questions are designed only to confirm our present views.

But one Pharisee wanted to learn, and that made him different. He came not governed by myth or superstition or cultural law or fad or fashion or pop psychology. He did not ask about the feel-good remedies but about the purpose of life. "Of all the commandments, which is the most important?" (Mark 12:28).

The first place of questioning is those things which are going on around us. The things we look past, like the institutions of mere human beings, are the things we should question first. We are here to question, but we are here to question like this Pharisee, because we seek the truth. This Pharisee sought the truth by looking beyond the cultural mandates of his age to see the truth.

How can we understand the founding of the United States if we do not understand the Great Commission? How can we understand the purpose of representative government if we do not understand original sin? How can we understand the Western political tradition unless we understand the doctrines of atonement and justification by faith which gave rise to the Reformation, the spawning ground of much of Western political thought? Can we understand the Arab-Israeli conflicts without an understanding of the Old Testament?

Closer to home, we must gain an insight into our everyday living by familiarity with and understanding of the Bible. We say that private ownership of property is dear to us. That principle was challenged by the Marxists. On what grounds do we refute the Marxists? Tradition? What are the grounds for our tradition?

We often claim to have certain rights in our culture. But what is the basis of those rights? We find the answers to those questions in Scripture. By reading and studying Scripture, we share with previous generations the wealth of the basis of our traditions and institutions. If we are unfamiliar with Scripture, we are living the unexamined life.

Relationships with People

Eugene Petersen wrote in *Leadership* magazine that

> The culture conditions us to approach people and situations as journalists do: see the big, exploit the crisis, edit and abridge the commonplace, interview the glamorous. The Scriptures and our best pastoral traditions train us in a different approach: notice the small, persevere in the commonplace, appreciate the obscure.[4]

The Bible contains practically every kind of personal relationship experienced on this planet. St. Augustine, in his preconversion years, said (paraphrasing) that the Bible could not be the Word of God because it contained crude stories of sex and violence set in a wild land. The Bible is particularly good for writers who want to learn the stories of human life. In the pages of the Bible, all human relationships are explored. The terms *lust* and *love* are defined and differentiated. David lusted for Bathsheba as he looked down upon her as she bathed on the roof of her house. Judah lusted after Tamar as she tricked him into a sexual liaison. On the other hand, Jesus loved Peter and James and John. Jonathan loved David and was loyal to him.

There are marital relationships which are exemplary and some which are not. David's wife Michal looked down on him with jealousy and disdain. Nehemiah and David exemplify leadership. Yet David succumbs to poor leadership in the case of Uriah the Hittite. Every human emotion is in the Bible. The Bible teaches us how to handle our emotions and what the consequences are of mishandling them.

When the stories are familiar to us, they take on an instructional purpose and guide our conduct. What would I do if I were in Joseph's position when approached by Potiphar's wife? What do present day television and film models do in those circumstances? How easy it is to default to the ways of the world. Many times we know them so much better.

Our failure to understand the meaning of human relationships leaves us emotionally and morally bankrupt. The lack of intellectual understanding of the relationships between people leaves us in a moral vacuum concerning our families, our neighbors, and our communities. Failure of the family unit, failure of social institutions, and failure of public education in twentieth-century America exploit that vacuum by focusing our understanding solely upon ourselves, leaving us tossed about on the emotional waves of a sea of situational ethics.

Through an understanding of Scripture we gain an intellectual appreciation for these personal relationships. Granted, these relationships can be found elsewhere in the great literature of the world. But great world literature, much of which finds its foundation in Scripture, is read less and less in an American educational environment more interested in pursuing trendy curricula than universal truths. The vacuum remains and the culture is weakened.

Instruction on Ethics

The higher critics' criticisms of the Bible have had more than a scholarly result. These criticisms have raised doubts about not only the Word, but Jesus Himself. The search for the historical Jesus raised doubts about the Jesus of the Gospels.

Yet putting all the academic pursuit aside and returning to the real world, the question still remains: What do you think about the content of Jesus' messages? The question is not the identity of the historical Jesus or the historicity of the miracles. The question concerns the teachings which are attributed to Him and appear in the Bible. The academics cannot dispute that the teachings appear and that they have content and meaning. The question to us is: Do we agree with the ethical structure set by Jesus?

Of course, to answer that question we have to be familiar with the content of His teachings. Even the uninterested observer cannot avoid the set of ethics revealed in the teachings of Jesus which are the foundation of the Judeo-Christian tradition. When it comes to family relationships, business relationships, neighborhood relationships, what do we believe about what He said? Scripture, then, becomes the Gibraltar by which all discussions of ethics must pass.

What guides us in our daily lives? In America in the last several generations, it has been personal advancement and personal improvement; in the generations before that, it was working for elevation in social status. In this generation in America, our chief end may be to gather the greatest benefits of our culture for ourselves with the smallest possible output.

Sixty-five percent of five thousand American high school students polled in a Girl Scouts survey say they would cheat on an important exam. Conducted by Louis Harris and Associates, the poll also revealed that 53 percent would lie for a friend who had vandalized school property. A report coauthored by Harvard psychiatrist Robert Coles and University of Virginia sociologist James Hunter, based on the survey, indicated discouragement at the small number of people and institutions which take moral education seriously.[5]

"In America in the last several generations, it has been personal advancement and personal improvement; in the generations before that, it was working for elevation in social status. In this generation in America, our chief end may be to gather the greatest benefits of our culture for ourselves with the smallest possible output."

Francis Schaeffer, in his book *True Spirituality*, found early in his ministry that he believed in the Christian faith; he knew what it was supposed to be. But he found that his own life exhibited very little of the joy and purpose the Christian life was supposed to bring.[6]

He engaged in a study of Scripture to find the answer to his problem. He found that his problem arose from failure to keep the tenth commandment: Thou shall not covet. That commandment, he says, is the converse of the greatest commandment. In it lies the very basic instruction of ethical living. Ecclesiastes 4:4 states: "And I saw that all labor and all achievement spring from man's envy of his neighbor. This too is meaningless, a chasing after the wind."

In his study, Schaeffer found the scriptural bedrock of ethical conduct. We are not to covet things from God; we are to love God. We are to trust Him and have faith in Him to the extent that we can live contentedly with what He has given us, relying on the faith that He and He alone knows what we need.

Now this does not mean that desire is sin. God gave us desires which should be properly directed. Desire becomes sin when it fails to include love of God and love of neighbor.

Schaeffer says that the test of covetousness is posed when we want something that our neighbor has, and we have a secret satisfaction at his loss of it, to us or to someone else. Schaeffer adds that if we speak too quickly and say that it is never so, we are not telling the truth.

The teachings of Jesus, even for non-Christians, sets forth the ethical framework which makes our society run. Few can argue that our society can continue to operate effectively if we are unfamiliar with the very basic ethics which guide us in our conduct in the culture. If we are unfamiliar with the basic ethical precepts of the Bible, we are reduced to a jungle environment in which our covetousness renders our lives barren of peace, joy, and happiness.

The Gospel of Hope and Salvation

Most importantly, the Bible expresses for our culture the meaning of hope and salvation. We live in a world that is unable to create perfection on its own, no matter how vociferously it claims that it can.

That tension between the images of man-made perfection, the American Dream, and our reality creates in the television age a sense of *angst*, of hopelessness. The Bible expresses to our culture and every other culture the human condition (which is well beneath the standard of perfection) and the hope of God for restoring us to Himself in a state of eternal perfection. The gospel tells us that God's plan for restoration is through Jesus Christ and that human history is the unfolding of that plan.

God's plan for restoration fosters in each of us hope, joy, and a purpose for our life and our world. Without that understanding and without hope, we are lost.

De-mythologize and Re-mythologize

We live in the modern age and are told by our diverse and purportedly tolerant culture that the Bible is a book which has lost its usefulness. The German critics of this century (and their British and American followers) claimed that the stories of the Bible must be de-mythologized, that is, stripped from their context so that only the meaning or

---

"Much of the Bible was written to pierce the cultural myths of the day and of each generation. Rather than being de-mythologized (as the critics have suggested), its power and function is to arm each human being to confront the cultural myths of his generation."

---

theme of the myth was left. Their contention was that the Scripture was written according to a certain set of cultural myths comprehended by pre-modern man. Once stripped of its mythological context, the message could be applied to the modern context where it would be more palatable to the modern, scientific mind of our age. But, of course, it is not that easy.

While the Bible is written in a variety of genres, some to be taken literally, some, like the poetry, to be taken figuratively, there is little indication, other than the cultural view of the observers, that portions of the Gospels are myths in the sense that they are fabricated by the early church to further its cause. Rather, the documents themselves in many instances purport to give accurate accounts of historical events.

But if we look at it the other way around, we find what the Bible does for us. Much of the Bible was written to pierce the cultural myths of the day and of each generation. Rather than being de-mythologized (as the critics have suggested), the Bible's power and function is to arm each human being to confront the cultural myths of his generation, to de-mythologize the cultural myths, and to find and apply God's will and wisdom to the cultural milieu.

As human beings (both then and now), we are like computers in that we default to the self mode. Regardless of what is booted up and what is entered at the prompt, we default to self. Whether we enter *Christian*, *yuppie*, or *businessman*, we always default to *self*. That is why the command to love our neighbor as ourself is so difficult.

Scripture, on the other hand, in de-mythologizing the cultural myths, challenges that default. When measured against Scripture, we are required to re-boot every time we default to our selfish interests, every time we build our own structures and institutions, every time we are off on our "own thing." And there is the constant struggle.

Karl Barth once said that Scripture is the Gibraltar by which all human endeavor must pass. That draws a vivid picture for us, but what does it mean? It means that the myths of life cannot go on without passing by the truth of Scripture. Scripture tests everything that we think, everything that we want, and everything that we do: our experience, our beliefs, and our ethics—not just Christians but all people.

Challenge from Scripture. Scripture in the Ancient Near East challenged the myths and the gods of the Canaanites, the Egyptians, the Assyrians, and the myths that grew up in the nation of Israel. The most feared creature in the Ancient Near East was leviathan, the mythical sea monster or serpent, who appears in a variety of ways in the Old Testament and occasionally in the New.

"Can you pull in the leviathan with a fishhook?" Job asks (Job 41:1). Leviathan was the enemy of God and appears as the beast in Revelation. Leviathan lived in the sea which was seen as a place of trouble and chaos. Leviathan was present at the creation, if not the cause of creation (the myths differ in different areas). Scripture pierces the myth of leviathan, the evil sea monster, and the Canaanite view of creation, by showing that God is in command, that God can pull in leviathan with a fishhook.

In Psalm 74:13–14, the psalmist praises God by saying,

> It was you who split open the sea by your power;
>   you broke the heads of the monster in the waters.
> It was you who crushed the heads of Leviathan
>   and gave him as food to the creatures of the desert.

In the New Testament, Jesus challenges the man-made laws of the Pharisees when His disciples cross the grainfield and pick several kernels of grain. The Pharisees claim that this violates the laws which had evolved from the Scripture passages concerning the Sabbath. Yet these laws were cultural laws ostensibly developed over the centuries by the Pharisees to ensure compliance with Scripture. But the man-made laws were often much stricter and at odds with the Scripture passages. Jesus appeals to Scripture in His rebuttal. "Have you never read . . ." He says (Mark 2:25). Then He cites the story of David and his men recorded in 1 Samuel 21 which is contrary to the cultural regulations of the Pharisees. Thus, Jesus uses Scripture to pierce the veil of pharisaic law and reveal the truth concerning the Sabbath.

In the Sermon on the Mount, Jesus speaks to His listeners and to generations of listeners through the centuries. Much of the sermon pierces the cultural veil prevalent in the Jewish culture of His listeners and in our culture today.

In Matthew 5:21–48, Jesus speaks directly to the cultural myths created by the Pharisees, prevalent in the cultural life of Jerusalem and the cities of Judea. He speaks of murder, adultery, divorce, honesty, pride, revenge, and love for enemies. He specifies the cultural view by beginning with the words, "You have heard that it was said . . ." or some variant (Matthew 5:21, 27, 31, 33, 38, 43). With that phrase He sets out the popular view, and our popular view today, because we all pay lip service to what we have heard. No one will seriously argue that we should commit murder in our culture or that we should commit adultery or divorce or dishonesty or vindictiveness or hatefulness.

But in our culture, as in the first century, people ingeniously circumvented these beliefs by reducing them to the personal and rationalizing their conduct as unavoidable. Adultery is a case in point. Most people in our culture will agree that as a general principle we should avoid adultery, particularly if our spouse is involved. Yet our culture has proffered virtually every reason conceivable for legitimizing adultery without regard for the consequences. Mythical conduct in the conquest of sexual partners abounds in our culture. The words of Jesus prescribe ethical conduct which pierces the mythical foundation of sexual promiscuity. He instructs His listeners through the ages that the warning against adultery is a warning against prideful lust and covetousness, against greed and selfishness, and against conduct which violates the commandment to love your God and your neighbor. For we do neither when we look at others as objects to satisfy and gratify our basest desires. Those words are as true today as they were in the first century and every century before and since they were spoken.

Today, thousands of years later, Scripture challenges the gods and myths of America in the same manner. As we worship at the altar of materialism, cynicism, and existentialism, we think we have discovered these for the first time. Human beings have been troubled by these phenomenon for millennia, and the Bible speaks directly to them.

Jacques Ellul writes:

> I am practically certain that only Jewish and Christian revelation [Scripture] is radically contrary to religion [as defined by Ellul, the institutional church and its worldview, as in civil religion or the American religion]. That is, every time one returns to the written word of that revelation [the Bible], to its always new Good News, one finds a challenge issued to all religious institutions, to all churches and religious philosophies, to all religious moralities, dogmas, and interpretations—Christian or otherwise. When we relearn how to take this revelation [Scripture] seriously and reacquire the habit of listening in silence, then a kind of earthquake occurs that brings on the collapse of all religion [mankind's traditions and myths and structures]. This is the great divide between all other revelations and the revelation of the God of Abraham, Isaac, Jacob, and Jesus Christ.[7]

The Bible provides the standard which pierces all philosophies, all actions, all the machinations of mankind, both individually and collectively. Scripture was designed to pierce the veil of mankind's institutions in order to show the way that God would have us live. The Bible is God's grace to all to give them the necessary groundwork to recognize their worldviews, to identify the myths of culture, and to reinterpret those myths when viewed passing the Gibraltar of God's truth. As Christians, we believe that all the doctrines of man, all of man's visions

of the limits of the world, are to be judged by the Word of God revealed to us in the Bible.

Jesus ends the Sermon on the Mount with a parable which warns
that those who build houses on the myths of the culture build those
houses on sand, and they will be washed away. But those who hear the
Word of God and put it into practice will have houses built upon rock
which will last forever (Matthew 7:24–27).

Challenge to Our Cultural Myths. It is the duty of both Christians
and non-Christians to de-mythologize our myths and to understand the
truth about our existence as we approach the twenty-first century. A
primary purpose of Scripture is to de-mythologize the myths of culture.
But what happens then? Each culture must have a set of beliefs to guide
its conduct.

Stephen Ausband writes:

> No society has existed that did not need some sort of structure, a
> system of belief, by which it could ask and answer questions about its
> relationship to the universal. Myths die as societies change, but the
> need for the myth does not die because man's need for order does not
> change or die.[8]

Scripture provides the structure by which we find order in our culture, by which we find the dreams that guide us.

The time will come when all of our earthly desires are challenged,
either from without or within. Halford E. Luccock, the New Testament
commentator of the earlier part of this century, wrote of the commencement address Rudyard Kipling gave years ago at McGill University in Montreal. As Kipling warned the students about ambition in the
accumulation of wealth or power or position, he said, "Someday you
will meet a man who cares for none of these things. Then you will
know how poor you are."[9]

Luccock adds that just such a thing has happened on a grand scale.
Jesus cared for none of these things, and for nineteen centuries He has
led many people to see how poor they are with only a collection of
things to show for their journey through life.

In Scripture we meet a God who cares for none of the things which
we as human beings hold dear. "As the heavens are higher than the
earth, /so are my ways higher than your ways /and my thoughts than

your thoughts" (Isaiah 55:9). In their stead, God puts forth things which we are to hold dear, things that are important to God and to life and not so important to mankind.

Charles Dickens wrote a book to his children entitled *The Life of Our Lord,* in which he sets out the Christian faith for his children. Dickens was well known for his lampooning of Christians in his culture, but the lampooning was aimed at an inability in many of them to practice what they preached. His criticism is aimed at people who followed the cultural myths rather than the Lord they professed to follow. In the book, he writes:

> My dear children, I am very anxious that you should know something about the history of Jesus Christ. For everybody ought to know about Him. . . .
>
> And when people seek ill of the Poor and Miserable, think how Jesus went among them and taught them, and thought them worthy of his care. . . .
>
> Remember!—It is Christianity to do good always—even to those who do evil to us. It is Christianity to love our neighbor as ourself, and to do to all men as we would have them do to us. It is Christianity to be gentle, merciful, and forgiving, and to keep those qualities quiet in our own hearts, and never make a boast of them, or of our prayers or of our love of God, but always to show that we love him by humbly trying to do right in everything.[10]

We can agree with Dickens on his description of Christianity. But if we substituted the word *American* for Christianity in this passage, would we be able to agree with the passage? Is it American to love your neighbor, to be gentle, etc.? That is the reason we must challenge our culture with the tenets of Scripture.

To de-mythologize the American myths is to strip them of their detail and return them to the one main theme in American mythology: the typology of people chosen by God for an exodus from the Old World and a mission to conquer the New World. This theme, brought by the Puritans to this country, has been differently adapted to the circumstances of each individual so that the American myths, in most applications, have become myths of selfish ambition and vain conceit.

When stripped of individualism and relativism, the de-mythologized myths are simply statements of the most basic human lusts: the basic need for purpose in life, the lust for self-identification and adulation, and the lust for power in the conquest of money, of the opposite sex, of material acquisition, and of political and business status. In Scripture, we meet the Man who cares for none of these.

To re-mythologize is to look at Scripture for the model God has given us to understand His will and to guide our conduct.

PIERCING OUR CULTURAL MYTHS

Why should we pierce the myths of our culture?

Paul says to the church at Colossae: "See to it that no one takes you captive through hollow and deceptive philosophy, which depends on human tradition and the basic principles of this world rather than on Christ" (Colossians 2:8).

Why does he tell them that? Because he knows that the hollow and deceptive philosophies, the human traditions, and the principles of the world which were pervasive in his culture—and the same in our culture—lead to strife, division, and heartache. What is his purpose for bringing his message to these people?

"My purpose is that they may be encouraged in heart and united in love, so that they may have the full riches of complete understanding, in order that they may know the mystery of God, namely, Christ, in whom are hidden all the treasures of wisdom and knowledge" (Colossians 2:2–3).

For the same purpose, the Scripture pierces the myths and deceptive philosophies of our day. Consequently, we can be relieved from the strife, division, and heartache which is so rampant in our culture; we can be encouraged in heart and united in love, knowing that it is love and encouragement which are found in Christ, in whom are hidden all the treasures of wisdom and knowledge.

What is the purpose? That we may be encouraged in heart and united in love with our spouses, with our children, with our neighbors and our fellow workers, so that we may know the treasures of wisdom and knowledge. We will be able to overcome the loneliness and heartache of divorce. We may never feel the anxiety of wayward children, tempted daily with drug and alcohol abuse by a culture ensconced in its own hypocrisy concerning sexual freedom and sexual abuse. We may live without the threat of property line disputes, loud and obnoxious noises, and vulgar threats and disruptions. Paul gives us a purpose of love and encouragement.

The Myth of the Christian Nation

How often we have heard that the United States is the promised land, that it was founded as a Christian nation. Such claims are the very basis of our American mythology. But if we de-mythologize the claim that the United States is a unique nation with a specific mission from God, we have left a worldview in which we are trying to legitimize our undertakings in the world.

We know that nations, empires, and races come and go. And we know that, while God uses nations and empires as He did Egypt and Babylon, He does not call people by nationality or race.

Paul defines God's nation:

> It is not as though God's word had failed. For not all who are descended from Israel are Israel. Nor because they are his descendants are they all Abraham's children. On the contrary, "It is through Isaac that your offspring will be reckoned." In other words, it is not the natural children who are God's children, but it is the children of the promise who are regarded as Abraham's offspring. (Romans 9:6–8)

The myth of the Christian nation is man-made and runs counter to the themes of Scripture which prescribe that God's grace goes beyond national boundaries and is shed upon persons who follow Him. When tested against Scripture, the myth comes up lacking. The Bible describes a nation of believers that constitute the invisible church.

Jesus did not preach about national loyalties nor did He suggest that the kingdom of God belonged to any certain group identifiable by physical means. The Apostle John gives us this view of heaven: "After this I looked and there before me was a great multitude that no one could count, from every nation, tribe, people and language, standing before the throne and in front of the Lamb. They were wearing white robes and were holding palm branches in their hands" (Revelation 7:9).

The gospel was not sent to a certain group or nation but was destined for all groups and all nations. "Then I saw another angel flying in midair, and he had the eternal gospel to proclaim to those who live on the earth—to every nation, tribe, language and people" (Revelation 14:6).

The United States has no greater claim to God's providence than any of the earlier empires and, indeed, any of the nations to come. In the end, there will be one nation, and that nation will be the nation of

---

"The myth of the Christian nation is man-made and runs counter to the themes of Scripture which prescribe that God's grace goes beyond national boundaries and is shed upon persons who follow Him."

---

believers, the nation of God which comes down from heaven and is called the New Jerusalem. "I saw the Holy City, the new Jerusalem, coming down out of heaven from God, prepared as a bride beautifully dressed for her husband" (Revelation 21:2).

The United States has provided much in the recent history of the world, but its presence does not authenticate it as a Christian nation or as God's elect. Washington is no more the eternal city than Rome was. That is not to say that the United States has not been a God-fearing nation and has not been used by God.

"It is too small a thing for you to be my servant to restore the tribes of Jacob and bring back those of Israel I have kept. I will also make you a light for the Gentiles, that you may bring my salvation to the ends of the earth" (Isaiah 49:6). The United States, not as a military power, but as the home of a nation of "lights," may be used to bring salvation to the ends of the earth. If that is our role we should zealously guard it and diligently carry it out. But we should also recognize that we are no more a Christian nation than present-day Israel is the Jewish nation. We are a secular state with a mythology which places us at the center of the universe. We should not fool ourselves into thinking that our mythology justifies our actions.

The Myths of the Restoration and the New Beginning

Very basic to the American mythology is the ideal that individuals can start over again as if nothing had happened in the past. Indeed, this myth has its basis in Scripture. We are told that we must be born again, that we shall become a new creation in Christ, and that a new world will come. But Scripture tells us that the new beginning can only be in Christ. We are not restored in this world but only in the hands of God. Mark tells us that what is impossible for man is possible for God (Mark 10:27).

The de-mythologizing of the restoration and the new beginning again shows that we are trying under our own power to guide our way in this world. It is an escape hatch for our imperfection; if we mess up the first time, we can always start over again. Our future is in our own power. Yet we find in that frame of mind that we are often at a loss to find the purpose for our existence.

But more importantly, these myths focus us on the present and away from the promises God has made concerning our eternal life. A congregation member in her eighties said, "The older I get, the more I understand and want to reach heaven, the more I understand what Paul meant when he said to die is gain." God has made *the* promise for restoration and a new beginning. Those in the older generation, those who have been through hardships in the Depression and the Second World War, understand the scope of what that means much better than the younger generations whose eyes are focused upon perfection here on earth. The older generation have had their faith tested and molded by hardships here on earth.

Our younger generation, many of whom have grown up in a comfort unknown in human history, have no need for God's restoration. They are told that they can find their own.

Jesus said that eye cannot see nor ear hear nor heart comprehend the treasures the Father has for us in heaven. The reason may very well be that we are too busy searching for and counting our blessings here on earth.

The view Jesus puts forth is directly in opposition to the view of the American myth. Our efforts to establish our own restoration run counter to the plan shown us in the Bible.

> Trust in the LORD with all your heart
>   and lean not on your own understanding;
> in all your ways acknowledge him,
>   and he will make your paths straight.
> Do not be wise in your own eyes;
>   fear the LORD and shun evil.

This will bring health to your body
and nourishment to your bones.
(Proverbs 3:5–8)

The Myths of Sacrifice and Dissent and Political Equality

When the United States revived the selective service system, the draft, there were demonstrations on college campuses across the country. The Associated Press carried a photograph of a Princeton University student carrying a sign which stated: nothing is worth dying for. In this age when cultural literacy is reduced to sloganeering, he registered his protest against the draft. Yet it was a sad comment when compared to the motto of the University: Princeton in the nation's service. Presumably, at Princeton, the nation's service is not worth dying for anymore.

The myth of sacrifice and dissent has become one of the major tenets of political discourse in our country today, merging with and devouring the myth of political equality. The myth of political equality presumed some reciprocity, some commitment to the common good. The myth of sacrifice and dissent, rejuvenated with the present myths of individualism, has done away with the need for commitment and requires no sacrifice but only dissent from anything that does not benefit the individual personally.

The quest for political equality through sacrifice and dissent, when de-mythologized and stripped of its political rhetoric, is the basest of quests for power, a quest motivated by personal pride. The stridency of today's street demonstrations says that we'll do it my way or not at all.

Nowhere have these myths been so strident as in the demonstrations of civil disobedience. Used effectively for political change in the civil rights movement of the 1960s and 1970s, the street demonstration has become the model for political expression in our generation—our generation's way of asserting our "rights." But the stridency which has come with the street demonstrations of this generation has replaced the biblical exhortation to love your neighbor, to be self-controlled, to control the tongue. "Speak to one another with psalms, hymns and spiritual songs. Sing and make music in your heart to the Lord, always giving thanks to God the Father for everything, in the name of our Lord Jesus Christ. Submit to one another out of reverence for Christ" (Ephesians 5:19–21).

Stridency is one of the fundamental debates in the pro-life movement. In a letter to the editor in *U.S. News and World Report,* a woman wrote in response to an essay by John Leo pointing out the strong bias of the American media in favor of the pro-abortion political forces. The letter gives some reason for that bias:

> When a local TV reporter asked our pro-life group to shout 'baby-killers' while she did an interview in front of an abortion clinic, we grudgingly obliged even though we had been praying quietly. Sadly, we would have leapt through flaming hoops to get any coverage at all. Many thanks to John Leo for exposing unworthy media tactics.[11]

This is an astounding example of how easy it is, in a second's time, to disregard all that we have learned from Scripture and seek the world's methods and the world's recognition, and then complain about the media's unfairness. The protesters were standing there praying quietly and along slithered the serpent and suggested that they disobey God's commandment, and they fell for it hook, line, and sinker. Surely, God did not say to love your enemy. That's why we need the Word of God, so we can challenge the methods of the world.

Granted, Christian methods often seem slow and unreliable; so people reach out for something which seems to be quicker and surer. Paul wrote to the church at Corinth:

> I beg you that when I come I may not have to be as bold as I expect to be toward some people who think that we live by the standards of this world. For though we live in the world, we do not wage war as the world does. The weapons we fight with are not the weapons of the world. On the contrary, they have divine power to demolish strongholds. (2 Corinthians 10:2–4)

We see the secular world's methods and we think that if they work there, they will work for us. But the church has a different agenda. "Be still before the LORD and wait patiently for him; /do not fret when men succeed in their ways, /when they carry out their wicked schemes" (Psalm 37:7). Scripture pierces the wisdom of the world by calling for a different way.

The Myth of the Self-Made Man

The myth of the self-made man is perhaps the dearest to the American heart. It has become in recent decades the focal point of individualism, resulting in a selfish mentality which elevates the individual in the public eye at the expense of all others. It goes without saying that the theme of this myth as it is interpreted in our day is personal greed. And it goes without saying that this myth, in most ways, flounders before the Gibraltar of all wisdom.

"We see the secular world's methods and we think that if they work there, they will work for us. But the church has a different agenda."

We live in a competitive society that seeps into our souls. The urge to be "the greatest among us" is strong. The cult of pre-eminence and the desires induced by profit-driven corporations shape the thoughts and ambitions of our citizens. Television advertising deliberately stimulates practically every selfish emotion known to humanity. When stripped of its context, the present myth of the self-made man is rooted in greed, envy, covetousness, pride, and vanity.

When the disciples asked who was the greatest among them, Jesus said: "If anyone wants to be first, he must be the very last, and the servant of all" (Mark 9:35). This is an unsettling statement in response to personal ambition. This tests the myths which guide us and makes us think. William Lane points out that this great reversal of all human ideas of greatness and rank is a practical application of the greatest commandment of love for one's neighbor.[12]

Jesus did not abolish ambition. What He is telling the disciples is not that ambition itself is negative. We read in Colossians 3:23–24: "Whatever you do, work at it with all your heart, as working for the Lord, not for men, since you know that you will receive an inheritance from the Lord as a reward. It is the Lord Christ you are serving."

William Barclay writes: "Rather he re-created and sublimated ambition. For the ambition to rule, he substituted the ambition to serve. For the ambition to have things done for us he substituted the ambition to do things for others."[13] Rather than quashing ambition, Jesus offers a call to battle. Barclay points out that so far from being "an impossibly

AMBITION TO SERVE   DO THINGS FOR OTHERS
AMBITION TO RULE – HAVE THINGS DONE FOR US

idealistic view, this is a view of the soundest common-sense. The really great people of history, the people who are remembered as having made contributions to life are those who have said not, 'How can I use society and government to my greatest advantage?' But 'How can I contribute most to society?'"[14]

Later Barclay says,

> Every economic problem we have would be solved if men lived for what they could do for others and not for what they could do for themselves. Every political problem we have would be solved if the ambition of men was only to serve the society and not to enhance their own prestige. . . . When Jesus spoke of the supreme greatness and value of the man whose ambition was to be a servant, he laid down one of the greatest practical truths in the world.[15]

Scripture tells us that "Whoever loves money never has money enough; whoever loves wealth is never satisfied with his income" (Ecclesiastes 5:10). And yet in our human condition, we continue to lust for more. That is why we must pass the Gibraltar which oversees all human ambition.

The Myth of the Search for the Soul

Arising recently in the culture of our country, the myth of the search for the soul has mushroomed through every nook and cranny until it calls each American to search for the self until satisfaction is reached.

The great irony is that Scripture says to find ourselves we must lose ourselves. "Whoever finds his life will lose it, and whoever loses his life for my sake will find it" (Matthew 10:39). The central thought in losing oneself is the great commandment: to love your neighbor as yourself. That's impossible! Maybe. But we are called on to try.

The search for the soul has led to a selfishness and a competitiveness which invites personal confrontation. Anglican Bishop Alexander 'Muge of Kenya, invited to speak at an Anglican church near San Francisco, suggested to his hosts over dinner that the reason the Anglican church in the United States was in decline was the number of homosexuals in positions of power. At that point, the rector of the host church and a female parishioner shouted furiously at their guest, proclaiming that they were homosexuals. The disturbance was such that several of the restaurant patrons left the premises. 'Muge said it was the shock of his Christian life. The Bishop of the diocese of California issued a statement defending the rector and the parishioner.[16] The invitation to speak was withdrawn and the Bishop of Kenya was introduced to love for one's neighbor, American-style.

Scripture calls upon Christians to treat each other in a brotherly manner, not in the manner of the world. "My dear brothers, take note of this: Everyone should be quick to listen, slow to speak and slow to become angry, for man's anger does not bring about the righteous life that God desires" (James 1:19–20).

How easy it is to default to the ways of the world and forsake the ways of the Word. The search for the soul overwhelms the basic Christian fellowship in the church. The right to voice your anger overcomes the brotherhood of Christ.

The Christian life is to understand what the Christian faith means, what the Cross means, and how it affects our way of life. It includes the extreme of laying down our life as a sacrifice for others, of giving mind, heart, time, and strength for the betterment of others. The Apostle Paul tells us that we are to support and encourage one another: "Do nothing out of selfish ambition or vain conceit, but in humility consider others better than yourselves. Each of you should look not only to your own interests, but also to the interests of others" (Philippians 2:3–4).

Scripture pierces the veil of the cultural myth that we shall find the truth when we find the soul. Scripture places before us another truth: That the search for the soul, the quest to find oneself, is another form of bondage. In our effort to be free of the perceived bondage of our culture, we seek a "freedom" which ironically enslaves us in a prison much worse than the first.

Martin Lloyd-Jones writes:

When we considered the man who is meek, we saw that all that really means is that he is free from self in its every shape and form—self-concern, pride, boasting, self-protection, sensitiveness, always imagining people are against him, desire to protect self and glorify self. That is what leads to quarrels between individuals, that is what leads to quarrels between nations; self-assertion. Now the man who hungers and thirsts after righteousness is a man who longs to be free from all that; he wants to be emancipated from self-concern in every shape and form.[17]

Now, unfortunately, that flies in the face of the "me-first" philosophy that we see in values classes in schools, portrayed daily on the television, and evident in our political processes. The American myths teach us to focus on ourselves. There is a story often told about the Wednesday evening prayer meeting which ended each time with a prayer by one of the men in the congregation. After a long, drawn-out prayer, the man always concluded with the supplication, "Lord, please clean all the cobwebs out of my life."

Finally, one Wednesday evening when he had taken about all he could take, one of the men in the back heard the final supplication to clean the cobwebs and shouted, "Lord, don't do it. Please kill the spider instead."

Scripture challenges the very essence of the search for the soul, of the American fascination with finding oneself to the exclusion of all others, and of the American pastime of gazing at one's navel. The call is to look away from oneself and focus upon the eternal, immovable object that gives the call. The call is to focus outward constantly and consistently, not just to clean the cobwebs but to kill the spider of self.

What does it mean to lose ourselves? It means knowing the kind of person God wants you to be and not doing what prevents you from being that person. If you do not know what God wants, get involved with the Bible, and you will find a description of life which is much different from any you have seen in this world.

Get involved with the people around you. Take up your cross. Get involved with the church. This is a call to battle in the Christian community and in the culture at large. It's a call to get involved with what's going on around you. It's a call to be the salt of the earth.

The American church has a great deal of talent. Nevertheless, in the age of instant gratification, it still takes time and effort to get things done. It takes getting involved with people.

CONCLUSION

The American myths repeatedly appear in daily life, in a variety of guises. Recently, a new movie was advertised as the story of a young man who prowled the streets in search of women to seduce, to add to his long list of trophies, to add more notches to his gun. The closing line of the advertisement was: "See it [the movie] with someone you love." This confused advertisement baldly exploits the American myth of election and conquest as it appeals to male sexual fantasies and exploits and demeans females. Moreover, it renders the term *love* meaningless by placing it in the context of lust as a mark of personal success.

The only reason this advertisement is worth mentioning is that it is symptomatic of the manipulation of individuals in our culture by appealing to cultural myths. The only way our culture can preserve the dignity of the individual is to challenge this manipulation with the principles passed down to us in Scripture.

This is not a call for conversion to Christianity. This is a call to become culturally literate, a call to be concerned about human dignity, about the welfare of our children.

Our cultural myths are often the opposite of what the Bible teaches. Presumably, we can say that for thousands of years people have been wrong about life and wrong in believing the Bible. We can say that in the last half of the twentieth century, we have finally found the key to life—self-gratification. But if we did, we would be making a grave mistake. As we examine our lives and search for the ultimate truth, we should remember the words of the carpenter from Galilee:

> Do not store up for yourselves treasures on earth, where moth and rust destroy, and where thieves break in and steal. But store up for yourselves treasures in heaven, where moth and rust do not destroy, and where thieves do not break in and steal. For where your treasure is, there your heart will be also. (Matthew 6:19–21)

14

AMERICANS AND THE SACRAMENTS

The entire law is summed up in a single command: "Love your neighbor as yourself." If you keep on biting and devouring each other, watch out or you will be destroyed by each other.

GALATIANS 5:14–15

The command to be the light of the world bore heavily upon the Puritans as they came into view of the North American continent. Aboard the ship *Arbella* off the coast of what came to be New England, John Winthrop reminded them that they were to be a city on the hill, a light to the world. And we know that Scripture provided the guide for their conduct as they left a culture whose myths were contrary to Scripture.

Today, we find ourselves in a position not that different from the Puritans. We are entering a new world in the twenty-first century, a world which is likely to be arrogant, hostile, and ignorant of the Christian faith as well as indifferent to the Christian church. We cannot fall back on our present situation, because it has guided us into a moral abyss.

Are we not at an impasse in our culture? The myths which made America have been perverted to the extent that they are meaningless beyond the goals of the most selfish and personal aggrandizement. In the inner cities there are no myths or models except those which hit the street today and the morgue tomorrow. In the schools we have lost touch with the culture, so that we do not understand the very basic communications.

Nor do we understand acculturation—the passing of knowledge from one generation to the next. Our freedom has led us to an impasse. Psychologist Erik Erikson wrote that the American is so rich in opportunities for freedom that he does not know what he is free from.

If the original American myths no longer pack the punch to guide our conduct, if they are obsolete in a nation of instant gratification, if they ignore and dismiss the wisdom of the ages, what do we do? We must fall back, not on the myths of our culture, but on the worldview in Scripture.

What is it that we all look for in our journeys here on earth? Psychologist Larry Crabb says that each person yearns for security and significance in his or her life. In the Christian faith we find that security and significance, but not in the culture's terms. We find it, like those in generations before us, in God's terms. For the twenty-first century, just as for each preceding century, the stories of the Bible are brought into context to provide guidance in our culture. The meanings are timeless and do not change; the cultures change. As we bring the stories into our culture, we must search for the unchanging meaning and apply it to our changing context. That is why Scripture is the Gibraltar by which all human cultures must pass—it does not change and its truth does not go away but looms constantly over all the endeavors of humanity.

The last chapter discussed the role of Scripture in piercing the American myths. This chapter will explore the context for the application of Scripture to our lives in the Christian community and in the community at large.

Our sacraments pierce the mythological tenet of exclusive mission, the tenet which calls us to a conformity through individualism and focuses us upon ourselves. The sacraments pierce the tenet of exclusive mission by calling Americans to holiness and community.

THE FIRST STEP

The first step in any course is to recognize our situation and to want to do something about it. In his book on discipleship, Eugene H. Petersen quotes Friedrich Nietzsche:

The essential thing "in heaven and earth" is . . . that there should be long obedience in the same direction; there thereby results, and has always resulted in the long run, something which has made life worth living.[1]

Petersen's book, based on the psalms of ascent, points out that the first step is to say no to the ways of the world. We must recognize that the culture around us, for all its strong points, does not permit us peace or joy or happiness in this world. True peace, joy, and happiness are found in our knowledge of God and in following His ways.

We must recognize that there are two ways in this world: the way of the culture or the way of the faith. That is not to say that a person at any given time is on one path or the other. That is to say that, in the end, we will follow one or the other.

But we are talking about the first step. And that first step lies in the answer *no*. The resounding *no* begins our journey from the culture and toward the truth. Petersen says that "the first step toward God is a step away from the lies of the world. It is a renunciation of the lies we have been told about ourselves and our neighbors and our universe."[2] Once that step is taken, the path of long obedience is before us.

Who may take that first step? We all must take that first step, Christians and non-Christians alike—all who yearn for a better world, all who dream of a life of peace and joy, all who wish to live an abundant life in harmony with neighbors and environment. We know that the road of the culture has not led to community but to fragmentation. Each of us must examine the myths and traditions of our culture and say *no*. That includes the Christian pastor as well as the American businessman; that includes the full-time Christian worker as well as the two-Sunday-a-month overachiever. All must say *no* to the myths which have isolated us and turn toward community and commitment if this world is to be a better place.

"If we really want to come into this way of life," Martin Lloyd-Jones writes, "we have to leave our 'self' outside. And it is there of course that we come to the greatest stumbling-block of all. It is one thing to leave the world and the way of the world; but the most important thing in a sense is to leave our self outside."[3]

To say *no* to the world is to say *no* to the preaching of the world that our purpose in life is elevation of "self." That is the foremost hurdle to be overcome in the first step. The elevation of self was the first obstacle for humanity and humanity fell on that hurdle. Each of us face that hurdle on a daily basis.

To say *no* is to say *yes* to the unique and independent path which leads to God. To follow Jesus, the first step is to obey by saying *no* to the old ways and *yes* to the new path.

Bonhoeffer points out that the first step is not belief or faith but obedience.

> If you believe, take the first step, it leads to Jesus Christ. If you don't believe, take the first step all the same for you are bidden to take it. No one wants to know about your faith or unbelief, your orders are to perform the act of obedience on the spot. Then you will find yourself in the situation where faith becomes possible and where faith exists in the true sense of the word.[4]

But what do we do after we take the first step?

THE SACRAMENTS

The second way God has given us His grace is through the sacraments. Scripture gives the basis of the sacraments. In the sacraments we find the methods by which God, through His Holy Spirit, channels His grace to our souls.

I do not wish to enter into a theological debate about the number of the sacraments or the efficacy of the sacraments. Rather, I wish to look at the sacraments as God's grace to us, as God's seal upon us, and as God's symbol for our lives. The sacraments symbolize something much larger than the purpose they fulfill in the Christian church today. The sacraments symbolize our commitment to holiness and to community. And it is these two things that I will discuss.

How can the sacraments symbolize holiness and community? The sacraments of baptism and the Lord's Supper are the outward signs of our commitments in life. When we are baptized we are set apart as holy. When we participate in the Lord's Supper, we are reestablishing our commitment to the community in the church. But, wait a minute! The average Protestant has been baptized once and participates in the Lord's Supper at a rate of less than once a quarter. How can these empty rituals symbolize anything in our real lives? How can that be the Holy Spirit working in our lives? Because part of God's grace to us is not only the symbol but the context in which the symbol is given. In Scripture, we see the context of the sacraments. In Scripture, we are given the contexts which will allow the sacraments to become operative in our lives.

The sacrament of baptism is a mark of holiness. Scripture gives us the context, the definition, and the examples of holiness. The Lord's Supper is the practice of community. Scripture gives us the context, the definition, the and examples of this as well.

The sacraments are the one-two punch of the greatest commandment. We are to love our God and love our neighbor as ourselves. The meaning of that commandment lies in holiness and community. The sacrament of baptism sets us apart for a life of holiness in God, and the sacrament of the Lord's Supper draws us together for a life of community with our neighbor.

Another way of saying that is:

> We have to keep two elements in mind here: first, if there is to be an authentic church, there must be "real" men. There have to be steadfast, vigorous people; there have to be individuals. . . . Second, the church is generated out of the encounter, the union, the friendship of unique "isolates" learning to recognize one another.[5]

In the church there must be individuals who have begun that long obedience in the same direction to find the meaning of life. They must walk on paths independent of all cultural bonds. They must be "real"

"The sacraments are the one-two punch of the greatest commandment."

---

people who are steadfast and vigorous, who are set apart as holy in this world—holy in that they see the meaning of life not in the myths of the culture but in the truth of God given to mankind. Secondly, there must be the union of the individuals "learning to recognize one another." There must be a unique fellowship of the "isolates" in which each loves the other as he loves himself.

The sacraments give us the model of meaningful living for the twenty-first century. The sacraments pierce that foundation of the American mythology which rests upon our sense of exclusive mission. That sense of mission has led our myths to be differently adapted into myths of selfish individualism.

We are called to a holiness that rejects the self-focused conduct prescribed in the myths of our culture and instead leads us to a life of peace in communion with God. Rather than follow the present-day myths of individualism that demand a perverse conformity to the standards of culture, our focus is outward, on God. We celebrate our personal uniqueness in the joy of walking with God. As we look at our neighbors, we are called from the American myths of exclusiveness and conquest which have produced the isolation and alienation of the post-industrial world. We celebrate communion in fellowship with our neighbors. In these celebrations of God and of neighbor, we find security with God and significance and purpose in our lives. This is a long obedience which makes life worth living.

The sacraments, as God's grace to us, lead us to a life which rejects selfish individualism and reestablishes our sense of holiness and community.

THE MARK OF HOLINESS

We should not confuse the terms *holiness* and *piety*. *Piety* means that we conduct ourselves in a certain way. *Holiness* means that we are set apart, that we are different from other people, that we walk a unique and independent path through this world. Although it is a long haul, it does not begin with a list of accomplishments. It begins with saying *no*, which starts our path toward God. It is the rejection of the bonds of the cultural myths and the freedom of following a different path.

The Westminster Shorter Catechism states that "baptism is a sacrament, wherein the washing with water in the name of the Father, and of the Son, and of the Holy Ghost, doth signify and seal our ingrafting into Christ, and partaking of the benefits of the covenant of grace, and our engagement to the Lord's."

Our ingrafting, our partaking, and *our engagement* are terms which set us aside at baptism for a different life. In the Old Testament, God set Israel aside and told them to be different from all the nations, not to engage in the corruption and misery and death which marked their neighbors and not to adopt their neighbors' ways of living. He set Israel aside as His treasured possession. "You yourselves have seen what I did to Egypt, and how I carried you on eagles' wings and brought you to myself. Now if you obey me fully and keep my covenant, then out of all nations you will be my treasured possession" (Exodus 19:4–5).

The seal of the covenant was circumcision, just as today the seal of the covenant is baptism. The act is a symbol of God's grace to us which sets us apart from the "nations," carries us on eagles' wings, and guides us on our paths though this life to Himself. It creates a new path for each of us, a path which leads us away from the wide path of the cultural myths and onto the narrow path toward God.

In the sacrament of baptism in the church, we admonish the congregation to look back on their own personal baptisms, to repent of their sins against their covenant with God, to recall and examine the faith, to recall and examine their covenant promises made concerning and during baptism to ensure daily living in the right manner before God, and to honor the covenant sealed between God and their individual souls. That admonition is a reminder that baptism is a mark of holiness and that we are to live lives set apart from the ways of the world.

In the Protestant church, the congregation serves as godparents to the baptized child, promising to assist in his growth and nurture. The parents are admonished before the congregation that they are to teach their child to read the Word of God, to instruct their child in the principles of holy religion, as contained in the Scriptures of the Old and New Testaments, to pray with their child, and to make every effort to bring their child up in the nurture and admonition of the Lord.

That is a solemn call to holiness.

The Apostle Peter issues such a call in his first letter. "As obedient children, do not conform to the evil desires you had when you lived in ignorance. But just as he who called you is holy, so be holy in all you do" (1 Peter 1:14–15).

Nobel Prize-winner Alexander Solzhenitsyn found his holiness in a different way.

It was only when I lay there on rotting prison straw that I sensed within myself the first stirrings of good. Gradually, it was disclosed to me that the line separating good and evil passes, not through states, not between classes, nor between political parties either, but right through all human hearts. So, bless you, prison, for having been in my life.[6]

It is difficult to find the line between good and evil which passes through all human hearts, but it is there in each of us. That means that Samson, David, Solomon, and each of us can understand holiness yet succumb to the ways of the world. Because of the human condition, we cannot avoid the lure and glitter of the desires of the world. But we are called away, called to travel that path God has given us to carry us to Himself. We are called to see that the line separating good and evil is in our own hearts. We are called to live in God's side of that line.

IN THE EXILE

Where do we find the stories that pierce the veil of the myths of exclusive mission? They are the stories of the exile. Instead of conquering our promised lands, the exile stories give us a model by which to live in this world *before* we get to the promised land. The Christian promised land is not here on earth but is in eternity with Jesus Christ.

The Bible is a book written for those in the exile, for those whose call is to walk with God, for those whose beat is to "a different drummer." God prepared the faithful for the exile by showing them models of people who lived by faith in hostile lands. The story of Joseph who was sold into slavery by his brothers is the prototypical story of the exile. Joseph's brothers are jealous of him and sell him into slavery in Egypt. He rises to a position of trust with the captain of the guard whose name is Potiphar. But Potiphar's wife has designs on Joseph. Joseph refuses and runs, but Potiphar's wife grabs his cloak, shouts that he sexually assaulted her, and Joseph is once again in prison. Through perseverance and faith in God, Joseph rises again to the second highest position in Egypt and becomes the most powerful man in the world. From that position, he can be reunited with his family and help many in the times of famine (Genesis 37–47).

Another model for the exile is the prophet Daniel. In exile in Babylon, Daniel is among those chosen to be in the court of the king.

During the training period, Daniel asks the overseer if he can eat vegetables rather than the food of the king. The overseer begrudgingly relents, and Daniel, by his own regimen, becomes healthier and stronger. Daniel's diligence in service to the king gains him a top spot from which he can prophesy and serve God.

"The Bible is a book written for those in the exile, for those whose call is to walk with God, for those whose beat is to 'a different drummer.' "

Esther is the story of the exile in which a young Jewish woman is called upon to help her people. When the king looks for a queen, her uncle persuades her to step forward. She is chosen, and through her beauty and her personality she is able to gain much power in the kingdom. Through her position she is able to avert the plot to slaughter the Jews and save her people.

There are others such as Nehemiah, who rose in the exile to the honored and trusted position of cupbearer for the king. Moses himself was raised in the original exile in Egypt, there to gain his education and upbringing at the hands of the Egyptians.

The Christians of the first century were all exiles, pilgrims in this world who were a strict minority. Yet they kept the faith even in the face of overwhelming odds. The church often met in the most oppressive of circumstances, yet the church prospered. The apostles, particularly Paul and Peter, and the church in the book of Acts provide us with models for action in exilic circumstances.

THE DIFFERENT DRUMMER

Our call to holiness is in living in exile. The sacrament is so much stronger as we approach the circumstances and the context of the twenty-first century, and God's grace to us takes on greater meaning.

As we look at the model of exile living we see that today in the United States we are moving closer to exile conditions. Indeed, many would suggest that the government, through the courts and through the vast bureaucracy of public education, has turned hostile to the Christian and Jewish faiths. The mark of the Christian community and the witness to the community at large is still holiness. Scripture provides a road map for holiness. It is up to us to follow that road map as God leads us.

Treated Unfairly

Each of the models for living in exile was treated badly in some way. The circumstances surrounding Joseph's life would justify the most extreme sociopathic behavior today. But Joseph did not turn away from God but found his strength in God to meet the most bizarre of reversals.

Ours is not a Christian nation elect of God but a nation of many diverse beliefs. Once a strong point in our culture, those diverse beliefs have become an angry tribalism which confronts rather than compromises, which accuses rather than accommodates.

Often in our culture, Christians find themselves being confronted, mocked, or looked down upon for the things they believe. *Christianity Today*[7] editorialized on the situation confronting John Cardinal O'Connor, Archbishop of New York City, when he suggested that heavy-metal music can be a contributing cause to experimentation with satanism. Rock performer Ozzy Osbourne, former singer for a group called Black Sabbath and who has gained notoriety for biting the heads off bats during his performances, telegrammed the Cardinal that his comments "insulted the intelligence of rock fans all over the world." According to the *Christianity Today* editorial, *Time* magazine joined the bandwagon. Once a respected news magazine, *Time* now plays upon the sensational as items of entertainment. The editorial response of *Time* was to ask "Was O'Connor seriously suggesting that demons were loose in the land?" While the answer to that may be revealed in the sensationalism found in its pages, *Time* gave an answer from a Catholic "scholar" who said that belief in the devil was a "premodern and precritical" superstition.

Not only confronted in writing, Cardinal O'Connor has been confronted during worship services by homosexual hooligans bent on imposing their views by terrorist acts, in this case, desecrating the church and disrupting the services.

"The irony of the Christian fulfillment, or indeed, any fulfillment, like the irony of happiness, is that we do not find it by pursuing it."

Cardinal O'Connor is but one notable example of the confrontation experienced by many Christian teachers, parents, and businesspersons in a culture increasingly antagonistic to the Judeo-Christian heritage.

Refused Self-Pity

Each refused to withdraw into self-pity when confronted with beatings, injustice, violent criticism, or circumstances which would have overwhelmed the average man or woman. Self-pity is not an honored characteristic for those who wish to survive the exile. While most of them no doubt felt bad about their enslavement and may have cried out like the psalmist to God, they did not cocoon and give up on life, hope, or God's saving grace.

In our walk of holiness we must refuse to withdraw in self-pity from culture or life. We have all seen people in our communities who are able to live their lives without bowing to peer pressure or to someone else's ideas of how they should live. We have friends who live in a fresh independence of life, refusing to compromise with the pettiness of the world around them.

The irony of the Christian fulfillment, or indeed, any fulfillment, like the irony of happiness, is that we do not find it by pursuing it. We do not establish our identities by finding the self. We establish our identities by living a life of holiness independent of the search for personal identity. We do not live in comparison to our neighbor; holiness demands that we love our neighbor.

Refused Compromise

Each refused to compromise his or her principles with the world when it would have been easy to do so. It would have been easy for Joseph to compromise with Potiphar's wife, to manipulate that situation to his own advantage. Nehemiah could have stayed with the king in comfort and, if he worked it right, had all the physical comforts that he ever wanted. Esther could have lived happily ever after with the king. Peter, James, and John could have been comfortable as fishermen. Paul could have avoided a great deal of discomfort had he rationalized his encounter with Jesus as a psychological aberration. But none of them turned his or her back on the principles of faith which set each of them apart from the culture at large.

We must refuse to compromise our faith with the ways of the world. Scripture gives us the model which says that the world does not dictate our lives. We are to be steadfast under all conditions. A term in vogue in the Christian community is that we are called to a *counterculture*— we are called to show the world the way of Christ. While that is basically true, I do not think we are called to be stridently at odds with the world. That connotes some judgmentalism. We are called to live our lives the best we can. We are to excel in the community in whatever we do. But we are to do it in a way that is true to the principles of God.

Holiness is a call to live life as God has planned it for us. I once heard the definition of *success* as the ability to establish your own set of values and to be able to adhere to them. The author said that not many famous people were successful and not many successful people were famous. Famous people adhere to the values of others and more particularly to the common values of the culture. Otherwise, they would not be famous.

Our holiness is most often affected by American mythology that compromises the principles of the Christian faith. Often, we are so imbued with the American religion that we do not see the Christian religion when it stares us in the face.

Worked Hard

Each worked hard and excelled, gaining honor in the secular world as well as in the community of the faithful. The picture of life in exile drawn in Scripture is the picture of the person who excels in the culture rather than hides in the ghetto. The prophet Jeremiah carried this word to the Israelites going into exile:

> This is what the LORD Almighty, the God of Israel, says to all those I carried into exile from Jerusalem to Babylon: "Build houses and settle down; plant gardens and eat what they produce. Marry and have sons and daughters; find wives for your sons and give your daughters in marriage, so that they too may have sons and daughters. Increase in number there; do not decrease. Also, seek the peace and prosperity of the city to which I have carried you into exile. Pray to the LORD for it, because if it prospers, you too will prosper." (Jeremiah 29:4–7)

This is an interesting concept: praying for the prosperity of those who are imprisoning you. On the other hand, it is loving your enemy. The Hebrew word *shalom*, which means a deep peace and contentment, is used three times and is translated as the word *prosper*.

We must live as productive members in the culture and excel in each position we hold, whether it be family member, employee, or simply neighbor. Christians have always believed that human technology, science, and all the endeavors of human discovery are tools for us to learn more of God and His creation. But we believe that finding out more about God's creation is finding out more about the nature of God. From the very beginning, Christians have been at the forefront of education, science, and all areas of life.

John Calvin called that the "cultural imperative." And we are to continue to learn about God from His creation and to interpret nature with the help of God's special revelation.

Remained Holy and Obedient

Each kept the faith with God; each remained holy and obedient to God and kept walking in communion with Him no matter how bad the circumstances. Each was a paragon of holiness, not giving in to the myths and the gods of the culture but holding back and remembering the promises of God. We must keep faith with God; we too must remain holy and obedient to God and keep walking in communion with Him no matter how bad the circumstances.

The 1960s borrowed the saying that we all know now: "If a man does not keep pace with his companions, perhaps it is because he hears a different drummer. Let him step to the music he hears, however measured and far away." Written by Henry David Thoreau a century earlier, it was soon distorted to walking to the beat of your own drum and became a banner for doing whatever you wanted, regardless of how destructive it was to others. Instead of a call to holiness, it was a call to selfishness.

We find holiness where we are, but it requires following the beat of the eternal drummer. It's not in the church or in the next county. Like unethical conduct, it's not confined to Wall Street. Like drugs, it's not confined to the big city. The world faces us each day. The question to us in the twenty-first century is what we do when we come face-to-face with it.

Legacy of Holiness

Each left a legacy of holiness and obedience for the following generations. They served as typologies for Jews and Christians in many circumstances, in many lands. God used them and their stories to prepare other people for holiness in times of trouble.

In the exile living, we must pass the faith on to the next generation. In Deuteronomy, Moses commands the Israelites to do this, but what they passed along was not the faith but a watered-down version of it. We must walk in the faith and raise our children to understand it. So many children in the church today are raised without an understanding of the faith. Their only model is their parents who are living the American Dream and are too exhausted from their hectic living to get up for church on Sunday morning.

In the book, *What Every Christian Should Know*, there is a passage about one of the authors whose uncle was a pastor. When the author was young, they used to stay up all night talking. Early one morning, when the sun was coming up and they had been talking all night, his uncle said, "Do you understand what Uncle has been telling you?"

And the author said, "Sure, I understand."

His uncle laughed. "No, you don't. But someday you will, and when you do, you will remember that Uncle has told you this."[8]

His uncle had introduced him to holiness. And his uncle knew the day would come when, amidst all the drumbeats that come out of our culture—out of the television and the radio, out of the news media and out of the schools—that one day, he would hear that faraway drumbeat.

What are the stories which we will someday understand? They are the same stories which have influenced the generations before us. They are the stories which pierce the veil of our cultural myths.

CHRISTIAN FELLOWSHIP

The second sacrament, the Lord's Supper, was initiated by Jesus at the fellowship of the Passover meal in Jerusalem shortly before His arrest, trial, crucifixion, and resurrection. Most Protestant churches celebrate the Lord's Supper at least once a quarter. In the celebration we are to remember Christ as we commune with His spirit.

As we draw near to the Lord's Table to celebrate the sacrament, we are genuinely reminded that Jesus instituted this sacrament for a number of reasons:

- For the perpetual memory of His dying for our sakes and the pledge of His undying love;

- as a bond of our union with Him and with each other as members of His mystical body;

- as a seal of His promises to us and a renewal of our obedience to Him;

- for the blessed assurance of His presence with us who are gathered here in His Name;

- as an opportunity for us who love the Saviour to feed spiritually upon Him who is the Bread of Life; and

- as a pledge of His coming again.[9]

The Apostle Paul gave this instruction in his letter to the Corinthians:

For I received from the Lord what I also passed on to you: The Lord Jesus, on the night he was betrayed, took bread, and when he had given thanks, he broke it and said, "This is my body, which is for you; do this in remembrance of me." In the same way, after supper he took the cup, saying, "This cup is the new covenant in my blood; do this,

whenever you drink it, in remembrance of me." For whenever you eat
this bread and drink this cup, you proclaim the Lord's death until he
comes. (1 Corinthians 11:23–26)

The Lord's Supper reminds us also that we are to love our neighbor
as ourselves and that we are to find our significance in our relationships
with our neighbors. The Lord's Supper is a call away from self-focus to
community. The Lord's Supper is a time for self-examination, but more
than that, it is a time of reaching out to others. In the Christian community and in the community at large, fellowship is a scarce commod-
ity. In the midst of our vain struggles to conquer our own promised
lands, we continually return to the point where we want to be reassured
that it is all worthwhile.

The Lord's Supper is a reminder that there is only one way that
struggle is all worthwhile—that is in fellowship with families, with
neighbors, and with Jesus Christ.

The Bible gives us many examples of Christian fellowship. There is
the caring and sharing attitude of Abraham when he parts with Lot and
bids him to select the finest land; the reunion of Jacob and Esau; the
close friendship of David and Jonathan; and the fellowship, reflected in
the Psalter, with the Lord and the congregation in the house of God.
But the New Testament gives us the primary example in the Upper
Room when Jesus instituted the sacrament. The fellowship of the Lord's
Supper is both a calling together and a bidding good-bye. Jesus has
called them together for the last time to express His love to them and
to comfort them. He knows what is going to happen to Him and to
them. So He gathers them for one last time, until He sees them again.

In the Gospel of John, the description of the Upper Room is five
chapters long. In John's discourses, Jesus uses the word *love* thirty-one
times. In the rest of the Gospel, it is used only six times. The Lord's
Supper is a time of love.

There is a contrast in the passage between the meal, which is a
time of fellowship, and the betrayal that is being planned by Judas
Iscariot. It has always been a tradition and still is among many Arabs
today, that if you sit with someone for a meal, you are bonding yourselves together. As we sit for the Lord's Supper, we are bonding ourselves together in the body of Christ. That's why we have family meals,
business meals, fellowship meals. In the mobster movies, they always

strike the deal in a restaurant while they are eating. You don't betray someone with whom you have just eaten. Yet, knowing of the betrayal, Jesus continues with the meal and with Judas.

This meal, called the paschal meal, commemorating the sacrifice meal in Exodus 13, is the meal in which the Jews in Egypt sacrificed the lamb and wiped its blood over their doorways to be saved from the angel of the Lord who was going to take the firstborn of each family. The blood of the lamb saved them.

The tradition for the Passover meal dictated that near the end of the meal itself a fourth cup of wine was passed around and Psalm 136 was sung—the psalm of praise with the refrain in every verse, "His love endures forever." However, the Lord's Supper in the Upper Room ended after the third cup of wine and did not include the fourth cup or the psalms of praise.

William Lane writes that the fourth cup from which Jesus abstained was a solemn oath that He would not share the festal cup until the messianic banquet at the Second Coming. "Jesus will drink the wine anew, and the newness refers to the mark of the redeemed world and the time for the ultimate redemption. That day refers to the return of Jesus and the triumph of the son of Man."[10]

He is pledging that the fourth cup will be extended and the unfinished meal completed in the consummation, when the Messiah eats with the redeemed sinner in the kingdom of God. This will be the time of full fellowship in the community of God.

The disciples did not understand it at the time. But as they traveled the world carrying the gospel, they lived not in the frustrations and trials of this world but in the great anticipation of the messianic banquet, the time when they would finish the Last Supper, the time when they would eat as redeemed sinners in the kingdom of God.

That was the new Passover.

It was customary in the celebration of the Passover to end with the singing of the Hallel. One person would sing the words antiphonally while the others around the table chanted hallelujah.

Lane writes that Jesus took the words of these psalms as His own prayer of thanksgiving and praise. He pledged to keep His vows in the presence of all the people (Psalm 116:12–19); He called upon the Gentiles to join in the praise of God (Psalm 117); and He concluded with a song of jubilation reflecting His steadfast confidence in His ultimate triumph (Psalm 118). "I will not die but live, and will proclaim what the LORD has done" (Psalm 118:17). Lane writes that when Jesus rose to go to Gethsemane, Psalm 118 was on His lips, providing an appropriate description of how God would guide His Messiah through distress and suffering into the glory that belonged to Him and to those who follow Him in Christian community. His love will endure forever.

A second picture of fellowship is in the early church. The early church grew so rapidly that the issue of fellowship must have been cumbersome. Yet we read that they prayed together, they looked after one another, they shared their possessions, and they carried one another's burdens. They were a strong fellowship that the power of Rome and of Jerusalem could not break. The book of Acts shows us the efforts made at fellowship as well as some of the failures of the fellowship. All the church is called to come together in the remembrance of Christ.

THE MISSING LINK

Where does the church as an institution stand in American culture? In a recent survey by Barna Research Group, four out of five Americans consider themselves Christians yet only 47 percent were church members. The same respondents see the church as outdated in our culture. Only 38 percent see the church as relevant today; only 40 percent turn to God in times of trouble; only 42 percent read the Bible on a weekly basis.[11]

What is the reason for this reversal? It springs from a lack of something we as human beings and as Christians need fundamentally in our lives: community.

> The neighborhood bar is possibly the best counterfeit there is to the fellowship Christ wants to give His church. It's an imitation, dispensing liquor instead of grace, escape rather than reality, but it is a permissive, accepting, and inclusive fellowship. It is unshockable. It is democratic. You can tell people secrets and they usually don't tell others or even tell you what to do. The bar flourishes not because most people are alcoholics, but because God has put into the human heart the desire to know and be known, to love and be loved, and so many seek a counterfeit at the price of a few beers.

With all my heart I believe that Christ wants His church to be . . . a fellowship where people can come in and say, "I'm beat!" "I've had it."[12]

The following models from Scripture show several criteria: fellowship, an outward focus for encouragement, forgiveness, friendship, and fitness.

"Fellowship comes when we know that Jesus Christ is with us as He promised He would be to the very end of the age. His fellowship with us allows us fellowship with our neighbor."

Fellowship

Fellowship is one of the basic needs in the alienated lives of our modern culture. And nowhere else does the fellowship appear as dramatically as in the Last Supper.

That's easy, we say. We like to fellowship. But, in fact, it is the hardest thing to do. Sometimes we go to church to get lost in the crowd. Sometimes we go to church to vent our weekly frustrations. Sometimes we go to have others' frustrations vented upon us.

William Barclay writes: "The essence of sin is pride; the core of sin is independence; the heart of sin is the desire to do what we like and not what God likes."[13]

Fellowship comes when we know that Jesus Christ is with us as He promised He would be to the very end of the age. His fellowship with us allows us fellowship with our neighbor. His fellowship with us dampens our lust for pride and independence and satisfies our desire to do what we like, cooling our rancor toward our neighbor and drawing us together.

But first we need His presence in our lives. That brings community.

In William Faulkner's book, *The Unvanquished,* the spirit of the Confederate cavalryman Colonel John Sartoris is always present. The reader comes to understand how a generation of Southern people felt about the war, how friendships and loyalties were bound together through hardship, and how the young characters lost their innocence in the violence of the day. The secondary characters reflect the qualities of purpose and commitment (rightly or wrongly) toward the myths which form their own ideals.

The book entitled *Sartoris* is set in the same place in Mississippi a generation later, and the ghost of John Sartoris is still around:

> As usual, old man Falls had brought John Sartoris [who had been dead for a generation] into the room with him, had walked the three miles in from the county Poor Farm, fetching, like an odor, like the clean dusty smell of his faded overalls, the spirit of the dead man into that room where the dead man's son sat and where the two of them, pauper and banker, would sit for a half an hour in the company of him who had passed beyond death and then returned.
>
> Freed as he was of time and flesh, he was a far more palpable presence than either of the two old men who sat shouting periodically into one another's deafness.[14]

The question we are asked everyday in Christian ethics is: Do we live like we believe that the spirit of the risen Lord is with us? Do we sit in the company of Him who has actually and physically passed beyond death and then returned? Or do we live like we believe that it's not true? Fellowship arises out of that distinction.

Do we have that today? No, and in the vacuum comes a variety of things, beliefs, and idols. Into the vacuum of our identity comes a variety of faiths and religions. Whether it be the rags-to-riches faith once prominent in America or the me-first, greed-is-good mindset common in some parts of our culture, each of us grabs something to give us an individual identity. And that is the search for the soul which destroys fellowship.

That's why Jesus tells His disciples, "Do this in remembrance of me," so that they will remember the fellowship and rely on the hope of the future fellowship which Jesus has promised in the fourth cup.

Focus for Encouragement

The second criteria is focus for encouragement. In Christian fellowship, we are to care for others as much as we care for ourselves; we are to encourage.

When I made the decision to go to seminary, I left a law practice of thirteen years, a nice house, and a comfortable situation to move my

family to Mississippi. A month after the move, I went to annual training with my Army Reserve unit. We had been in the field a while when
the commander told us that an active component major assigned to
Germany would like to speak to each of the staff officers. He caught me
just after dawn one morning when I was sitting on the ground—dirty,
unshaven, hungry, and down in the dumps. It had just dawned on me
that I had left a law practice, a good income, and a lot of comfort to
move my family to Mississippi.

"Mind if I sit down?" he asked. I did not answer because I knew he
would anyway.

"I'm going to be assigned to Fort McClellan," he said, "but I didn't
think I would like it here." I did not blame him.

"I understand you're going to seminary?" That's the last thing I
wanted to talk about at that point. I did not respond. "I'm a Christian,"
he said. "I think God does everything for a purpose. I think He brought
me here to Fort McClellan to show me that I would like it here."

No, God brought him to Fort McClellan for encouragement. God
brought him there to encourage a fellow Christian who was engaged in
self-pity and doubt, who was struck by the awesome thought that the
promises of the American Dream were floating out the window. He
focused on me while I was focused upon myself. And that is Christian
community.

> One of the highest of human duties is the duty of encouragement. . . .
> It is easy to laugh at men's ideals; it is easy to pour cold water on their
> enthusiasm; it is easy to discourage others. The world is full of discour-
> agers. We have a Christian duty to encourage one another. Many a
> time a word of praise or thanks or appreciation or cheer has kept a
> man on his feet. Blessed is the man who speaks such a word.[15]

When we focus on others, truly focus, and not consider others in
comparison to ourselves or in competition with our goals, we find fellowship and encouragement. We find the way of community with others which Jesus sought for us.

Forgiveness

The third criteria of community is forgiveness. All were to betray Jesus
that night after the paschal meal. He knew it. Yet He was telling them

that He would forgive them. He was telling them that He would have compassion upon their human frailties.

There's a story about Abraham Lincoln in which several of the defeated Confederate politicians once came to him to complain about certain events. Lincoln listened to them complain and shout. He spoke softly and calmly to them and explained his position. Soon, the others listened to him speak, and the former Confederates left with a great respect for Lincoln.

Later, some of Lincoln's advisers came in and criticized him for befriending what they considered to be traitors. They said he should have run them off and destroyed them before they had the chance to do anything more to him. Lincoln smiled and said, "Am I not destroying my enemies by making them my friends?"

Forgiveness is the act of Jesus Christ and the grace of God which touches all men who come to Him. It is celebrated in the Lord's Supper and is a foundation of the Christian community. The community cannot live without it. In the Christian faith, we are to forsake pride and ambition and seek to commit ourselves to the welfare of others and the community.

Friendship

The fourth criteria of Christian community is friendship.

There was a sign on a church in Philadelphia: If you don't find me in your neighborhood, you won't find me in here.

There are many definitions of friendship. Aristotle said that my best friend is the man who in wishing me well—wishes it for my sake and not his.

Robert Louis Stevenson once said so long as we live, we serve. No man is useless while he is a friend. But he fails to be a friend when he ceases to serve and begins to be served.

In the Christian community, friendship is a service, a reaching out to those around you. A man named Kent Amos moved with his family to Washington D.C. He was a middle management employee for Xerox Corporation who saw the blight of the black neighborhoods. He saw that the children had no male role models and no hope in the inner city. So he started taking kids into his house, feeding them and making them study, and teaching them about things like table manners. All he required was that they use good table manners, speak good English, shake hands firmly, and look him in the eye when they spoke. He made them study when they came on school nights, and he helped them get college scholarships when they deserved it. He helped pay for them to go to school and to college. And in ten years, a girl from Detroit wrote him a letter saying that she had seen a picture of all these kids, and they looked so happy. She had no father and would he allow her to call him father for just this one letter. He took her in, and she graduated from Delaware State.

Now, one of the kids he helped through college is working in Washington D. C. and has opened his house to the street kids so they can learn the things he learned.[16]

Friendship and community go together. But there must be true friendship to start the community.

Fitness

The fifth criteria of Christian community is fitness. By that I mean fitting in. The artist James Whistler was once told by one of his patrons that a certain painting would not fit into a room. Whistler replied: "You can't make the picture fit the room. You must make the room fit the picture."

When do we act like Judas and betray Jesus? We betray Him when we try to make Him fit into our world instead of changing our thoughts and ways to fit into His. We cannot simply fit Jesus into our lives. Our life must be arranged to fit Him. Let me tell you, that's radical. If we look at the way we live our lives now and think about changing them to fit Jesus, that's a radical change.

Halford Luccock says in his commentary on Mark that we betray Jesus when we show a distrust of love as the supreme motive and method of life, when we become infected with the poisons of the world and we elevate our interests and deny the interests of our families and neighbors.

In the end, Barclay suggests that Judas joined with Jesus not so much to become a disciple, not so much to contribute his gifts to the group, but to work out the plans and desires of his own ambitious heart. In his pride, independence, and desire, he wanted to take from this community rather than give to it.

That is our problem today. But the Lord's Supper bids us to forsake pride and individualism and desire and to join the fellowship of the community of Christ.

CONCLUSION

The life of Christ and the Christian walk are a stirring summons to that long obedience in the same direction. After piercing that short obedience to each of the many directions we see in our culture, Scripture spells out the models which we are to follow in our lives in the community at large and in the Christian community. The theme of this Scriptural model is the integration of Christian experience (what we are), Christian theology (what we believe), and Christian ethics (how we behave). These three components emphasize that being, thought, and action belong together and must never be separated.[17] It is simply the Christian faith. And it is the call of the sacraments—to holiness and community, to love God and love our neighbors.

The myths of our culture stick to us and are hard to shake. They pit wealth and status against holiness and community. Those who choose the life of holiness, those who seek the communion of God, those whose obedience yearns for the purpose of life are a minority in our culture and in our church. But they always have been a minority. The Bible gives us the strong sense that we are to live the holy life even though we are in the minority, even when we live in the exile.

It is there and there alone that we find security and significance.

EXPERIENCE (WHAT WE ARE)

BEING

THEOLOGY
(WHAT WE BELIEVE)
THOUGHT

ETHICS
(HOW WE BEHAVE)
ACTION

15

AMERICANS AND PRAYER

The meaning of the earthly existence is not, as we have grown used to thinking, in prosperity, but in the development of the soul.

ALEXANDER SOLZHENITSYN, *The Gulag Archipelago*

Robert Novak has confessed that he was wrong about communism. Novak, a newspaper columnist who has been a witness of world affairs for nearly forty years now, said in a speech to the Notre Dame Club of Chicago that the liberals are scoffing and saying that communism never was a threat to the United States. Novak denies that, saying that there was a time when the Communists were a grave threat to the United States. He believed along with many others that governments had gotten so big the ordinary man could never again prevail against the established governments of the world.[1]

Novak says that fear of communism was not his mistake. No, his mistake was something much deeper. He says that where he went wrong was lack of faith—the lack of faith in God who is overseeing this struggle here on earth. He points out that in Poland it was the Catholic church which stood alone against the Communists for decades. In Czechoslovakia and Hungary, it was the church which was the rallying point against communism. In Romania, where for over twenty-five years it was a crime to say Merry Christmas to your neighbor, the Greek Orthodox Church held public services, and people flocked to them.

231

Novak continued: "It is a revolt against the forces that have re-placed God with man, substituting the religion of power and the gospel of omnipotent government. So in the streets of Prague and Berlin, the words of Thomas Jefferson are read out. It would seem, then, that it is not God after all who is dead, but Marx and Lenin."

The point is well taken that our isolation and alienation lead us to believe that one man can do nothing against the established govern-ments or the multinational corporations of the world. The only place where we may overcome our increasing sense of meaninglessness, it seems, is in the fantasy world of the commercial arts, which still pan-ders the myths of our culture into one large meditation upon self-gratifi-cation. The fact is that the individual, for all our individualism, is get-ting smaller and smaller and smaller.

A friend of mine was the lawyer for a well-known country music star who was indicted by a federal grand jury for cocaine possession. The entertainer and the lawyer appeared for arraignment in the federal court. As the court was gaveled to order, the bailiff read the style of the case: The United States of America versus . . . , and there coldly read the entertainer's name. The entertainer leaned over to his lawyer and said: "Whew! Those are bad odds, ain't they?"

Often, when we look at the world around us and we think of how we are going to be faithful and still survive in this world, we say, "Whew, those are bad odds, ain't they?"

God gives the ordinary person the grace to persevere against isola-tion and alienation, against the corrupting forces of culture and against the conforming power of our mythology. He gives that grace through prayer.

Christians are called to seek the guidance of the Holy Spirit in daily life as they evaluate and critique the American Dream and the Ameri-can culture. Recognizing that we are both American and Christian, we must seek once more to be the witnesses for Christ in a dark world. As Christians view the arts, science, politics, and education, we must seek the strength and the wisdom of the Holy Spirit so that we may under-stand and contribute and excel as if unto the Lord. Our vision must not be blurred by the glitter of the world nor must our perseverance fail in the face of helplessness and discouragement. As the apostles discovered in the early church, their kingdom was not of power but of love. The only way they could deal with the culture was through reliance on the Holy Spirit.

We have discussed the Word and the sacraments as God's means of grace to us. Now we look at the third means of grace: prayer. Prayer sets the soul in relationship to God and to the rest of the world.

PRAYER AS A MEANS OF GRACE

God's grace to us in prayer overcomes the American mythology that tells us that the individual self is the center of the universe. The American mythology has evolved to the stage that its basic assumptions are aimed at elevation of self over God, neighbor, even family. We see ourselves upon a conquest in this world to bring the individual self to the state of perfection. The conquest of the American mythology is, in the end, the subjugation of all things to the self—the final victory of self over the soul.

Charles Hodge says that the means of grace are "those institutions which God has ordained for the end of communicating the life-giving and sanctifying influences of the Spirit to the souls of men. . . . Not only does it lead to the end for which it was appointed—the bestowal of the blessings of God—but it brings us near to God who is the source of all good."[2]

Charles Colson writes about the time he boarded an airplane and as he came down the aisle, a Filipino jumped up and said, "Charles Colson, Charles Colson. I have wanted so much to meet you."

> **"The conquest of the American mythology is, in the end, the subjugation of all things to the self—the final victory of self over the soul."**

Colson saw that they were blocking the aisle so he ushered him to the side and talked to him. The man said, "I have served seven-and-a-half years in prison in my native country, the Philippines, because I was a radical Marxist. While I was there, I read your book *Born Again*. I did the same thing you did. I got on my knees and said to God, 'If you're there, God, please let me know.' I struggled all night long but by morning, God had told me He was there. Now I am a Christian and have accepted Jesus as my Lord and Savior. I am going back to the Philippines."

The man's name was Benigno Aquino.[3]

Colson cautioned him that Marcos was a pretty tough customer and that maybe he shouldn't go back.

He laughed and said, "They no longer have any control over me. When I go back only three things can happen. They can hold free elections, in which case I will be elected the new president of the Filipinos. Secondly, they can throw me in jail, in which case I will start a Prison Fellowship Ministry. Thirdly, they can murder me, in which case I will be with Jesus."

Wouldn't it be nice to be able to face the world like that? Aquino must have known what was going to happen. He landed in the Philippines as a hero to a reception of thousands of Filipinos, hundreds of Marcos's security guards, and dozens of television cameras from around the world. As he moved into the airport terminal amidst the crowds, he was shot to death by Marcos's men. The world did not see it, but the world heard the gunshots on the evening news.

Marcos is gone now. The murderers are in prison. Aquino's wife, Corazon "Cory" Aquino, a devout Roman Catholic educated in the United States, became the president of the Philippines.

It was only the grace of God which allowed Benigno Aquino to return to the Philippines; it was only the hand of God which calmed him and guided him; and it is into the arms of God that Aquino went after his appointment in the Philippines.

ASSUMPTIONS ABOUT PRAYER

As we approach the topic of prayer in the lives of Americans, there are certain assumptions we have to make about prayer and what it means.[4]

The first assumption is that God has personality, that is, God is a person. I have heard people say that they pray on occasion, but I have wondered whether they believed that God actually existed in a personal way. In order to pray to God, we must see Him in terms of His personality. God is a person who can hear prayers and respond to them.

I was once approached by a man seeking advice who began his explanation by saying, "I know that God is not worried by the little things in life." The "little things" in this particular case were problems that greatly bothered this man. If God is concerned enough to know the number of hairs on your head—as Jesus told us in the Sermon on the Mount—He can take care of the little things in life. We frame our thoughts and our prayers in that context.

The image of God as a huge spiritual Buddha sitting atop a spiritual mountain refusing to look down and be bothered by the trivialities of the world is not the God of the Bible. The image of God as an impersonal force driving the world is no God at all.

The second assumption is that God is near us. Only if we believe that God is near us in terms of hearing us and seeing us and communing with us will we be able to commune with Him. This is a belief in the God of the Bible, a God who is a person, a God whose image was the prototype for ours. This God is a spirit who is eternal and omnipresent, a power far greater that we can fathom. This God is infinite, and we are finite. In His infinity, He is near us always. Anything less is not God.

The third assumption is that God has personal control of all nature. For God to control all things, He must be omnipotent.

There is an often-told story on the subject of prayer. Colonel Gracie, aboard the *Titanic*, was among the many who helped the women and children aboard the lifeboats and then prepared for his own death. As he was sucked under with the great ship, he called upon God to save him from his imminent death. At the same time, thousands of miles away in the United States, his wife awoke in the dark of night with an overwhelming dread that her husband was in serious trouble. She prayed for him fervently until, at about five A.M., she felt a reassurance that he was safe, and she went back to sleep. In the Atlantic, Colonel Gracie bobbed to the top, clung to a capsized lifeboat, and at about five A.M. (his wife's time), he was pulled aboard a lifeboat and saved. At the time of tragedy, their hearts and their minds held the right perspective that God and God alone could help them in that situation.

A God with any less power is not the God who has created all things.

The fourth assumption is that God's government extends over the minds of all persons. God can work through the believer and the unbeliever. He used Pharoah in the history of the Israelites, He used King George in the history of America; He can use your neighbor in your history. More importantly, He has the power to change the minds and the hearts of unbelievers and draw them to Himself. His government of all things gives us assurance that His providence will be complete—and that is reason for great hope in a culture of alienation and hopelessness. A God who is a God of the Christians alone is only a tribal god without the power or the grace to give us hope and to save us from the plight of the human condition.

THE REQUISITES OF PRAYER

The assumptions of God concern the character of God. But what about our character as we seek and approach God in prayer? There are a number of requisites to approaching God in prayer, and I will mention a few.

The first requisite of prayer is a heart and a mind in the right mood for communing with God.[5] This requires a perspective upon prayer and upon God which reflects the right relationship to Him. Recognizing that God is God and we are mere mortals, that God is infinite and we are finite, that God is spirit and we are spirit encased in the flesh, is the first step to communing with God. In our culture, racked by the effects of existentialism and relativism, we must come to God with the recognition of His reality in our lives.

The second requisite of prayer is that we pray for only what God allows, that is, we pray within His will. Certain things are clearly against the will of God. We are not to pray for the murder of our enemies or for the stealing of certain goods for our benefit or for gaining of the property of others at the others' loss. We are to pray in God's will. To do that we must know the character of God. That is an impossible task on this earth, but we are called upon to begin the long trek toward the understanding of the will of God.

I knew a fellow who was an ordained minister. He ordained himself. He had his own denomination, his own church, and his own church property. He had five members in his church: himself, his wife, and three kids. He just wasn't going to pay any taxes. He said if they ever caught him, he would just haggle with them in court, then settle. But the statute of limitations has run out on several years of taxes so he had already gotten off scot-free.

This man, by all outward appearances, is not dealing honorably with the government and is not representing the Christian faith. His actions and his thoughts are not in accord with God's will or plan and not within what God allows. Scripture directs us to ask. Our sanctification is the road to asking with His will, the road to becoming more like His Son in thought and practice.

The third requisite of prayer is to rid ourselves of all vain conceit and selfish ideas. This may be the most important of the requisites in the context of the American experience because we come to prayer from a world that is replete with models and directions for vain conceit and selfish ambition. We can only overcome those models and directions and come near to God when we follow the command to love our God and love our neighbor. Only then will we find true relationship with God and live joyfully in the human experience.

Jesus tells us that our prestige is based upon what we are in our spirits, not our outward appearances. Nevertheless, we still focus upon our outward appearances. We all want to look our best. The ABC news program "20/20" had a feature recently about fourteen-year-old girls getting cosmetic surgery—plastic surgery, not for birth defects, but to straighten their noses a bit or to tuck their chins a little. Why? Because their mothers had done it and because they wanted to change the way they looked. Now, the "20/20" interviewer was put off by this sheer vanity. He interviewed some other students about all this, and one of them made the comment that these girls ought to work as hard on beautifying themselves on the inside as they do on the outside.

But if we find our identity in our outward appearances, if we find our identity in how slim we are or whether we have wrinkles in our faces, or in our physical prowess, someday soon we are going to be without an identity. But if we follow the Lord Jesus, read the Word of God, and pray that the Holy Spirit will beautify us on the inside by sanctification, then we won't have to worry about identity or about self-esteem or about anything else the "me-generation" swoons about, because our identity will be established by God, focused upon Him and upon our neighbor and not upon the vanity of self.

The fourth requisite of prayer is confidence in the success of prayer, confidence that God will answer the prayer in His time and in His way. More than that, this is the confidence that God lives and controls His creation. If that statement is so, God is big enough to answer the prayers in accordance with His Providence and to guide us by His grace through our lives.

The confidence in God to be there is a gift of the Holy Spirit that comes from communing with God in prayer.

John Calvin writes:

> This claims our attention, that every man, remembering his own weakness, may earnestly resort to the assistance of the Holy Spirit; and, next, that no man venture to take more upon himself than what the Lord promises.
>
> Believers ought, indeed, to be prepared for the contest in such a manner that, entertaining no doubt or uncertainty about the result and the victory, they may resist fear; for trembling and excessive anxiety are marks of distrust. But, on the other hand, they ought to guard against that stupidity which shakes off all anxiety, and fills their minds with pride and extinguishes the desire to pray. . . .
>
> For those who forgetting their weakness and not calling upon God, feel assured that they are strong, act entirely like drunken soldiers, who throw themselves rashly into the field, but, as soon as the effects of strong drink are worn off, think of nothing else than flight.[6]

There is a middle ground, of course, and Calvin points that out by referring to Philippians 2:12–13: "Therefore, my dear friends, as you have always obeyed—not only in my presence, but now much more in my absence—continue to work out your salvation with fear and trembling, for it is God who works in you to will and to act according to his good purpose."

Prayer is the grace of God to us that replenishes us when we struggle with our place in the world.

THE POWER OF PRAYER

What is the power of prayer? What is the power of God's grace in our lives? Does God have the power to change us from the ways of our culture into the ways of the riches of His blessings? Yes, and He does this work through prayer.

Prayer is the great irony in our culture. Our myths project a strong people whose primary reliance is upon self. Our conquest, at least in theory, is a result of our own initiative and cunning. But prayer makes us subservient to God, and subservience is not a treasured characteristic in the American culture. The great irony is that only in the weakness of subservience to God does the great power of God show itself in prayer; only in reliance upon God and not upon self do we find His overwhelming power. In Mark 12, as Jesus and the disciples leave the Temple, Jesus speaks of the parable of the fig tree. He stands on the

---

"Prayer is the great irony in our culture. Our myths project a strong people whose primary reliance is upon self."

Mount of Olives which was covered with fig trees and looks across the Kidron Valley to the Temple Mount. The view of the Temple from the Kidron Valley was one of the most spectacular views because the Temple, with all its white marble and bright gold and silver, appeared like a great white snowcap on Mount Zion. The disciples were very impressed with the feats of mankind in the building of this monument to man's ingenuity, this monument which had become a Tower of Babel.

Jesus says to them, "Do you see these fig trees? Do you see that Temple over there?" He is saying, "Let me tell you which is stronger."

John Calvin writes that the fig tree would have been ready to bloom at the time of the Passover. Like most trees, its bark is hard and strong in the winter. But in the spring, at the time of blossoming, the bark becomes very soft and pliable, weak, so that the blossoms and new twigs can sprout through the bark. That's when the tree is seemingly at its weakest moment. And yet life is just about to spring forth.

On the other hand, He has told them that the Temple, which appears to be at its strongest time, will fall before the end of the generation. That the Temple would be destroyed was as foreign to the disciples as the thought that the streets of our nation's capital would be physically unsafe would have been to the generations before us.

When we appear to be our weakest, God gives us the strength to be our strongest. That is the power of prayer, the power of God's grace in our lives.

Calvin applied that power to the churches of the Reformation when it looked as though the Christian church was coming apart at the seams. Calvin cautioned that it was just the feeble look of all life before the growth begins. It was simply the darkness before the dawn.

> It is as if he said, 'So long as the church shall continue its pilgrimage through the world, there will be dark and cloudy weather; but as soon as the end shall be put to those distresses, a day will arrive when the majesty of the church shall be illustriously displayed.[7]

Today, the American church seems to be in dark and stormy weather, splitting from within and assaulted and insulted from without.

Discouragement overtakes us, and we think we shall never see the day when things will get better. We lose faith that things can change. We give up on the power of God to change not only the circumstances around us but to change our lives. Jesus says to hang in there. Have faith. It is darkest before the dawn, but God promises that the dawn will come. Isaiah 40:29–31 states:

> He gives strength to the weary
>   and increases the power of the weak.
> Even youths grow tired and weary,
>   and young men stumble and fall;
> but those who hope in the LORD
>   will renew their strength.
> They will soar on wings like eagles;
>   they will run and not grow weary,
>   they will walk and not be faint.

PRAYER AND THE AMERICAN DREAM

Can we overcome the trend of cultural affairs? This is not the first time in history that the Christian faith has seemed to be overcome by the mass inhumanity of humanity. This is not the first time in history that economic materialism has made the pursuit of money more attractive than the pursuit of God.

Each time the Holy Spirit has worked among the remnant of Christians in the culture to call the church back on course. This is done by the work of the Holy Spirit in a small number of Christians in all walks of the culture. God gives His grace to a small number of Christians through communicating, as Charles Hodge states, the life-giving and sanctifying influences of the Spirit to the souls of men. Not only does it lead to the end for which it was appointed—the bestowal of the blessings of God—but it brings us near to God who is the source of all good.

The sanctifying influences of the Holy Spirit overcome the self-loving influences of the American Dream. The individual soul is allowed to gaze through a window much larger than that which focuses on the self. The soul gazes upon a world much, much larger and more meaningful than the New York Stock Exchange. The soul is allowed to see the life-transforming changes possible in the individual life as well as the culture as a whole.

The Public Broadcasting System aired a documentary on the history of the hymn, "Amazing Grace." It was the story of the hymn and the power the hymn and God's grace have had in the lives of people who have sung it, people like Judy Collins and Johnny Cash. It was the story of the power of God to transform the disappointment in their lives into good. Bill Moyers narrated the program and showed several children from the Harlem Boys Choir singing the song in Japan. He asked the choir director if the boys knew what grace meant.

The director's response was insightful. He said, "No, you have to be a certain age before you really understand that God can change things in your life."

You have to be a certain spiritual age before you can understand how God's grace works, how His perfect goodness enters your life, how His transforming power defeats the conforming power of the culture. His grace works through prayer. God uses prayer in the culture. Through His grace, the trends evident in our culture will be reversed.

Christians should not encounter our culture with hostility or stridency. Christians should meet the culture and the cultural myths with a reliance upon the Holy Spirit to enable us and encourage us to critique the culture and to cross-examine the culture's claims. Each Christian should view each cultural expression, including those expressions within the church, with the question: What is the basic assumption or presupposition about life underlying this expression? Each Christian should ask God to enlighten him or her through the Holy Spirit.

A seminary classmate once asked me if I had seen the movie *Top Gun*. When I told him I had not, he excitedly told me all about it. It was the best movie he had ever seen. He concluded by saying, "It just made me want to join the Navy and fly those airplanes."

When I had the opportunity to view the movie and see it from a frame of reference of many more years than my friend, I had a completely different view. The main character was a rather selfish, egotistical young man whose defiance of his superiors caused the death of his best friend and whose conduct would not have been tolerated in any military organization. The supporting female character, a government employee, was selfish, ambitious, and without the slightest moral character or integrity.

Yet the themes of character had gone unnoticed and unchallenged by my friend, covered in the glitter of the bouncy music, artistically filmed dogfights, and the bedroom scene which was designed "to take your breath away." Three years of seminary had not helped him challenge the underlying assumptions or presuppositions of the film maker.

As we engage the cultural expressions, we must address the questions of worldview and search for the American myths which underlie the expressions. We must examine the tenets of the expressions against what they say about humanity, about the value and dignity of human life, and about the purpose of life. Only then will we understand the expressions.

The Apostle Paul wrote to the Corinthians:

> For though we live in the world, we do not wage war as the world does. The weapons we fight with are not the weapons of the world. On the contrary, they have divine power to demolish strongholds. We demolish arguments and every pretension that sets itself up against the knowledge of God, and we take captive every thought to make it obedient to Christ. (2 Corinthians 10:3–5)

Through His grace, God has given us the means to discern His will and knowledge when confronted by the will and knowledge of the world. As Christians we must be sensitive to God's will and knowledge in the world, and we must use the means He has put at our disposal.

THE ARTS

The arts have been a strong point in the overall history of the church. But lately, Christians have looked down upon the arts as a way of expressing themselves. Consequently, the arts have become an expression of various sectors of the culture, many of which are destructive to human dignity. The term *art*, it seems, has become paramount to license to vent upon the public the most deviant of human behavior. As a result, our government debates the effort to control the expenditure of public funds to support a variety of art programs. This is most unfortunate because art is a vital part of expression not only of the culture but of the Christian faith.

E. M. Forster wrote in *Two Cheers for Democracy*, that "To make us feel small in the right way is a function of art; men can only make us feel small in the wrong way."[8]

Control of the arts will result in a degradation of the arts for everyone; it will make us—indeed, it has made us—feel small in the wrong way. In the same manner, government funding of the arts will result in the degradation of the arts for everyone. The influence of the church in the field of the arts is sorely needed. The church has turned its back on the arts and left a vacuum to be filled by the government. The arts express the innermost longings of mankind and are a valuable contact between the church and the culture. Presently, however, the television and film industries have turned the power of the arts against the Christian church and, in some instances, against the Jewish faith.[9]

The challenge to the church is to return to the arts, to reach out to the lost who are yearning for answers but not finding them in drugs, alcohol, and the lust for money, sex, power, and domination. The church must support the arts through funding, through foundations, through exhibits. The church has been woefully inadequate in this area in the past century.

We are born blind, but we think we can see when the myths of our culture lead us on a path of conquest. The only ways that our eyes will be opened, like those in the first century whom Jesus touched, is by the grace of God. The arts have the power to convey that grace as God uses individual human beings to help their neighbors.

We must see again a future of hope in which the gospel meets the longing of the human heart. There is no better place than in the arts.

THE SCIENCES

Probably in no other area has the Christian church come under greater fire than in the area of the science-faith split as portrayed by the American news and film media. And probably no other portrait foisted upon our culture by the American news and film media is further from the truth.

The understanding of science and the understanding of the faith go hand in hand. Pearl S. Buck wrote in *A Bridge for Passing*, "Science and religion, religion and science, put it as I may, they are two sides of the same glass, through which we see darkly until these two, focusing together, reveal the truth."[10]

In looking at the portrayal by the cultural media, we must recognize the limitations of newspapers and television news to delve with any depth into any topic. Therefore, the news must be reduced to slogans in order to be conveyed to a mass audience. Truth, as the saying goes, is the first casualty.

The debate over the theories of evolution is the most dramatic example of this situation. Depicted in the media as a debate with irreconcilable differences, there has been little real debate among those in the theological and scientific communities. Douglas Spanner writes, "The view of the debate over evolution as a battlefield on which the armies of faith and science fought is hardly true to history."[11] Science and faith are locked together in the pursuit of the knowledge which God has revealed to us in His Scripture and His creation.

Martin Luther King, Jr., wrote in his book, *Strength to Love*, "Science investigates; religion interprets. Science gives man knowledge which is power; religion gives man wisdom which is control."[12] And that is the balancing power of the Holy Spirit. Science investigates God's creation. The Holy Spirit interprets that for us so that we come to know more of God and His creation.

Albert Einstein wrote, "Science without religion is lame, religion without science is blind." Therein lies the danger of the media portrait of the relationship of science and the Christian faith. Faith gives strength to the culture—sight into moral visions and interpretation of

---

"The church must support the arts through funding, through foundations, through exhibits. The church has been woefully inadequate in this area in the past century."

---

the actions of mankind, which is lost when we close our ears and our hearts to the work of the Holy Spirit.

We say, well, what's the big deal? I'm getting along pretty well in this world on my own. Why should I really be concerned about this?

One big reason occurred recently. In Michigan, a retired doctor assisted a fifty-four-year-old woman to commit suicide. This doctor was on a television program discussing his "suicide machine." The woman, who was diagnosed with Alzheimer's, contacted him and they met over dinner one evening. Her husband was present. The next day, they crawled into the back of his old van, and he hooked her up. Moments later she was dead. She had played two sets of tennis a week before she died.

The doctor professes that he was compassionate. She wanted to be put out of her misery, although she apparently had few outward symptoms of the disease.

On the "McLaughlin Group," a television news program, John McLaughlin asked the panel about the theological ramifications of this conduct. He reported that the American Bar Association and the American Medical Association have both condemned this action. But, he enjoined his panel of news reporters and commentators, the church has been silent.

Panelist Pat Buchanan stated that he had asked this doctor what he would have done if this woman had been suffering from depression and wanted to end it all. The doctor said he would not have done it. Another panelist pointed that the doctor would have used his suicide machine fifty years ago for people suffering from tuberculosis.

Buchanan stated that his concern was that this thinking is found in the clash of the post-Christian mindset and the Christian faith. In the post-Christian era, the common belief is that the wishes of the individual human being are the highest reference of man. Christians believe in the dignity of a life created in the image of God. Buchanan warns that by the year 2000, our country will be like the Netherlands where, Buchanan says, the elderly are afraid to enter the hospital for risk that some young intern will determine that they are no longer worthy of living, and shoot them with a needle and end their life.

What happened in Michigan will be one of those events which marks a watershed in the history of our country. Martin Niemoller, who led the German church against the Nazis and went to a concentration camp for his efforts, said:

> In Germany, they came first for the Communists, and I didn't speak up because I wasn't a communist. Then they came for the Jews and I didn't speak up because I wasn't a Jew. Then they came for the trade unionists and I didn't speak up because I wasn't a trade unionist. Then they came for the Catholics and I didn't speak up because I'm not a Catholic. Then they came for me and by that time, no one was left to speak up.[13]

Fifty years from now, will we say: In America, they came first for the viable fetuses and I didn't speak up. Then they came for the terminally ill, then the quadripalegics, then the elderly, then the Jews, then the Christians?

In our country, it is the duty of each Christian to speak up: to express his or her views in a lawful way. But it is also our duty to speak in our actions: to love our God and love our neighbor. Then we will walk near the kingdom of God. And we will find the value and goodness of human life that is lacking in large segments of the American culture. We will find that value and goodness through the grace of God given in prayer.

Science and the Christian faith are at odds only where one jettisons the other. Robert Jastrow once wrote, "For the scientist who has lived by his faith in the power of reason, the story ends like a bad dream. He has scaled the mountain of ignorance; he is about to conquer the highest peak; as he pulls himself over the final rock, he is greeted by a band of theologians who have been sitting there for centuries."[14]

Likewise, the person with faith who seeks the knowledge of God without the exploration of God's creation is ignoring the character of God Himself.

"We have allowed the cultural institutions—predominantly the legislatures, the education lobbies, and the cultural bias in the television and film media—to convince us that the government should have a monopoly on education."

EDUCATION

Historically, education has been one of the strong points, if not the province, of the church. The Christian church has been the social leader in education for centuries, but now we have given that to the government. Not only that, we have given up the parental role of education to the government. We have allowed the cultural institutions—predominantly the legislatures, the education lobbies, and the cultural bias in the television and film media—to convince us that the government should have a monopoly on education. If we were to suggest that in, say, car manufacturing, we would be hooted out of the country. Earlier chapters have traced the course of public and private education in this country and concluded that the course of education has led this nation to a serious crisis. A variety of social scientists, politicians, and educators have drawn the same conclusion.

In the Christian community and in the culture at large, we must arrive at a balance in education. It is much too important, to quote a cliché, to leave it to the government.

The church must take the lead in education; it is its greatest mission. The church began the education business and must return to it, not as a mere imitation of the defunct public school systems based upon the teaching of John Dewey, but as a purveyor of hope and love in a world lacking in both.

GOVERNMENT

I read not long ago about a situation at Arizona State University. The ACLU brought suit against the state to remove a cross from the top of the chapel on the campus. The judge ruled that the university had to remove the cross, saying that it did not have a significant secular purpose.

The government of Oregon runs its own gambling business on sporting events. In fact, the National Football League has brought suit against the state of Oregon to prohibit them from running a legalized gambling operation involving NFL games. It's a new twist—a private corporation suing the government to keep the private corporation from being soiled and tainted by the actions of government.

Charley Reese, a columnist for the Orlando paper, said recently that government's basic job is to provide a safe environment—free from foreign and domestic bandits—in which individuals may seek their own fortunes to the best of their abilities. Now, you can argue about the sufficiency of that definition, but the role of government does not include bookmaking.

For some of us, the words of Romans 13 grate on our ears; you might as well be scratching a blackboard. The point of Romans 13 and "Render unto Caesar . . ." is not what man requires but what God requires. The point here is not to view what is Caesar's and what is God's as equal or mutually exclusive. They are not two separate spheres, unrelated to each other. Everything is subservient to the will of God. Government is there to bring about God's purpose. Sometimes it's there to kick us. Sometimes it's there to wake us up when we need to be awakened. That may be what is going on now in our country. The actions of the government are shaking the slumbering remnant in the church.

Yet, nowhere in Scripture are we enjoined to oppose the government actively. And that has posed a problem over the centuries. Nowhere does Jesus suggest that the disciples should meet persecution or tribulation with force. To do so would be to deny the life-changing power of Jesus in our enemies and in us and would deny us the opportunity to make God's Word complete. That power gives us hope for the future.

Halford E. Luccock writes in his commentary:

Throughout the ages, Caesar has generally gotten the lion's share and God has taken the leftovers. We often laugh about government and make jokes—I have repeated some of them today. But then we quietly let the primary questions of culture be answered by the government: questions of right and wrong; questions of life and death. The moral imperative of God is often surrendered with limp words, "Here, Caesar, this is your business."[15]

And the ruling powers in this and every country will take that moral imperative if it is given to them or abandoned before them. Frederick Wilhelm I of Prussia once said: "Salvation is of God. Everything else is my affair."[16]

We are stuck now in a situation where people have looked to the government for the past fifty years to provide services the government has been unable to provide. People have become skeptical, disenchanted, or simply uninterested. The 1990 census forms are an interesting example of citizen apathy. Voter participation in elections in this country are a national disgrace. We have had things shoved off on the government for so long that we have lost faith.

Jesus made it clear that His chief concern was not to establish an earthly kingdom, to stir up a revolt, or to settle the relations between the Jews and the Romans. He refused to allow His authority to be used merely to support a temporal partisan cause.

Luccock continues: "His mission was to preach the kingdom of God and to prepare men for its coming, heart, soul, mind, and strength. It was not enough to be against Caesar; they had to be for God—without limit."[17] They had to know the role of government and not expect to find there the answers to eternity.

Samuel Johnson said two hundred years ago, "I would not give half a penny to live under one form of government over another. It doesn't make any difference to a person's happiness."

Our happiness does not come from what the government can give us; our government does not have that capability. We can understand the situation only when we recognize the limited capacity of government.

British Prime Minister Margaret Thatcher spoke to the General Assembly of the Church of Scotland some time ago. She was explaining to them the limits of politics and of government.

> The truths of the Judaic-Christian tradition are infinitely precious, not only, as I believe, because they are true, but also because they provide the moral impulse which alone can lead to that peace . . . for which we all long. . . . There is little hope for democracy if the hearts of men and women in democratic societies cannot be touched by a call to something greater than themselves. Political structures, state institutions, collective ideals are not enough. We parliamentarians can legislate for the rule of law. You the church can teach the life of faith.[18]

The church must not rely upon the government as it has for the past two centuries in this country. We are to participate but we are not to hide behind it. The church has a mission and the government has a mission. In the church, we are to do our work, relying on the power of prayer and the strength of God. Through prayer, we will forsake our yearning for strength and look to Him who has all strength.

CONCLUSION

The means of grace which God has given us are sufficient for us. They give us the wisdom and the courage to face up to the cultural myths, to pierce the lie of culture, and to return to the fold of the community of Christ. The challenge of the next century is to spur the revival of the church and the culture. Being salt and light does not mean circling the wagons; it means relying on the power of God to transform the church and the culture into God's image.

The church must reach out in the next century and not rely upon the ways it has taken in the past three centuries. It must not forsake the wife of its youth as it looks forward in the darkness of a new era, but it must boldly meet a culture filled with individuals yearning for security and significance. The church must boldly re-enter the fields of the arts, sciences, education, athletics, government, and the fields of individual lives to bring the truth of God for all people.

The means of grace provide us with those things which we are all seeking in the world: significance and security. They come to us in the form of God's hope and love.

All we must do is see it. Christ gave us the vision. We must simply open our eyes.

FOCUS ON OTHERS OPTIMISM
FOCUS ON SELF - PESSIMISM

16

POSTSCRIPT

He who testifies to these things says, "Yes, I am coming soon." Amen. Come, Lord Jesus. The grace of the Lord Jesus be with God's people. Amen.

REVELATION 22:20–21

This book, not unlike our nation, began with a relatively optimistic outlook. As the book—and the nation—progressed, pessimism began to appear. That pessimism appeared at a rate proportionate to the growing focus of individuals upon themselves and the resultant decline in social morality.

The second half of the book, and, I think, the twenty-first century, are not without hope. My intention has been to be more optimistic in the second half of the book, for the Christian vision is much more hopeful than what we have seen recently of the American Dream.

We must remember that the Christian faith and the Christian church have flourished at the times when the cultures of this world have tumbled. There is a correlation. The Christian faith flourishes when mankind recognizes that it cannot build perfection on this earth.

As we stumble into the twenty-first century, there are several things the church must do. I would like to propose these as a summary to what has been said in this book.

REDISCOVER THE FAITH

A substantial impact of the modernist movement in theology has been to strip the meaning from much of the faith, taking faith out of daily life. The faith has become a confused amalgam of reactions to secular attacks. We must remember that the faith is not a philosophy in that we can think one thing and do another.

Professor Thomas Oden describes the impact of modernism in four fundamental values: "moral relativism (which says that what is right is dictated by culture, social location, and situation), autonomous individualism (which assumes that moral authority comes essentially from within), narcissistic hedonism (which focuses on egocentric personal pleasure), and reductive naturalism (which reduces what is reliably known to what one can see, hear, and empirically investigate)."[1]

Such is the impact of the myths of individualism and relativism upon our culture and the Christian church. Only by being grounded in Scripture and in the traditions and the history of the church will we overcome these destructive forces in our culture. The antidote is in Scripture and in the work of the Holy Spirit in the church through the centuries.

We must know the Christian faith and not what others say the faith is. We must not take our direction concerning the faith from the world but must, individually and collectively, arrive at the faith through our individual examination of the Scripture, our community within the church, and through prayer. Faith is a matter which each of us must address in our individual conscience; to allow another to decide for us is to abdicate our most precious freedom to the world.

Our faith includes our experience, our beliefs, and our ethics. Through all three, we must communicate the faith to those around us. In these times, people are looking for answers. In these times, people are grasping at straws to find meaning in life. The shame of the church is that many are looking right past the truth of Jesus Christ to cling to the New Age, to cling to dubious ways to reach a perfection they cannot attain, to cling to the faith of a culture in ruins.

Lech Walesa said to U.S. Secretary of State James A. Baker that "sooner or later, we will have to go back to our fundamental values, back to God, the truth, the truth which is in God. . . . We look to

America, and we expect from you a spiritual richness to meet the aspirations of the twentieth century."[2]

To find that richness takes time and inquiry and priority. It is not
easy but only comes as we experience it, believe and think about it, and
act it out in the ethics of our daily lives. Only then will we as individuals and we as a nation live up to the expectations that all Christians
have in the faith.

RELY ON GOD'S WORD

Second, we must rely on the Word of God to pierce the veil of our
cultural myths. In Acts 17:11, Luke writes, "Now the Bereans were of
more noble character than the Thessalonians, for they received the
message with great eagerness and examined the Scriptures every day to
see if what Paul said was true."

> *"We must know the Christian faith and not
> what others say the faith is. We must not take
> our direction concerning the faith from the
> world but must, individually and collectively,
> arrive at the faith through our individual
> examination of the Scripture, our community
> within the church, and through prayer."*

Each day Americans are bombarded with messages from the culture.
We should receive many of them eagerly, but we should also examine
the Scriptures to see if what is said is true. Some of it, indeed, much of
it, may be true. But without examining the Scripture and testing the
message against the truth of Scripture, we will not know the truth.
Scripture and the faith must be a part of our daily lives.

Religion not only moves a man to think deeply but it also moves him
to make up his mind about the universe and his own place in it.
Especially is this true of Christianity. There was never a man who

thought more clearly than Jesus. He made observations; he drew con-
clusions, he revised old ideas; he challenged prejudices—all of which
call for mentality of a high order. His followers through the centuries
have included some of the greatest thinkers of the world: Paul, Augustine, Thomas Aquinas, Luther, Pascal, Temple.[3]

We must return to an appreciation and an understanding of the Bible.
We must understand not just the proof-texts but the grand themes which
have guided our predecessors through the centuries. Yes, we must understand doctrine, and we must apply the doctrine lovingly to our daily lives.
That requires time, inquiry, and priority. It is not easy, but requires deep
contemplation and independence of mind. When confronted with daily
obstacles, we must be free and independent of the chains of the world.
Only then will we be able to address the deepest currents of our culture
and to understand truth in our world.

OBEY THE CALL TO HOLINESS AND COMMUNITY

Third, we must reassert the commitment of our sacraments to the holiness and community which were at the forefront of the early American
experience and at the forefront of the Christian faith. We can do that
only by following the great commandment to love God and love our
neighbor. This, also, takes time, inquiry, and priority. When we say we
are too busy for church or for our neighbors or for our family, we are
stating our priorities in life. And those priorities are wrong. It takes
time to know our neighbors and our spouses and our children. It takes
inquiry to learn their likes and their dislikes and their problems. It takes
priority to be of service to them rather than to ourselves. We must
strive for holiness. We must overcome pride and discouragement to find
true community.

Our American myths have eaten at the foundations of our culture.
The only antidote to individualism is the call to holiness and to community. Implicit in this reassertion is the commitment to rediscover the
history and traditions of our country—and to recognize them as history
and traditions, mythical thought and conduct.

As Christians, we are once again called to be a light to the world,
to hold out the hope of life. We cannot do that by circling the wagons.
We cannot do that in a "counter-culture." We must reach out. And we

must reach out in love. We must reach out in the belief in God's transforming power through Jesus Christ.

We would do well to recall Paul's direction to the Corinthians in 1 Corinthians 13 that love is the most important quality. We would do well to recognize that we cannot change souls by legislation or by force or by anything short of the greatest commandment to love our God and love our neighbors. We would do well to remember the admonition of Martin Luther King, Jr.:

> To our most bitter opponents we say, "We shall match your capacity to inflict suffering by our capacity to endure suffering. We shall meet your physical force with soul force. Do to us what you will and we shall still love you."[4]

We can only communicate the faith through love. In today's world, there is so much talk about love but so little action. There are so many hearts with doors open, searching for meaning in life. That is an invitation to the Christian faith and to the love of Christ.

PURSUE GOD THROUGH PRAYER

Fourth, we must return to a relationship with God through prayer in which we rely on God's power in this world and not solely on our own. We must regain a balance between the spiritual and the physical in American life, and the only way we can do that is through the relationship with God that comes with prayer. This takes time, inquiry, and priority. It is not easy. Yet, when we try to do things on our own strength, when God is banished from our lives, we focus on the physical rather than the spiritual.

This is most egregiously seen in the diminishing dignity of human life which is pervasive in our culture. This goes beyond the debate over abortion to include the social concerns that are glaring before the shrinking eye of the public. Christians must be concerned about the homeless, the orphans, and the elderly. Christians must be concerned about those things which devalue human dignity, like pornography, drug and alcohol abuse, and the sky-rocketing crime rate all over our country.

There is very little question that these cankers in our culture have
arisen from the long trend in America to emphasize the material and
hide the spiritual. In our efforts to conquer our promised lands, to find
our own perfection, we have destroyed ourselves. That is the irony of
America. We do it at home; we do it abroad; we do it in government
and in the private sector. I recall the quip attributed to a European
army officer about working with Americans in NATO: You have to
watch the Americans. Every time you turn around, they will stab themselves in the back.

Without the recognition and understanding of the spiritual principles in our lives—both our collective lives and in our individual lives—
we have no basis for experience, belief, and ethics. Without that basis,
we will continue to stab ourselves in the back.

We live in a country with double vision. One vision calls us to the
American Dream with its seductive myths and siren song of selfish success. The other calls us to a faith in God and His truth. One is a call to
status and wealth; the other a call to holiness and community. We
often want to compromise by following the American religion. But that
is no compromise at all; that is a sellout.

Each of us has a choice in this world. And each of us must make
the choice. There is no middle ground.

> In our historical present we make our individual decisions with free-
> dom and in faith; but we do not make them in independence and
> without reason.
>   We make them in freedom because we must choose. We are not
> free not to choose. Choice is involved in the resolution to wait a
> while before we commit ourselves to a line of action; it is involved in
> the decision not to interfere in action but to be a spectator; it is pres-
> ent in our consent to accept an authority that will regulate all our
> lesser choices. Yet, though we choose in freedom, we are not indepen-
> dent; for we exercise our freedom in the midst of values and powers
> we have not chosen but to which we are bound.[5]

There is no non-choice. In our human condition, we are bound to
values and powers we have not chosen.

In making our choice, we would do well to look back to the first
century church, to look to the apostles, particularly Peter and John as

they stood before the Sanhedrin, a hostile governmental body (Acts 5). Powerless, helpless, weak, they were not without hope.

I am reminded of the scene in the movie, *Gardens of Stone*, in which an eager young soldier is talking with a senior sergeant, a har-

---

"In our efforts to conquer our promised lands, to find our own perfection, we have destroyed ourselves."

---

dened veteran of the war. It is still early in the war, and the eager young man wants to go to combat. The conversation is paraphrased as follows.

"You know what they say? They say that the Vietcong shoot bows and arrows at our helicopters. How can we lose against a people who shoot bows and arrows at helicopters?"

And the hardened veteran replies in a fatherly manner, "How can we win against a people who have the courage to stand up and shoot bows and arrows at helicopters?"

In a culture which boasts of more helicopters than our minds can fathom, we must stand up dressed in the armor of God. In the twenty-first century, we must meet the hostility of government, of the culture, and of our neighbors with the love of Christ and the grace given to us by God.

> Therefore put on the full armor of God, so that when the day of evil comes, you may be able to stand your ground, and after you have done everything, to stand. Stand firm then, with the belt of truth buckled around your waist, with the breastplate of righteousness in place, and with your feet fitted with the readiness that comes from the gospel of peace. In addition to all this, take up the shield of faith, with which you can extinguish all the flaming arrows of the evil one. Take the helmet of salvation and the sword of the Spirit, which is the word of God. And pray in the Spirit on all occasions with all kinds of prayers and requests. With this in mind, be alert and always keep on praying for all the saints. (Ephesians 6:13–18)

In the face of hostile myths and even more hostile forces of government, the apostles "never stopped teaching and proclaiming the good news that Jesus is the Christ" (Acts 5:42).

John Calvin comments on this passage, "Therefore, woe be unto our daintiness, who, having suffered a little persecution, do by and by give up the torch to another, as if we were now old worn soldiers."[6]

Peter never became an old worn soldier. Peter's job to spread the word about the kingdom of God was just getting started. Peter's job was to stand up to helicopters armed only with the love of Christ and the power of the Holy Spirit. It was a job he welcomed. He was not about to give up the torch to someone else.

In the church today, we are not old worn soldiers. We are not asked to give up the torch to anyone else. We are not to quit when we see secular opposition, to keep our mouths shut for fear of being embarrassed, to duck away from the noise of the world. Our job is to summon the courage given us by the Holy Spirit and to have the courage of our convictions:

- to witness for the faith of our Lord and Savior, whether it be in the family, on the job, whatever the opposition;
- to obey the Word of God rather than the myth or fad or whim of human beings;
- to commit ourselves to the love and community of Christ and the human dignity for which He stood;
- to rely on the strength and power of God through a relationship of prayer and to forsake the pride of our own strength; and,
- to disregard the daintiness of old worn soldiers and hold fast to the torch which is given to each of us.

That is what Peter was doing with the Sanhedrin—he was standing up against helicopters with the armor of God. And that is what the Lord expects of each of His apostles and disciples.

His purpose, like the purpose of Paul, is that we all may live with encouragement in our hearts, united with God, our families, and our neighbors in love, so that we may have and enjoy the full riches of complete understanding, in order that we may know the mystery of God, namely, Christ, in whom are hidden all the treasures of wisdom and knowledge.

That is our vision.

NOTES

Introduction

1. Justo L. Gonzalez, *The Story of Christianity*, Vol. 1 (San Francisco: Harper and Row, 1984), xvii.

Chapter 1: An American Image

1. I am indebted to Laurence J. Peter, *Peter's Quotations: Ideas for Our Time* (New York: William Morrow and Company, 1977), 49.

2. Quoted in Sidney Mead, "The 'Nation with the Soul of a Church,'" *American Civil Religion,* eds. Russell E. Richey and Donald G. Jones (New York: Harper and Row, 1974), 45.

3. I am indebted to Dr. Os Guinness who cited this in a lecture at Christ Presbyterian Church, Nashville, Tennessee, March 23, 1985.

4. James Cornman, *Philosophical Problems and Arguments: An Introduction* (New York: Macmillan Publishing Company, Inc., 1982). Quoted in Michael Green, Ed., *Illustration for Biblical Preaching* (Grand Rapids, Michigan: Baker Book House, 1982), 287.

Chapter 2: An American Dream

1. Joseph Campbell with Bill Moyers, *The Power of Myth*, ed. Betty Sue Flowers (New York: Doubleday, 1988), 5.

2. Stephen C. Ausband, *Myth and Meaning, Myth and Order* (Macon, Georgia: Mercer University Press, 1983), 111.

3. Richard Slotkin, *The Fatal Environment: The Myth of the Frontier in the Age of Industrialization, 1800–1890* (New York: Atheneum, 1985), 16.

4. Ibid., 19.

5. G. B. Caird, *The Language and Imagery of the Bible* (Philadelphia: The Westminster Press, 1980), 220–222.

6. Ibid., 223.

7. Ronald E. Yates, "Japanese Aren't Computer-Wise," *Chicago Tribune*, Reprinted in *Jackson Clarion-Ledger*, January 22, 1989.

8. Ibid.

9. Robert Fulghum, *All I Really Need to Know I Learned in Kindergarten: Uncommon Thoughts on Common Things* (New York: Villard Books, 1988), viii.

10. I am indebted to Colonel Phillip W. Childress for this quote and have taken it from "From the Editor," *Military Review*, vol. LXIX, no. 7 (July 1988), 1.

Chapter 3: The Myth of Our Christian Origins

1. Robert Bellah, Richard Madsen, William L. Sullivan, Ann Swidler, and Steven M. Tipton, *Habits of the Heart: Individualism and Commitment in America* (New York: Harper and Row, 1988), 28.

2. James Reichley, *Religion in American Public Life* (Washington, D. C.: The Brookings Institution, 1985), 53.

3. Sacvan Bercovitch, *The Puritan Origins of the American Self* (New Haven: Yale University Press, 1975), 185–186.

4. Mason I. Lowance, Jr., *The Language of Canaan: Metaphor and Symbol in New England from the Puritans to the Transcendentalists* (Cambridge: Harvard University Press, 1980), 14–15.

5. Quoted, Ibid., 15.

6. Charles Mabee, *Reimagining America: A Theological Critique of the American Mythos and Biblical Hermeneutics* (Macon, Georgia: Mercer University Press, 1985).

7. The text is printed as an appendix in Sacvan Bercovitch, *The Puritan Origins of the American Self* (New Haven: Yale University Press, 1975).

8. Quoted in Bellah, *Habits of the Heart*, 28.

9. Quoted in Reichley, *Religion in American Public Life*, 62.

10. Quoted, Ibid., 62.

11. I am indebted to Dr. Os Guinness who cited this in a lecture at Christ Presbyterian Church, Nashville, Tennessee, March 23, 1985.

Chapter 4: The Myth of Restoration and the New Beginning

1. Ernest G. Bormann, *The Force of Fantasy: Restoring the American Dream* (Carbondale: Southern Illinois University Press, 1985), 3.

2. Robert Bellah, *The Broken Covenant: American Civil Religion in Time of Trial* (New York: Seabury Press, 1975), 5.

3. Richard T. Hughes and C. Leonard Allen, *Illusions of Innocence: Protestant Primitivism in America, 1630–1875* (Chicago: University of Chicago Press, 1988), 3.

4. Dag Hammarskjöld, "1956", *Markings*, Trans. Leif Sjoberg and W. H. Auden (1964) in *The International Thesaurus of Quotations*, Comp Rhoda Thomas Tripp (San Francisco: Harper and Row, 1970), 226.

Chapter 5: The Myth of Sacrifice and Dissent

1. Ernest G. Bormann, *The Force of Fantasy: Restoring the American Dream* (Carbondale: Southern Illinois University, 1985), 240.

2. James Reichley, *Religion in American Public Life* (Washington, D. C.: The Brookings Institution, 1985), 56.

3. Artemus Ward, "Is Introduced at the Club," *Artemus Ward in London* (1872), in *The International Thesaurus of Quotations*, Comp. Rhoda Thomas Tripp (San Francisco: Harper and Row, 1970), 523.

4. Justo L. Gonzalez, *The Story of Christianity*, Vol. II (San Francisco: Harper and Row, 1984), 217.

5. Quoted in Edwin S. Gaustad, *Faith of Our Fathers: Religion and the New Nation* (San Francisco: Harper and Row, 1987), 31.

6. Sacvan Bercovitch, *The Puritan Origins of the American Self* (New Haven: Yale University Press, 1975), 137.

7. Richard Slotkin, *The Fatal Environment, The Myth of the Frontier in the Age of Industrialization, 1800–1890* (New York: Atheneum, 1985), 66.

8. Ibid. Slotkin has a detailed and fascinating account of the Custer legend in the growth of the United States.

Chapter 6: The Myth of Political Equality

1. James A. Reichley, *Religion in American Public Life* (Washington D. C.: The Brookings Institution, 1985), 85.

2. Ibid., 95.

3. Ibid., 94–95.

4. Charles Mabee, *Reimagining America: A Theological Critique of the American Mythos and Biblical Hermeneutics* (Macon, Georgia: Mercer University Press, 1985), 42–43.

5. Ibid., 43, note 9.

6. Ibid., 48.

7. Quoted in Robert N. Bellah, Richard Madsen, William M. Sullivan, Ann Swidler, and Steven M. Tipton, *Habits of the Heart: Individualism and Commitment in American Life* (New York: Harper and Row, 1986), 37.

Chapter 7: The Myth of the Self-Made Man

1. Sacvan Bercovitch, *The Puritan Origins of the American Self* (New Haven: Yale University Press, 1975), 185.

2. Melvin H. Buxbaum, *Benjamin Franklin and the Zealous Presbyterians* (University Park: Pennsylvania State University Press, 1975). Quoted in Charles Mabee, *Reimagining America: A Theological Critique of the American Mythos and Biblical Hermeneutics* (Macon, Georgia: Mercer University Press, 1985), 57.

3. Quoted in Mabee, *Reimagining America*, 56–57.

4. Ibid., 54–55.

5. Edwin S. Gaustad, *Faith of Our Fathers: Religion and the New Nation* (San Francisco: Harper and Row, 1987), 65.

6. Mabee, *Reimagining America*, 51.

Chapter 8: The Myth of Individualism I

1. I am indebted to *World Book Encyclopedia* for a portion of these portraits and quotations.

2. Sacvan Bercovitch, *The Puritan Origins of the American Self* (New Haven: Yale University Press, 1975), 176–77.

3. An interesting chapter on the meaning of "Moby Dick" in the transformation of American mythology appears in Charles Mabee, *Reimagining America: A Theological Critique of the American Mythos and Biblical Hermeneutics* (Macon, Georgia: Mercer University Press, 1985).

Chapter 9: The Myth of Individualism II

1. John Steinbeck, *East of Eden* (New York: Bantam Books, 1950), 151.

2. Francis Schaeffer, *The God Who Is There* (Downer's Grove, Illinois: InterVarsity Press, 1968), 6.

3. Joseph Campbell with Bill Moyers, *The Power of Myth*, ed. Betty Sue Flowers (New York: Doubleday, 1988), 4.

4. Ibid., 8.

5. James Reston, "Staffing Should Be Priority," *Jackson Clarion-Ledger*, 1 July 1988.

6. Robert N. Bellah, Richard Madsen, William M. Sullivan, Ann Swidler, and Steven M. Tipton, *Habits of the Heart: Individualism and Commitment in American Life* (New York: Harper and Row, 1986), 284.

7. Allan Bloom, *The Closing of the American Mind: How Higher Education Has Failed Democracy and Impoverished the Souls of Today's Students* (New York: Simon and Schuster, 1987), 34–35.

8. Robert N. Bellah, et. al., *Habits of the Heart*, 147–148.

9. Sacvan Bercovitch, *The Puritan Origins of the American Self* (New Haven: Yale University Press, 1975), 5.

10. Quoted in John R. W. Stott, *Between Two Worlds* (Grand Rapids, Michigan: William B. Eerdmans Publishing Company, 1982), 174.

11. Ibid., 194.

Chapter 10: The Myth of Relativism

1. This passage includes a portion of a testimony appearing under the title "Story," in *Critique, A Publication of the Ransom Fellowship*, Special Issue, no. 3.87. I include it, adapted and paraphrased, because it represents the story of many in similar circumstances.

2. Carl F. H. Henry, *Twilight of a Great Civilization* (Westchester, Illinois: Crossway Books, 1988), 15.

3. Allan Bloom, *The Closing of the American Mind: How Higher Education Has Failed Democracy and Impoverished the Souls of Today's Students* (New York: Simon and Schuster, 1987), 143.

4. E. D. Hirsch, Jr., *Cultural Literacy: What Every American Needs to Know* (Boston: Houghton-Mifflin, 1987).

5. Bloom, *The Closing*, 42.

6. Ibid., 26.

7. Quoted in John R. W. Stott, *Between Two Worlds* (Grand Rapids, Michigan: William B. Eerdmans Publishing Company, 1982), 55.

8. Bloom, *The Closing*, 26.

9. Quoted in Charles Colson, *Against the Night: Living in the New Dark Ages* (Ann Arbor, Michigan: Servant Publications, 1989), 80.

10. Malcolm Muggeridge, *The End of Christendom* (Grand Rapids, Michigan: William B. Eerdmans Publishing Company, 1980), 17.

11. Alexander Solzhenitsyn, *A World Split Apart: Commencement Address Delivered at Harvard University, June 8, 1978* (New York: Harper and Row, 1978). Cited in Muggeridge, 17.

12. Colson, *Against the Night*, 44.

13. Oliver Wendell Holmes, *The Common Law*, 1881, Reprint Ed. (Boston: Little, Brown and Company, 1964).

14. Cited in Francis Scheaffer, *A Christian Manifesto* (Westchester, Illinois: Crossway Books, 1981, rev. ed. 1988), 41.

15. Ibid., 41.

16. Quoted in Charles Colson, *Kingdoms in Conflict* (n.p.: William Morrow/Zondervan Publishing House, 1987), 211.

17. Quoted in Ibid., 211.

18. Quoted in Schaeffer, *A Christian Manifesto*, 42.

19. Bloom, *The Closing*, 143.

20. Ibid., 143.

21. Quoted in Malcolm Muggeridge, *The End of Christendom* (Grand Rapids, Michigan: William B. Eerdmans Publishing Company, 1980), 20.

22. Charley Reese, "'Traditional' Religion Under Attack," *The Orlando Sentinel*, published in the *Jackson Clarion-Ledger*, 2 July 1990.

Chapter 11: The Myth of the Christian Nation

1. Quoted in Robert D. Linder and Richard V. Pierard, *Twilight of the Saints: Biblical Christianity and Civil Religion in America* (Downers Grove, Illinois: InterVarsity Press, 1978), 135.

2. Martin Lloyd-Jones, *Studies in the Sermon on the Mount*, Combined Volume (Grand Rapids, Michigan: William B. Eerdman's Publishing Company, 1979), II:95.

3. Linger and Pierard, *Twilight*, 21.

4. Will Herberg, "America's Civil Religion: What It Is and Whence It Comes," in *American Civil Religion*, ed. Russell E. Richey and Donald G. Jones (New York: Harper and Row, 1974), 77–78.

5. Robert Bellah, "Civil Religion in America," in *American Civil Religion*, ed. Russell E. Richey and Donald G. Jones (New York: Harper and Row, 1974), 40–41.

6. Malcolm Muggeridge, *The End of Christendom* (Grand Rapids, Michigan: William B. Eerdmans Publishing Company, 1980), 13–14.

7. Jacques Ellul, *The Subversion of Christianity*, trans. Geoffrey W. Bromiley (Grand Rapids, Michigan: William B. Eerdmans Publishing Company, 1986), 48.

8. Halford E. Luccock, *Exposition of the Gospel of Mark*, Interpreters Bible (Nashville: Abingdon Press, 1951), 899.

9. I am indebted to Carroll E. Simcox, *3,000 Quotations on Christian Themes* (Grand Rapids, Michigan: Baker Book House, 1975), 205.

10. Quoted in John Stott, *Involvement: Being a Responsible Christian in a Non-Christian Society*, vol. I (Old Tappan, New Jersey: Fleming H. Revell Co., 1984), 100.

11. Martin Lloyd-Jones, II:102.

12. Charles Colson with Ellen Santilli Vaughn, *Kingdoms in Conflict* (n.p.: William Morrow/Zondervan Publishing House, 1987), 208.

13. Charles Mabee, *Reimagining America: A Theological Critique of the American Mythos and Biblical Hermeneutics* (Macon, Georgia: Mercer University Press, 1985), 57.

14. Robert Bellah, *Habits of the Heart*, 221.

15. Linder and Pierard, *Twilight of the Saints*, 74.

16. Charles Colson, *Kingdoms in Conflict*, 223.

17. Dietrich Bonhoeffer, *The Cost of Discipleship*, rev. ed. (New York: Collier Books, 1960), 169–170.

18. Martin Lloyd-Jones, I:135.

Chapter 12: Americans and the Christian Faith

1. Arthur Gordon, *A Touch of Wonder: A Book to Help People Stay in Love with Life* (Carmel, New York: Guideposts Associates, Inc., 1974), 69ff.

2. Quoted in "North American Scene," *Christianity Today*, vol. 34, no. 10 (16 July 1990): 44.

3. Dietrich Bonhoeffer, *The Cost of Discipleship*, rev. ed. (New York: Collier Books, 1963), 38.

4. This discussion is based upon H. Richard Niebuhr, *Christ and Culture* (New York: Harper and Row, Harper Torchbooks, 1975), 234ff. This book is a classic work which should be studied by anyone interested in ethics and culture.

5. Ibid., 256.

6. Jacques Ellul, *The Subversion of Christianity* (1986; reprint, Grand Rapids, Michigan: William B. Eerdmans Publishing Company, 1987), 54–173. These five items are drawn from Ellul's discussion.

7. Cf. Martin Lloyd-Jones, *Studies in the Sermon on the Mount* (Grand Rapids, Michigan: William B. Eerdmans Publishing Company, 1959).

8. John Calvin, *Commentary Upon the Acts of the Apostles*, trans. Henry Beveridge, Esq. (Grand Rapids, Michigan: Baker Book House, n.d.), 559.

9. Bonhoeffer, *Cost of Discipleship*, 38.

10. Ibid., 39.

11. Niebuhr, *Christ and Culture*, 238.

12. Some of these items are suggested in John R. W. Stott, *The Message of Ephesians*, The Bible Speaks Today Series (Downers Grove, Illinois: Inter-Varsity Press, 1979), 195ff.

13. R. V. Pierard, "Pascal's Wager," *Evangelical Dictionary of Theology*, ed. Walter A. Elwell (Grand Rapids, Michigan: Baker Book House, 1984), 828.

14. Stott, *The Message of Ephesians*, 205–209.

15. William Barclay, *The Gospel of Mark*, The Daily Study Bible Series, rev. ed. (Philadelphia: The Westminster Press, 1975), 57.

16. John Leo, "The Heartbreak That Is New York," *U.S. News and World Report*, vol. 109, no. 12 (24 September 1990): 37

17. Bonhoeffer, *Cost of Discipleship*, 40.

18. Charles Hodge, *Systematic Theology*, ed. Edward N. Gross (Grand Rapids, Michigan: Baker Book House, 1988), 478.

Chapter 13: Americans and the Word

1. Quoted in Cal Thomas, *The Death of Ethics in America* (Dallas: Word Publishing, 1988), 134.

2. Charles Hodge, *Systematic Theology*, ed. Edward N. Gross (Grand Rapids, Michigan: Baker Book House, 1988), 480.

3. E. D. Hirsch, Jr., *Cultural Literacy: What Every American Needs to Know* (Boston: Houghton-Mifflin, 1987).

4. Quoted in "Reflections," *Christianity Today* (16 July 1990): 33.

5. Reported in "North American Scene," *Christianity Today* (16 July 1990): 44.

6. Francis A. Scheaffer, *True Spirituality* (Wheaton, Illinois: Tyndale House Publishers, 1971).

7. Jacques Ellul, *Living Faith: Belief and Doubt in a Perilous World*, trans. Peter Heinegg (San Francisco: Harper and Row, 1980), 155–156.

8. Stephen C. Ausband, *Myth and Meaning, Myth and Order* (Macon, Georgia: Mercer University Press, 1983), 111.

9. I am indebted to Carroll E. Simcox, *3,000 Quotations on Christian Themes* (Grand Rapids, Michigan: Baker Book House, 1975), 113.

10. Charles Dickens, *The Life of Our Lord,* quoted in Stephen Rost, "The Faith Behind the Famous: Charles Dickens," *Christian History,* vol. IX, no. 3, 41.

11. "Letters to the Editor," *U.S. News and World Report* (6 August 1990): 4. The author's identity is not listed here for obvious reasons.

12. William Lane, *The Gospel According to Mark,* New International Commentary on the New Testament (Grand Rapids, Michigan: William B. Eerdmans Publishing Company, 1974), 339.

13. William Barclay, *The Gospel of Mark,* rev. ed., The Daily Bible Study Series (Philadelphia: Westminster Press, 1975), 223.

14. Ibid., 223.

15. Ibid., 224.

16. Reported in "North American Scene," *Christianity Today* (16 July 1990): 44.

17. Martin Lloyd-Jones, *Studies in the Sermon on the Mount,* Vol. I (Grand Rapids, Michigan: William B. Eerdmans Publishing Company, 1959), 79.

Chapter 14: Americans and the Sacraments

1. Eugene H. Petersen, *Long Obedience in the Same Direction: Discipleship in an Instant Society* (Downers Grove, Illinois: InterVarsity Press, 1980), 9. This is an excellent book by an excellent writer.

2. Ibid., 25.

3. Martin Lloyd-Jones, *Studies in the Sermon on the Mount,* Vol. II (Grand Rapids, Michigan: William B. Eerdmans Publishing Company, Combined Volume, 1971), 224.

4. Dietrich Bonhoeffer, *The Cost of Discipleship,* rev. ed. (New York: Collier Books, 1963), 73–74.

5. Jacques Ellul, *Living Faith: Belief and Doubt in a Perilous World,* trans. Peter Heinegg (San Francisco: Harper and Row, 1980), 107–108.

6. Alexander Solzhenitsyn, *The Gulag Archipelago.* Quoted in Charles Swindoll, *Encourage Me: Caring Words for Heavy Hearts* (Portland, Oregon: Multnomah Press, 1982), 43.

7. Michael G. Maudlin, "Satan Makes Headlines," *Christianity Today,* 14 May 1990, 15.

8. Jo H. Lewis and Gordon A. Palmer, *What Every Christian Should Know,* Christianity Today Series (Wheaton, Illinois: Victor Books, 1989), 32.

9. Taken from "The Preface to the Lord's Supper," in the Book of Common Worship (Revised), as cited in Robert Rayburn, *O, Come Let Us Worship* (Grand Rapids, Michigan: Baker Book House, 1980), 260–261.

10. William L. Lane, *The Gospel According to Mark*, The New International Commentary on the New Testament (Grand Rapids, Michigan: William B. Eerdmans Publishing Company, 1974), 508.

11. Quoted in "North American Scene," *Christianity Today*, 20 August 1990, 41.

12. Bruce Larsen and Keith Miller, *The Edge of Adventure* (Waco, Texas: Word Books, 1974), 156. Quoted in Charles Swindoll, *Encourage Me: Caring Words for Heavy Hearts* (Portland, Oregon: Multnomah Press, 1982), 18.

13. William Barclay, *The Gospel of Mark*, The Daily Study Bible Series (Philadelphia: The Westminster Press, 1975), 330.

14. William Faulkner, *Sartoris* (New York: New American Library, 1964), 19.

15. William Barclay, *The Letter to the Hebrews*, The Daily Study Bible Series (Edinburgh: St. Andrews Press, 1955), 137–138. Quoted in Charles Swindoll, *Encourage Me: Caring Words for Heavy Hearts* (Portland, Oregon: Multnomah Press, 1982), 49.

16. Peter Michelmore, "The Kids of Kent Amos," *Reader's Digest*, September 1990, 117.

17. John Stott, *The Message of Ephesians*, The Bible Speaks Today Series (Downers Grove, Illinois: InterVarsity Press, 1979), 193.

Chapter 15: Americans and Prayer

1. Reprinted as Robert Novak, "I Was Wrong About Communism," *Reader's Digest*, June 1990, 99–101.

2. Charles Hodge, *Systematic Theology*, ed. Edward N. Gross (Grand Rapids, Michigan: Baker Book House, 1988), 505.

3. This passage is derived from a passage in much more depth on the remarkable conversion and faith of Benigno Aquino in Charles Colson with Ellen Santilli Vaughn, *Kingdoms in Conflict* (n.p.: William Morrow/Zondervan Publishing House, 1987), 313–318.

4. These assumptions are taken from Charles Hodge, *Systematic Theology*, 498–499.

5. This discussion is drawn from Book III, Chapter 20 of John Calvin, *Institutes of the Christian Religion*, ed. Tony Lane and Hilary Osborne (Grand Rapids, Michigan: Baker Book House, 1987), 202 ff.

6. John Calvin, *Commentary on the Harmony of the Evangelists*, vol. III, trans. William Pringle (Grand Rapids, Michigan: Baker Book House, reprint 1984), 220.

7. Ibid., 146.

8. E. M. Forster, "A Book that Influenced Me," *Two Cheers for Democracy* (1951) in *The International Thesaurus of Quotations*, comp. Rhoda Thomas Tripp (New York: Harper and Row, 1970), 35.

9. Michael Medved, "Does Hollywood Hate Religion?" reprinted in *Reader's Digest*, July 1990, 99.

10. Quoted in *The International Thesaurus*, 564.

11. Douglas Spanner, "Are Christians and Scientists Friends?" *Christianity in Today's World*, ed. Robin Keeley (Grand Rapids, Michigan: William B. Eerdmans Publishing Company, 1985), 288.

12. Quoted in *The International Thesaurus*, 564.

13. Quoted in Laurence J. Peter, *Peter's Quotations: Ideas for our Time* (New York: William Morrow and Company, 1977), 53.

14. Quoted in *Christianity in Today's World*, 288.

15. Halford E. Luccock, *Exposition of the Gospel According to St. Mark*, Interpreters Bible (New York: Abingdon Press, 1951), 841.

16. Ibid., 841.

17. Ibid., 841.

18. Quoted in Charles Colson with Ellen Santilli Vaughn, *Against the Night* (Ann Arbor, Michigan: Servant Publications, 1989), 119–120.

Chapter 16: Postscript

1. Christopher Hall, "Back to the Fathers: An Interview with Thomas Oden," *Christianity Today*, 24 September 1990, 29.

2. Quoted by James A. Baker, III, in *Decision*. Quoted in "Reflections," *Christianity Today*, 16 July 1990, 31.

3. Theodore P. Ferris, *Exposition of the Acts of the Apostles*, Interpreters Bible, vol. IX (Nashville: Abingdon Press, 1954), 232.

4. Quoted in *Christianity in Today's World*, ed. Robin Keeley (Grand Rapids, Michigan: William B. Eerdmans Publishing Company, 1985), 364.

5. H. Richard Niebuhr, *Christ and Culture* (New York: Harper and Row, 1951), 249–250.

6. John Calvin, *Commentary upon the Acts of the Apostles*, trans. Henry Beveridge, Esq. (Grand Rapids, Michigan: Baker Book House, n.d.), 228.

SUBJECT INDEX

ABOUT THE AUTHOR

Pat Apel was graduated from Princeton University and Vanderbilt Law School. After thirteen years, he left the practice of law to attend Reformed Theological Seminary in Jackson, Mississippi. He is a Presbyterian minister.

He and his wife, Katherine, and their three children, Therese, Mary, and Jeep, reside in Hazlehurst, Mississippi.

The typeface for the text of this book is *Goudy Old Style*. Its creator, Frederic W. Goudy, was commissioned by American Type Founders Company to design a new Roman type face. Completed in 1915 and named Goudy Old Style, it was an instant bestseller. However, its designer had sold the design outright to the foundry, so when it became evident that additional versions would be needed to complete the family, the work was done by the foundry's own designer, Morris Benton. From the original design came seven additional weights and variants, all of which sold in great quantity. However, Goudy himself received no additional compensation for them. He later recounted a visit to the foundry with a group of printers, during which the guide stopped at one of the busy casting machines and stated, "Here's where Goudy goes down to posterity, while American Type Founders Company goes down to prosperity."

Substantive Editing:
Michael S. Hyatt

Copy Editing:
Susan Kirby

Cover Design:
Steve Diggs & Friends
Nashville, Tennessee

Page Composition:
Xerox Ventura Publisher
Linotronic L-100 Postscript® Imagesetter

Printing and Binding:
Maple-Vail Book Manufacturing Group
York, Pennsylvania

Cover Printing:
Strine Printing Company
York, Pennsylvania

If Atheists Don't Believe in God, Then What or in Whom Do They Believe?

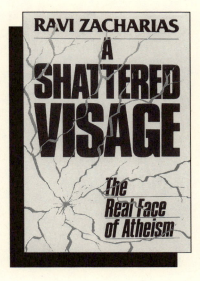

A *Shattered Visage*
The Real Face of Atheism
Ravi Zacharias
ISBN:0-943497-20-5
Trade Paper, 206 pages
Apologetics

DOES GOD REALLY EXIST? There are atheists who would argue the nonexistence of God as vehemently as Christians would argue His reality.

In the tradition of C. S. Lewis' *Mere Christianity*, Ravi Zacharias presents a concise apologetic showing the glaring contradictions in this bankrupt world-view. In an easy-to-read style, he provides us with a basic knowledge of atheism and its fundamental tenets, revealing it to be a "philosophy of despair." He contrasts the emptiness of atheism with the hope and fulfillment of Christianity, illustrating that atheism is a house divided against itself, destined for collapse.

The Government Has Lost
The War on Poverty

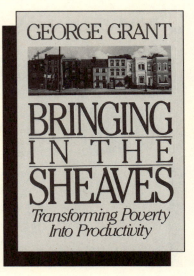

Bringing in the Sheaves:
Transforming Poverty Into Productivity
George Grant
ISBN:0-943497-34-5
Trade Paper, 222 pages
Practical Christianity/Contemporary Issues

IN 1964 THE FEDERAL GOVERNMENT declared an all out "war on poverty." Unfortunately it appears that poverty has won that war. Despite billions upon billions of dollars poured into the massive welfare system, the number of destitute, dependent, and dispossessed citizens continues to grow through recession and recovery alike. But the situation is not hopeless according to author and relief worker George Grant. There are answers to the poverty problem. And those answers can be found in the Bible. In this book, Grant outlines what those answers are and how families, churches, and communities can practically implement them.

There Are Biblical Issues That Christians Have Misunderstood

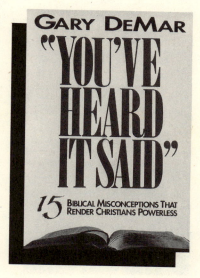

"You've Heard It Said:"
15 Biblical Misconceptions That Render Christians Powerless
Gary DeMar
ISBN 1-56121-049-8
Trade Paper, 242 pages
Christian Living

YOU'VE HEARD IT SAID: The world is evil—Christians should be neutral—You cannot legislate morality—Christians should not be involved in politics.

These are issues of doctrinal importance that Christians have been hearing and believing for years. They are also things that Christians have misunderstood. And their misunderstanding has trapped Christians in sinful inactivity.

Gary DeMar focuses on these and eleven other issues. Issues that many Christians have accepted as truth, and yet a close look at Scripture reveals that the Bible actually teaches the opposite.

With insight into the scriptural text, DeMar realigns the perspective on these points and encourages Christians to answer the call to action presented by the Word of God.

What Could the First Five Books of The Old Testament Possibly Have to Do With Jesus Christ?

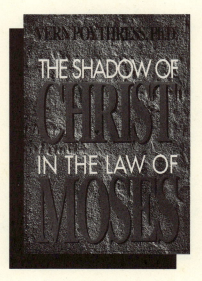

The Shadow of Christ in the Law of Moses
Vern Poythress, Ph.D.
ISBN 1-56121-054-4
Trade Paper, 424 pages
Theology

DR. VERN POYTHRESS shows you how the Old Testament points to Christ as he dramatically explores Genesis through Deuteronomy, demonstrating how the sacrifices and traditions of the Hebrew people foreshadow the relationship of Christ to His people. With crisp insight, Poythress explains that the punishments and penalties of the Law prefigure the destruction of sin and guilt through Christ.

With remarkable clarity, Poythress opens the door to understanding the Old Testament and its relationship to the New Testament. This book is for everyone who studies the Bible.

Dr. Poythress is a professor of New Testament Interpretation at Westminster Theological Seminary and has written four other books. He lives with his wife Diane and their two sons in Pennsylvania.